Dickens'
DREADFUL
ALMANAC

Dickens' DREADFUL ALMANAC

a TERRIBLE EVENT for Every Day of the Year

edited by CATE LUDLOW

The History Press

For Iona, my favourite twin

First published 2010

The History Press
The Mill, Brimscombe Port
Stroud, Gloucestershire, GL5 2QG
www.thehistorypress.co.uk

© Cate Ludlow, 2010

The right of Cate Ludlow to be identified as the Author
of this work has been asserted in accordance with the
Copyrights, Designs and Patents Act 1988.

British Library Cataloguing in Publication Data.
A catalogue record for this book is available from the British Library.

ISBN 978 0 7524 5828 1

Typesetting and origination by The History Press
Printed in Great Britain
Manufacturing managed by Jellyfish Print Solutions Ltd

Foreword

Everything wonderful and horrible in Victorian literature, from detective fiction and ghost stories to 'underworld tourism' and grisly true-crime reports, owes something to Charles John Huffam Dickens. Dickens had a long-standing interest in the strange, the paranormal, the criminal and the macabre. Today his letter to *The Times* describing the execution of the Mannings – 'When the sun rose brightly – as it did – it gilded thousands upon thousands of upturned faces, so inexpressibly odious in their brutal mirth or callousness, that a man had cause to feel ashamed of the shape he wore, and to shrink from himself, as fashioned in the image of the Devil' – is hailed as one of the best descriptions of the scenes attending an execution ever published. His books are filled with thieves and murderers, and with strange events (such as the spontaneous combustion of Krook in *Bleak House*), and his interest in crime and in the paranormal was quite genuine – he was, for example, one of the first men to join The Ghost Club, the oldest organisation of its kind in the world.

The sanguinary reports collected in this book were written by the man himself (and by his staff) as part of the monthly supplement to *Household Words*. I'm delighted to say that they include some of the most horrible incidents I've ever come across. (The cardinal rule when choosing these stories was that any tale involving rats, especially if it included the words 'horrible' or 'melancholy', was guaranteed a place; murophobic readers might want to avoid the entries for February 9th and March 7th.) I would suggest that anyone with a less than iron-clad stomach read it only in small doses ... These stories, every one of which is true, often made me roar with laughter; some, I confess, made me cry. Together they provide a vivid picture of life in Victorian London. The underworld institutions that inspired many of his novels can also be seen here: I defy anyone to read January 21st without thinking of *Oliver Twist*.

Above all, I hope that you enjoy reading them. Only the most incredible, gruesome or ridiculous stories have been included: January alone contains Byron's son, two dens of thieves, a shipwreck and a suicide, five murders, four explosions, a girl who was nearly killed by a Christmas tree and a tiger attack – and that's before you get to the death caused by a noxious cesspool ...

Cate Ludlow
May 2010

January

A case of Murder Long Concealed has come to light near Kilkenny. Mary Fleming, a widow, informed the police that one night between the 25th December 1847 and 1st January 1848, she chanced to pass the door of John Walsh, at Castlegannon; she turned for the purpose of going in, but drew back in terror upon beholding the body of Walsh's brother-in-law, Thomas Ball, a cowjobber, lying dead and covered with blood on the floor, and Walsh and his daughter making ready to remove it by the back-door. She contrived to get away without being observed; and upon reaching home, informed her husband of what she had beheld. He strictly enjoined her never to divulge the circumstance; and during his life she kept the pledge. Ball had been suddenly missed at the time referred to by the woman Fleming, but it was supposed that he had gone to America: he had a large sum of money in his possession. Walsh and his daughter have been arrested. A search was made at their house in Castlegannon, and a skeleton was found buried in the earth a few yards from the back-door. A coroner's inquest has returned this verdict:– 'That the said deceased was discovered dead in an old yard, late in the occupation of John Walsh, on the lands of Knockmoylan; that said deceased's skull was extensively fractured on both temples, with a blunt or some such weapon, feloniously and of malice aforethought, by him the said John Walsh, late of Castlegannon, aided and assisted therein by a person or persons unknown; and that the said murder appears to have been perpetrated on or about the close of the year 1847.' (1851)

💀 *January 2nd* 💀

A Serious Railway Accident occurred on the 2nd inst., on the Runcorn Gap Railway … [The engine of the luggage train] struck a passenger engine, shattering it almost to pieces, causing a great concussion of the carriages, and severely injuring several passengers. The Revd Dr. Burton, of St. Helen's, sustained a severe injury to his nose. A young lady had a severe contusion on her lip, and was taken to the hotel, where she had a succession of fits. One man was in the act of taking a pinch of snuff when the collision took place, and his teeth striking against the carriage, two of them were knocked into his snuff-box. Both engine-drivers escaped unhurt. (1854)

Meanwhile, at the Warwickshire Sessions, on the 2nd, Holloway, a turnkey in the County Gaol at Coventry, was found guilty of procuring a key to be made which would fit ninety of the locks in the gaol, with the object of facilitating the escape of Thompson, a prisoner awaiting trial for forging Bank of England notes. Thompson had promised Holloway 100*l.* if he should escape. The treacherous turnkey is sentenced to transportation for fourteen years. (1851)

💀 *January 3rd* 💀

A dreadful accident from the Explosion of a Patent Spirit Lamp occurred on the 3rd inst. Two young gentlemen, named Edwards and Foster (the latter a son of Sir William Foster of Norwich) law-students, resided at Highgate. They had dined together, and had a lamp on the table. Mr. Foster rose to supply the lamp with spirit; and just after he had done so, he was proceeding, candle in hand, to relight it, when a terrific explosion arrested his movements. On recovering a little from the shock, he beheld his friend, Mr. Edwards, enveloped in flames, the liquid having been scattered over his chest and entire person, and the saturated clothes having then ignited. Mr. Foster, who was himself fortunately unhurt, immediately rushed to his friend's assistance, and endeavoured with all his might to extinguish the flames. Not succeeding, he caught hold of his companion, and, by a desperate exertion of strength, almost carried him first down stairs, and then into a small garden at the back of the house, where by rolling him on the ground, he at length succeeded in extinguishing the flame; having, however, been himself sadly burnt through his generous efforts. Notwithstanding the prompt application of remedies, Mr. Edwards died ten days afterwards. Mr. Foster, however, is recovering. This accident shows how much caution should be exercised in the use of lights of this description. (1852)

January 4th

A middle-aged married woman, named Elizabeth Poole, committed Suicide on the 4th. From an inquest held on her body, in University College Hospital, it appeared that she and her husband, who had been twenty-one years married, were mutually jealous of each other, and that during those jealous ebullitions she had frequently threatened suicide. On the above day one of those love quarrels between them took place, during which the husband struck her. Soon afterwards she went to a female friend named Hancock, to whom she related the circumstance of the quarrel, gave her some money to hand to her husband, and told her that when she was next seen it would be a corpse in a hospital. The same evening she was found insensible and lying on the steps of a gentleman's house in Seymour Street, Euston Square, whence she was conveyed to the hospital, and it was found that she had swallowed oxalic acid, of which she died the following day. A verdict of insanity was given. (1851)

January 5th

A Den of Juvenile Thieves was discovered by the police on the Monday of the 5th, under one of the arches of the South Western Railway, nearest the vacant piece of ground in the York Road. The cave, which had a fireplace in it, was most ingeniously fitted up, having a cooking apparatus, and nearly every article required for domestic purposes. A place to keep the victuals in was sunk in the ground, and secured from dirt by a lid similar to the iron-grating over the area coal-vaults in the public streets. By fastening boards and canvas to the cave, they succeeded in keeping out the weather, whilst a quantity of straw served the gang for a bed. How it was possible for any one to live in the place seems incredible, for neither of the officers were able to stand upright in the cave, and to enter it they were obliged to force their way backwards, the opening being too small to admit of their going in, in the regular way. Five of the youths were apprehended and conveyed to the station. Next day they were brought up before the Lambeth Police Court, and sentenced to terms of imprisonment from six to three weeks. (1851)

January 6th

Frost having set in during the early part of the month, the ice on the waters in the Parks was sufficiently strengthened to tempt thousands of sliders and skaters. The ice broke repeatedly, and many persons were immersed. On Sunday, the 6th, a young man was skating on the Serpentine, when the ice broke, and he was Drowned. He had been warned by an iceman not to venture on the part of the ice where he perished – the rash young man instantly glided into the very centre of the dangerous spot. (1850)

On the 6th, a respectable-looking young woman was charged at the Southwark Police Court, on her own confession, with Stealing a Gold Watch from a gentleman in the city. On the previous night she had come up to a policeman on duty, and confessing the crime, told him she was impelled by remorse to give herself up to justice. On inquiry, it appeared that there was no foundation for this self-accusation; and the girl, questioned by the magistrate as to her motive in making it, said that she was out later than she was in the habit of being, and unwilling to disturb the family with whom she lived, and rather than remain in the streets, walking about all night, and subject herself to insult, she brought the whole accusation against herself, with a view of being taken to the station house. The magistrate dismissed her with a lecture on the folly and impropriety of her conduct. (1851)

🕱 January 7th 🕱

An accident, fortunately not serious in its results, occurred on the evening of the 7th at the residence of W.O. Bigg, Esq., of Abbot's Leigh. There was a large party at the house, and during the night a 'German Tree', about five feet high, with its branches covered with bon-bons and other Christmas presents, and lit with a number of small wax tapers, was introduced into the drawing-room for the younger members of the party. While leaning forward to take some toy from the tree, the light gauze overdress of one young lady, Miss Gordon, took fire, and blazed up in a most alarming manner. One of the lads present, whose quickness and presence of mind were far superior to his years, with much thought and decision threw down the young lady, and folding her in a rug that was luckily close by, put out the flame before it had done any serious damage beyond scorching her arms severely. (1850)

🕱 January 8th 🕱

A boy named George Ruby, who appeared about fourteen years of age, was put in the witness-box at Guildhall, on the 8th, to Give Evidence in a Case of Assault on a police-officer, when the following dialogue took place:– Alderman Humphery: Well, do you know what you are about? Do you know what an oath is? Boy: No. Alderman: Can you read? Boy: No. Alderman: Do you ever say your prayers? Boy: No; never. Alderman: Do you know what prayers are? Boy: No. Alderman: Do you know what God is? Boy: No. Alderman: Do you know what the devil is? Boy: I've heard of the devil, but I don't know him. Alderman: What do you know? Boy: I knows how to sweep the crossings. Alderman: And that's all? Boy: That's all. I sweeps a crossing. The Alderman said that in all his experience he had never met with anything like the deplorable ignorance of the poor unfortunate child in the witness-box. (1850)

A Little Chimney Sweeper has Perished at Manchester in the flue of a manufactory. It appeared at the inquest that there was a great want of caution in the engineer and the master sweeper: the flue had not been sufficiently cooled and ventilated, and the poor boy was suffocated by the heated gases, as well as burnt by falling on the hot soot. The coroner's jury directed that a copy of the depositions be sent to the Watch Committee, with a request that the parties concerned should be prosecuted for using climbing-boys contrary to law. (1851)

🕱 *January 9th* 🕱

A young man named Crook, a nailmaker at Birmingham, Accidentally Shot his Wife on the 9th. Having returned home in the evening from his work, he affectionately saluted her, and asked her to get him a nice cup of tea. She was busy in this duty, stooping before the fire toasting some bread, when her husband took up a gun that had just before been placed against the wall by Lockley, their fellow tenant in the house, who had been shooting birds in the garden. As Crook lifted the gun the charge exploded, and his wife sank quietly forward as if fainting; Mrs. Lockley ran and clasped her in her arms, and found her dead – the shot had entered her brain. The poor husband, who had been married only a fortnight, became frantic with grief, tearing his hair and uttering self-accusations. A coroner's inquest was held, and found that this lamentable occurrence was entirely accidental. (1851)

🕱 *January 10th* 🕱

At the Central Criminal Court on the 10th inst., Sarah Drake was indicted for the Wilful Murder of her male bastard child by strangling it with a handkerchief. The prisoner, of whose previous history little was known, had been recently engaged in the service of Mr. Huth, of Harley Street, as cook and housekeeper. From the evidence it appeared that in 1848, when three months old, the child was placed with Mrs. Johnson of Shorley Common, to nurse. Payment was regularly made for its maintenance for some time, but gradually fell off. On the 27th of November 1849, the nurse received a letter from the prisoner, stating that she was going with a family to Madrid, and regretting her inability to pay her the arrears owing at present. In consequence of this the nurse took the child the same day to the prisoner in Harley Street, and left it with her, refusing her entreaty to take him back for a week. The child was carried into the housekeeper's room, and nothing further was seen of it. At the usual dinner hour the prisoner absented herself under the pretext of writing a letter, and having a box of clothes to pack for her sister. She did not appear again until three o'clock, when one of the servants entering her bedroom saw the box packed in a wrapper and corded. It was carried down stairs next morning and sent to the station, addressed to her brother-in-law, Mr. Theophilus Burton, North Leverton, near Retford. A letter, which has since been burnt, was sent advising the forwarding of the box.

Mr Burton went the day following with her brother to East Retford and received it. On forcing the lock, the dead body of a child was discovered. On the box being searched by the police an apron was found slightly stained with blood, and marked S. Drake. Various articles of clothing were identified by the nurse. At the Marylebone station, in answer to the inquiries of the female searcher, she stated that, afraid of losing her place, she had hung it and sent it to her sister to be buried. The counsel for the prisoner made an eloquent and feeling defence, endeavouring to prove that the crime had been committed in a temporary frenzy of insanity. He urged the jury to look at the situation of the prisoner. After her seduction – after receiving the greatest injury that could be inflicted upon her by one of the other sex – she had been abandoned and left with limited resources, and suffering from bad health, to provide for this unhappy child. She had done so. She had struggled to preserve her reputation, which was all she had to depend upon, to protect her from utter destruction, and there was no doubt that the manner in which the child was suddenly thrown upon her hands, and the dreadful consequences which she foresaw must result from it, had for the moment unsettled her reason, and drove her to the commission of the dreadful act. A verdict of 'Not guilty, on the ground of insanity' was returned by the jury, and the prisoner ordered to be detained in safe custody during Her Majesty's pleasure. (1850)

January 11th

On the 11th, at Chatham, Ellen Bright, a girl of seventeen, known as the 'Lion Queen,' attached to the menagerie of her uncle Mr. George Wombwell, was Killed by a Tiger. An inquest was held on her body. She had been in the habit of entering the dens several times daily for the last twelve months. On that evening she entered a den in which were a lion and a tiger; she had only been in two or three minutes when, the tiger being in her way, she struck it slightly with a small whip she carried in her hand. The beast growled as if in anger, and, crouching close to the bottom of the den, stretched out its paw as if at her leg or dress, causing the deceased to fall sideways against the cage; the animal at the same moment sprang at her, and, seizing her ferociously by the neck, inserted the teeth of the upper jaw in her chin, and in closing his mouth inflicted frightful injury in the throat with his fangs. He then appeared to change his position, making a second gripe across the throat of his victim. A keeper who was standing on the step of the den, armed with a whip, immediately rushed to her assistance; but the animal did not loose its hold until struck over the nose violently with an iron bar; and whilst the keeper held the animal, the unfortunate girl was removed from the cage, bleeding profusely, and life all but extinct. She was taken into one of the caravans, where she was immediately attended by two medical gentlemen who happened to be present at the time of the occurrence. She died in a few minutes after she was taken from the den, from the wounds and from the shock to the system. The jury returned a verdict to the effect that deceased was killed by a tiger whilst exhibiting in its den; and expressed a strong opinion against the practice of allowing persons to perform in a den with such animals. (1850)

🕱 *January 12th* 🕱

An act of Horrible Cruelty, by which the whole livestock of a farmer was destroyed, was perpetrated on Sunday the 12th, at Dagnell near Dunstable. Mr. Cutler, a small farmer residing in the above village, was roused from sleep during the night, by the moaning noise of one of his pigs, and on going into the yard found the poor animal mutilated in a most shocking manner, being, in appearance, chopped in two across the loins with a bill or axe. Fearing that more mischief had been done to his stock, he went round his premises, and discovered, to his horror, that all his cows, six in number, had been cruelly cut about the hind-legs, the hamstrings completely separated, and the tail of one of the animals cut off. Mr. Cutler immediately sent for a butcher, and had the poor animals slaughtered.

Suspicion fell upon a man who had recently been working for Mr. Cutler. This man had disputed with his employer at the time of settling on Saturday night, and when he left the premises held out a threat that he would serve him out for it. Information was given to the police, who went to the cottage of the man and apprehended him while in bed. His clothes were marked with blood, and there were other suspicious appearances. He was taken before the magistrates and remanded for further examination. After the hearing, the man, whose name is Norman, and described as a labourer, was taken to Ivinghoe cage, but on the police officers going to the place on the following morning it was discovered that he had fled. It is supposed the prisoner had been assisted to escape from his confinement by persons on the outside, for, on examining the building, the wall was found to have been undermined, and a hole made large enough to admit a man's body. (1851)

🕱 *January 13th* 🕱

On Sunday the 13th, a large portion of the ice broke in the Victoria Park, Bethnal-green, and nearly a hundred people were plunged into the water. The scene was frightful; and when all had been pulled out that could be seen, it was feared that some persons had been lost under the ice. (1850)

🕱 *January 14th* 🕱

A distressing accident, resulting from the Incautious Use of Fire-arms, occurred at Walsall on the 14th. A youth about fifteen or sixteen years of age, son of Mr. Swanwick, relieving officer, was on a visit with a relation, of that place, and in the morning went out with two or three young companions to shoot birds. On their return home, two of them put their unloaded guns in the corner of a room, and shortly afterwards the third put his gun with the others; but unhappily this one was loaded. The young men were soon after playing with the servant-maid; and Swanwick, laying hold of one of the guns, and under the impression that they were all unloaded, presented it at her, and said he would shoot her. Thinking to frighten her, he pulled the trigger and fired; when, in an instant, the poor girl dropped dead at his feet. (1850)

🕱 *January 15th* 🕱

A Singular Trick has been played by the butler of Mr. Hudson, of Frogmore, in Hertfordshire. The man had been threatened with dismissal; and thought he could regain his master's favour by the exhibition of valour in defending his property. The family were roused in the night by the report of a pistol-shot. Appearances at first denoted that robbers had visited the place; the butler was found lying partly in an adjacent river, apparently insensible. When he had somewhat recovered, he said he had disturbed three robbers who were on the premises. He had had an encounter with them. They fired, and he fired; then they beat him, and thrust him into the mud on the river-bank. His watch was smashed, his coat torn to ribands; there was a hole in his straw hat, caused by a bullet. But a number of circumstances were observed which led to a suspicion that there had been no robbers there at all; and eventually the butler confessed to the police that he had concocted the whole affair.

In reward for all this trouble, Mr. Hudson dismissed his too clever and valiant servant. (1853)

🕱 *January 16th* 🕱

As Mr. Leffler, the singer, was going along the Kennington Road, about twelve o'clock at night on the 16th, he was run up against by a woman, and a man behind her, exclaiming, 'What do you mean by insulting my wife?' immediately made a violent attack on him, in which the woman joined. He defended himself with his umbrella till a constable came up, when they were both taken into custody. Next day they were brought before the Lambeth Police Court, and remanded. (1851)

🕱 *January 17th* 🕱

A Dreadful Explosion of Naphtha took place about six o'clock, on the evening of the 17th, on the premises of Mr. Moffett, 61, John Street, Tottenham Court Road, which resulted in the death of a youth named Moore; and the serious injury of a younger brother. They were alone in the shop at the time. It was very dark; and the deceased was going to fill the lamp, which usually burnt naphtha. The deceased held the can which contained the naphtha, and the lamp in the other hand. His brother stood at his side, with a lighted match in his hand, while the deceased was pouring the spirit into the lamp; he drew the lamp close to the light, and the spirit immediately exploded. (1850)

At the Worship Street Police Court, Susan Nunn, a showily-dressed young woman of thirty, was charged with Robbing Young Children of their Clothes in the streets of St. George's-in-the-East. A swarm of little girls and boys, estimated by the gaoler to be nearly fifty in number, and varying in age from six to thirteen, appeared under the care of their parents or friends to establish two or three score of cases. The prisoner had been placed in a room with several other women, and a number of the children brought in: they all consecutively and without the slightest hesitation identified Nunn as the person who robbed them. The officers arrested her by stratagem. Six cases were proved, and she was sent to Newgate for trial. (1851)

January 18th

Mr. Henry Francis Seymour, a retired military officer, was walking homewards to Hackney through Shoreditch late on the night of the 18th, when four men set on him at the corner of a street and tried to overpower him. He was struggling desperately when a policeman scared them, and they fled; but Mr. Seymour caught one, and held him fast. When the constable came up this ruffian audaciously charged Mr. Seymour with odious conduct; but the constable knew the accuser too well, and took him to prison. (1851)

January 19th

An extraordinary ease of obtaining goods, or 'Living on the Public' was disclosed in the Insolvent Debtors' Court, on the 19th, when Joseph William Williams, late of Fenchurch Street, ironmonger, was opposed by various creditors. The insolvent made on the present occasion his fourth appearance before the court, besides having figured as a bankrupt ... For the last eighteen years he had gone on getting into debt of 6400*l.*, or living on the public at the rate of 350*l.* a year. Mr. Commissioner Phillips, in giving judgment, held that the debts had been fraudulently contracted. For the protection of the public, he was bound to mark such a case with an imprisonment for twelve months. (1850)

January 20th

A dreadful Boiler Explosion, with loss of life, took place at the Ebley Clothing Mill, near Stroud, on the morning of the 20th inst., about nine o'clock. The workmen and women had been to breakfast, and were beginning to work, when a loud explosion, followed by a crash, which was distinctly heard in the town of Stroud, announced a catastrophe. The engine boiler had burst, and the building in which it was contained was found to be almost a heap of ruins. The end of the factory where the boiler had been placed was completely blown out, and a wall forming the boundary of the premises next to the canal was also blown down, the debris being blown into the canal. On removing the rubbish the body of the engineer was discovered, dreadfully mutilated and dead. Three women were also found to have sustained serious injuries, and were removed to Stroud Hospital, where they are now lying. It is a most providential circumstance that the accident happened at the moment it did, for in a quarter of an hour after there would have been some 500 people in the mill, and some 30 in the floor immediately over the boiler. One boy had a very narrow escape. He acted as stoker or attendant to the engineer, and just before the accident had been sent by him to fetch a hammer. He was returning with it to the building when the explosion took place. A coroner's inquest has been opened, but adjourned to give time for the attendance of a government inspector. (1853)

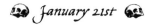

January 21st

William Bristol, a young ruffian, was tried on the 21st, at the Middlesex Sessions, for having Attempted to Steal from a person unknown. The prisoner, in company with a notorious thief and prostitute, had been detected by a police officer one evening, in Gray's Inn Lane, putting his hand into the pocket of a person passing by, but before he had time to take anything his companion gave the alarm and they ran away, but the man was captured. From the evidence given by the police officer it appeared that the prisoner was a member of a gang of daring thieves, and the 'deputy' or sub-landlord of a notorious den in Fox Court, Gray's Inn Lane, which was known as the 'Thieves' Kitchen,' and which was the rendezvous of burglars, pick-pockets, prostitutes, and pot-stealers; a regular receptacle of stolen property, and where nightly could be seen thieves, prostitutes, and beggars, of all ages and of both sexes, huddled together indiscriminately, there being in some instances eight or ten men, women and children, all in one bed together.

Some short time before, the officer had been on duty near Fox Court, and on contriving to peep into the 'Kitchen' through a window, he saw the prisoner in a room with a line tied across it, and from this line was suspended a coat, in the pockets of which were placed pocket-handkerchiefs. A dozen little boys surrounded the prisoner, and each in turn tried his skill in removing a handkerchief without moving the coat or shaking the line. If he performed the manoeuvre with skill and dexterity, he received the congratulations of the prisoner; if he did it clumsily or in such a manner as would have led to detection, had the operation been performed in the usual manner in the street, the prisoner beat them with severity, having on the occasion in question knocked down and kicked two of the boys for not having exhibited the requisite amount of tact and ingenuity in extracting the handkerchief. The learned judge said he regretted that the court had not the power of passing such a sentence as would rid the country of the prisoner, but sentenced him to be kept to hard labour for eighteen calendar months. (1851)

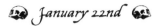

January 22nd

An important Coroner's Inquest was held in the Bethnal Green Road an the 22nd inst., on the body of a child of three years old, who died from typhoid lever, caused by the Noxious Exhalation of a Cesspool. The child's mother said that her husband was a hawker of crockeryware, and they, with three children occupied a lower room on the ground floor. She had another child lying ill, which the surgeon gave no hopes of. There was an overflowing privy connected with the house, at the back, which passed under their bed-room. It was a cesspool, as there was no drainage to the houses. Every morning the soil came through the flooring boards of the room, and witness was compelled to wipe it up. The coroner asked if any complaint had been made to the Board of Guardians respecting the horrid place? Mr. West (the medical officer) – No, sir, it is down in my last report, to come before the Guardians on Monday night next, and I have 14 more cases of a similar kind in the same district, where the privies were overflowing and the soil was to be seen several inches deep in the back-yards, or gardens, adjoining the closets. (1853)

January 23rd

A singular Omnibus Robbery was committed on the 23rd. A lady residing in the Liverpool-road, having received some money at one of the banks in the neighbourhood of Regent-street, took an omnibus there, into which she was followed by a quiet, respectable, and gentlemanly-looking young man, dressed in a suit of black. During the journey towards the Angel at Islington several changes of passengers occurred, which apparently gave occasion for the gentleman to change his seat, and finally to place himself at that side of the lady on which lay her dress pocket containing her money. On arriving at the end of Baron-street, the lady alighted; the gentleman also very politely assisting her. She proceeded a few yards, and feeling for her money found it gone. Her suspicion immediately fell upon the gentlemanly young man, and turning back, she proceeded towards the

Angel, and caught sight of him just coming out of a passage. She seized him and charged him with the theft, which he very coolly denied and threw her off, trying to escape. Fortunately he came in contact with a gentleman to whom the lady was known, and by whose assistance his escape was prevented. A scuffle now took place, when the gentlemanly thief drew a knife, crying 'Life or death!'; but on the assurance of the lady that if he would give up the money she would not give him in charge of the police, he threw the money on the ground and was allowed to escape, although by this time nearly 100 persons had collected on the spot. (1854)

January 24th

At the Clerkenwell Police Court, on the 24th, Ann White, a miserable, dissipated-looking young woman, was put at the bar for final examination on the charge of having Murdered her Infant Child, of nine months old. On her first examination, it appeared that she had resided in Somers-town, with her two children, one seven years old, and the deceased; that they were frequently left by her without food, fire, or clothes, and otherwise so utterly neglected that her landlord eventually deemed it his duty to call in a constable, with whose assistance the poor sufferers were removed to St. Pancras workhouse, and she was shortly afterwards found rolling about drunk and taken into custody. The deceased and the other child were speedily examined by Mr. Robinson, the parochial surgeon, who found them sinking rapidly from the combined want of food and general neglect; that they were in a state almost impossible to describe, and swarming with vermin. Everything which humanity could dictate was immediately bestowed on the little helpless creatures; but death happily terminated the sufferings of the one, and the other is recovering. The board of St. Pancras, on the former inquiries, had declined to prosecute, and were severely censured by the magistrate, who said that, in a matter of such atrocity, importance, and nicety, a meanness ought not to exist, especially with a parochial body, and he wished them to review their decision. It now appeared the parish-officers had profited by the recommendation of the magistrate, as the clerk to the vestry appeared as public prosecutor, and called another witness, who proved almost unheard-of brutality by the accused towards her poor children. The magistrate, at the conclusion of the examination, said it was a most painful case, and committed the prisoner to Newgate to take her trial. (1852)

January 25th

Iacchimo Guiccioli, who stated himself to be the Natural Son of the late Lord Byron, was placed before the Marylebone police magistrate on the 25th, very nearly naked, and shivering from head to foot, charged with being Drunk. He told the magistrate he had but just returned from the Archipelago, and had fallen in with some land sharks, who had stripped him of all his worldly goods and garments. The magistrate cast a pitying glance at the unfortunate man and dismissed the case. (1851)

January 26th

Elizabeth Vickers, a middle-aged woman, was examined at the Lambeth Police Court on the 26th ult., on the charge of Murdering her master. It appeared that she had been housekeeper to Mr. William Jones, a gentleman 84 years old, who lived in Acre Lane, Brixton. She had been fourteen years in his service, and had obtained a complete control over him, excluding his relatives and friends from his house, or only allowing them to see him in her presence. Whenever she threatened to leave him, the old man was greatly alarmed. He purposed that she should succeed to his property. He had transferred 1000*l.* in the funds to the joint names of himself and Vickers. Yet this woman treated him with the greatest cruelty. She would go out for hours, locking him in the house, and return very drunk. On these and other occasions she savagely beat the old man; the neighbours heard quarrels, cries, sounds of blows and falls; and Mr. Jones was seen with marks of frightful blows on his head and face. When Vickers announced that her master was dead, a surgeon found the body extended on a couch; she told an improbable story of his sudden death after drinking some water. A post-mortem examination detected the marks of numerous blows or falls and cuts on the face, head, and body; death had been caused by a blow or fall on the temple, which had produced an effusion of blood on the brain. The marks were not of wounds just inflicted; they had probably been received from six days to a fortnight before the surgeon saw them. Clothes that were bloody were found in the house, though attempts had been made to wash out the stains. All the circumstances detailed by the witnesses led to the conclusion that the old man had been murdered. When a policeman attempted to arrest Vickers, a woman of great strength, she fought so furiously, that but for the aid of a second constable the officer would have been worsted. She was remanded, and re-examined on the 8th inst., when additional evidence was given. She violently interrupted the witnesses, reproving them, and sometimes exclaiming that they lied. Articles pawned by her she declared were her property, not Mr. Jones's. The house at Brixton was found in a shamefully dirty state, and amid the piles of foul linen were articles stained with blood. Under his will, which has been proved by the executor, Jones left 1400*l.* in legacies, and made Vickers residuary legatee. Her solicitor offered no defence and she was fully committed for trial. (1853)

🕱 *January 27th* 🕱

A Dreadful Murder was committed on Saturday night, the 27th of January, at Rochester. The victim was Mrs. Bacon, an old lady who lived with a maidservant, in Ordnance-road. On Sunday morning, a man named Pearson, who is in the daily custom of calling with vegetables, while so engaged at the adjoining house, heard a rattling at the door, as of some one endeavouring to force his way out, and, on going to the spot, the servant-girl made her appearance in such a state of agitation as to lead him to apprehend she was in a fit, and he ran for assistance to a chemist's close by, who directed him to Dr. Gamine, at Fort Pitt, surgeon of the 94th regiment. On his arrival she was found to have her throat cut, and by his directions was removed on a stretcher to Fort Pitt. In the course of the day she expressed a wish to make a statement, and Major Boys, a county magistrate, attended for the purpose of taking her deposition. What the nature of the disclosure made, if any, was, did not transpire. On a policeman entering the house, the girl said her mistress had been murdered in the cellar by two dustmen. On going into the cellar he found a pail full of water, with a flannel in it stained with blood, and which appeared to have been used in washing the deceased's face. Close by this he found a hatchet and a knife, both stained with blood; he observed blood on the floor, and the fagot wood was also sprinkled with blood. On going up stairs he found Mrs. Bacon lying on her back inside the door on the second floor, and traces of blood from the cellar to where deceased lay, showing that the body had been dragged from the cellar to the spot where it was found. The skull was beaten in, there were two large gashes on the temple, and the face greatly disfigured from the blows which had been inflicted. The knife with which the girl's throat had been cut was found on the kitchen dresser, and there was a pool of blood just within the front door, where she had stood. She had been in the service of Mrs. Bacon for about seven weeks, having previously lived in service at Stroud, where her friends also reside. Mrs. Bacon was the widow of Mr. Bacon, formerly in her Majesty's dockyard, and was seventy-eight years of age. The servant-girl is about nineteen. A coroner's inquest has been held, and the jury have returned a verdict of wilful murder against Elizabeth Lawes, the servant-girl, who has been committed for trial. (1855)

January 28th

At the Mansion House, on the 28th, Alderman Humphery expounded a point in Omnibus Law, when a conductor of a Camberwell omnibus was summoned for having refused to admit a gentleman as a passenger into his omnibus. A few days before, at a quarter before five, the complainant went to the door of the omnibus, being desirous to be driven as far as Walworth, and requested the conductor to allow him to enter. The evening was extremely wet, but the conductor refused to admit the applicant, and excused himself upon the ground that all the seats were engaged, at the same time that there was abundance of room in the vehicle. The complainant represented the unfairness of the refusal, and determined to have the decision of a magistrate upon the subject. A gentleman who regularly takes a seat in the defendant's omnibus stated that the defendant was expected by his regular 'whole of the way' customers to keep seats for them, especially in wet weather, during which alone the passengers to Walworth or the Elephant and Castle were disposed to ride. The conductor stated he considered himself bound to reserve seats for his regular 'whole of the way' customers, and had acted accordingly. The Alderman admitted the reasonableness of the defence, but the law was positive on the subject. No seat could be reserved so as to prevent any applicant being refused admission into the omnibus. No penalty was inflicted. (1850)

January 29th

An inquest was held on the 29th, on Martha Joachim, a Wealthy and Eccentric Lady, late of 27, York-buildings, Marylebone, aged 62. The jury proceeded to view the body, but had to beat a sudden retreat, until a bulldog, belonging to deceased, and which savagely attacked them, was secured. It was shown in evidence that on the 1st of June, 1808, her father, an officer in the Life Guards, was murdered and robbed in the

Regent's Park. A reward of 300*l.* was offered for the murderer, who was apprehended with the property upon him, and executed. In 1825, a suitor of the deceased, whom her mother rejected, shot himself while sitting on the sofa with her, and she was covered with his brains. From that instant she lost her reason. Since her mother's death, eighteen years ago, she had led the life of a recluse, dressed in white, and never going out. A charwoman occasionally brought her what supplied her wants. Her only companions were the bull-dog, which she nursed like a child, and two cats. Her house was filled with images of soldiers in lead, which she called her 'body-guards.' When the collectors called for their taxes, they had to cross the garden-wall to gain admission. One morning she was found dead in bed; and a surgeon who was called in, said she had died of bronchitis, and might have recovered with proper medical aid. The jury returned a verdict to that effect. (1850)

January 30th

At the Marylebone Police Office on the 30th, J. Gammage, master of a National School at Paddington, was charged with having Cruelly Ill-used a William Taylor, one of his pupils, a delicate little boy, 10 years of age. The witnesses examined proved the boy had been so severely caned for a breach of school discipline, that large wheals, from one of which blood flowed, were produced on his shoulders and sides. In reply it was alleged that the boy had behaved with great impropriety while in attendance on a lecture in the school, and required correction, and also that he was generally unruly; and a number of testimonials from clergymen, which set forth that the defendant was a man much respected, firm of purpose, and kind towards his pupils, were produced. The Rev. Mr. Boone spoke in the highest terms of the defendant, whose salary had recently, in consequence of his valuable services, been raised. The magistrate considered that the chastisement was of much too severe a nature, and inflicted a penalty of 40*s.* The amount was paid by the Rev. W. Boone, who considered it a very hard case. (1850)

January 31st

Letters received from the British fleet in the Pirteus mention a fatal accident to Lieutenant Breen, and part of a crew under his command, on the 31st of January. Lieutenant Breen, and Mr. Chatfield, midshipman, with sixteen men, were returning from the shore to the *Ganges* in a boat laden with water; they were swamped by the rough sea, and their boat turned over just halfway between the ship Queen and the east point of the island of Lypso. Mr. Breen, Mr. Chatfield, and most of the men, immediately struck out for the island, and reached it. The gale increased, and the cold became so intense that their clothes were frozen stiff upon them. In the morning they could see the fleet, but were unable to catch attention by signals. One of the men suffered so much from the cold that Lieutenant Breen generously stripped off his coat and put it over him. As the day closed, most of the men retired into a cave; but Mr. Breen separated himself from the others, and was no more seen.

On board the *Ganges* it was thought they had not put off from shore; but next night it was known that they had set out, and a boat was sent to search. As it was passing by the island of Lypso at dawn of the third day, the wrecked boat was accidentally descried on the beach. Mr. Chatfield and half-a-dozen men were found in the cave, in a torpid state; Mr. Breen was found dead, crouched under a bush; and ten seamen are missing. There is little doubt that poor Mr. Breen lost his life from his generous act in favour of the suffering seaman. The survivors found in the cave have all recovered. (1850)

February

[During this month] a fatal and distressing Accident happened at Leith. A party had assembled in the house of an eminent merchant, and while amusing themselves in the drawing room, at a late hour in the evening, two young gentlemen, one of them, the son of the host, commenced in dalliance to fence with a couple of swords, when either by an awkward thrust, or some accidental slip or push, the short sword used by the latter entered his friend's side under the right bowel, and inflicted a mortal wound. He lingered for some days before he expired. The unfortunate young man was also the son of a most respectable merchant in Leith; he had only lately entered on business, and gave high promise of becoming one of the foremost mercantile men of the place. (1855)

🕭 *February 2nd* 🕭

Edmund Francis Hunt, a plasterer, of Bath, Drowned Himself and an Infant Child on the 2nd. Hunt was industrious and well-conducted, but his wife wasteful, drunken, and dishonest: she had several times been imprisoned for theft. This preyed on the husband's mind: in autumn last, when she was in gaol, where she was delivered of a child, he threatened that if she ever again committed a robbery, he would destroy himself. On the 2nd she was taken into custody for shoplifting, and a neighbour informed Hunt of this at night. Hunt, who had been drinking a little, became excited, and hastened home. At the inquest, his son deposed: 'As soon as father came home, he asked, 'Where's mother?' and I told him I did not know. My little sister, who was up stairs in bed, then called out 'Father!' My father told me to go up stairs and fetch her. I gave him my sister, and asked him to come up to bed. He told me to go up to bed, and said he should not see my face any more. When in bed I heard my father go out and shut the back-door. I then heard him say something to my sister, but I could not understand what it was. My sister was two-and-a-half years old. She was my only sister, and my father was particularly fond of her. He liked her better than all the rest of us, and often had her brought down stairs to him when he came home.' The river Avon flowed at the back of the house, and thither he proceeded with his child. Their bodies have since been found in the stream – the child's near Bristol. The verdict of the coroner's jury was 'Temporary Insanity'. (1850)

🕭 *February 3rd* 🕭

An investigation took place at the Kent Petty Sessions on the 3rd inst., respecting the Treatment of the Patients in a Lunatic Asylum at West Mailing, belonging to Dr. Maddock. The proceedings were instituted by the Commissioners in Lunacy. The complaint, framed under the Act of Parliament of the 8th and 9th, Victoria, Cap. 59, was against Dr. Maddock, the proprietor, and Mr. Perfect, the medical officer of the establishment, and charged them with having made false entries in the medical visitation book, and falsely represented that there were no persons in the asylum who were under restraint, when, in point of fact, it had been the constant practice for a considerable period to subject a great number of the patients, both male and female, to almost continual restraint. Two male and a female attendant were examined, and from their evidence it appeared that it had been the constant practice to restrain the patients; some of them by spring body-belts and handcuffs, others by iron leg-hobbles, and some were fastened to staples fixed in the floor.

Other patients, in addition to the iron belt, had gloves attached to straps, by which the hands were fastened to the sides. Some of the patients when in bed were also secured by leg-hobbles, which were strapped to the bedstead. Similar restraint was made use of with the female patients; and it was stated that in July, 1849, one of them was fastened by her ankle to a staple in the floor, and that in the spring of 1850 another female patient was confined by means of a strait-waistcoat and leg locks, or hobbles. It appeared in the course of the evidence that upon the occasions when the establishment was visited by the magistrates, or by the Commissioners in Lunacy, Dr. Maddock ordered all the patients to be released, and all the instruments of coercion to be put out of sight. The witnesses, however, admitted that some of the patients had been violent and dangerous, and that Dr. Maddock treated the patients generally with humanity. The magistrates called upon both the defendants to enter into recognisances of 200*l.*, with two sureties in 100*l.* each, for their appearance at the next Kent Assizes. (1851)

February 4th

A Shipwreck has taken place attended with Appalling Circumstances. The vessel was the *Bona Dea* of Liverpool, from Savanna. She was found at sea on the 4th inst. by the brig *Cuba*, water-logged, with several people on board, in a dreadful state, having been eleven days without food (except what they obtained by horrible means) or water. The following painful account is given by the survivors.

...The horrors of starvation now broke upon them, and their thirst was almost maddening. They at night discovered a kitten, which had crawled out from below; it was instantly killed and greedily devoured. Symptoms of insanity presented itself among some of the men ... Most of them now began to despair; some were delirious; and others commenced talking about sacrificing one of the number to save the rest from being starved to death. The men proposed that they should draw lots to decide who it should be ... Wednesday, Feb. 1:– One poor fellow, James Lilley, who appeared to be in a dying state, offered himself to save the rest. Mr. McLeod interfered, and cheered them up with the prospect of being soon relieved. No water. Thursday:– The weather moderating. The men were now become unmanageable. They were determined to have the dying man sacrificed. The poor fellow had offered to do the deed himself, and he cut his arms in two places, to bleed to death, but no blood came. The men afterwards surrounded him, and one of them cut his throat. Mr. McLeod says the scene that followed was most horrible – too horrible to detail. Friday:– Many of the men frantically mad, and crawling about the deck in a shocking state; the remainder nearly prostrate and unable to move ...

At about nine o'clock [on the twelfth day at sea] a vessel was observed through the haze. Their situation had been observed, and the vessel was running down to the wreck, and in about an hour she hove to and sent a boat to them. The vessel proved to be the *Cuba*, of Sunderland, bound to Swansea from Coquimbo, Capt. F.G. Organ master. By the *Cuba* the poor men were relieved, as already reported. (1854)

🕱 *February 5th* 🕱

George Wild, a policeman of the M Division, was tried on the 5th for Stealing Rabbit-Skins. Much interest was excited on account of the antecedents of the accused: he had been in the police ten years, had held a high character, and was very active in detecting crime; through his means thirty persons have been transported, and more than a hundred summarily convicted for robbery. Mrs. Sinnetts, a furrier, occupied some cellars in Southwark as warehouses for skins; it was suspected that the place was robbed; application was made to Wild, and he undertook to investigate the matter. To attempt to catch the thieves, he and one of Mrs. Sinnett's sons watched at night; and eventually Wild was left in the place by himself. An air-hole communicated from one of the cellars with the Crossbones burial-ground. The prisoner appears to have thrust a number of skins through this hole; then he got admission through a house into the ground, and took away a bag-full of skins; but as the tenant of the house suspected and questioned him, he took the bag and part of the skins to Mrs. Sinnett's son, pretending that a robber had thrust them into the grave-yard, and that he had noticed the articles through the railings. A number of skins were found in a yard near Wild's lodging, and there was no doubt he threw them there. (1850)

☠ *February 6th* ☠

A gang of burglars attempted to Break into Windsor Castle on the night of the 6th. Colonel Hood, Clerk Marshal to Prince Albert, arrived at Windsor at midnight. He took a short cut to the Castle by way of the Slopes; as he was walking forward, he encountered seven or eight men with their faces blackened, and who seemed to have their feet muffled. On perceiving Colonel Hood they ran off. It turned out that the band had been seen by a sentry on the terrace, who threatened to fire, and they answered they would blow his brains out if he did, or if he gave an alarm. At this moment Colonel Hood came up, and the burglars fled. The police turned out, but no traces of the band could be found. (1854)

Meanwhile, Jean Marie Courtoil, a foreigner, has been committed by the Marlborough Street magistrate for a singular Robbery. At midnight he entered Mr. Tyrell's cigarshop in the Haymarket; and, as he pretended to the woman in charge that he was a surgeon, he was allowed to pass on to a parlour. Mrs. Tyrell happened to have fallen asleep in her chair in the parlour; she was aroused by a tickling sensation about her ears; when she awoke, the prisoner was standing over her, and he dropped the earrings which he had just disengaged. He attempted to escape; pushed Mrs. Tyrell down in the shop, and ran into the street: but a policeman seized him. (1854)

☠ *February 7th* ☠

Mr. W. H. Apperley, a land-agent, was Attacked by Highwaymen on the 7th. Whilst returning in the evening from Abergavenny towards Hereford in his gig alone, he was stopped by three men in a lonely part of the road. Perceiving that resistance was useless, and having a sum of money upon his person, he leaped from the gig over the fence down into a strip of land adjoining the river, the field being here many feet below the road; almost before he regained his feet, he heard the horse and gig roll over the fence also. He ran for assistance, and found three men at home in a cottage not three hundred yards distant, who immediately returned with him; they found the horse and gig (the latter doubtless upset in its passage over the fence) near the river. The highwaymen had followed the gig down the place, and ransacked the contents; but the only booty they obtained was a letter-case, and about five or six French coins. Not the least damage was sustained by either horse, gig, or harness. (1850)

🕱 *February 8th* 🕱

At the Central Criminal Court, on the 8th, Margaret Higgins and Elizabeth Smith were indicted on a charge of robbing Mr. Frederick Hardy Jewett, a solicitor, after having Stupefied him with Chloroform. Between nine and ten o'clock on the evening of Jan. 10th, whilst proceeding slowly along the Whitechapel Road, he felt somebody, he believed a woman, touch his left side, and a rag or handkerchief pressed over the lower part of the face. He became insensible until the following morning, when he slowly revived, and found himself lying on a very dirty bed in a wretched apartment, and in a complete state of nudity, with the exception of an old piece of rag which had been carelessly thrown over him. Some of his clothes were in the room; other articles had been stolen, with his watch, jewellery, and money. His trowsers were muddy, as if he had been dragged through the streets. The door of the room was fastened by a padlock outside; he found the key on the floor; he pushed it under the door to a potman who happened to be in the house, and was thus liberated. He found that he had been conveyed to a low lodging-house in Thrall Street, Spitalfields. Policemen and other witnesses gave evidence. The women rented the room; when arrested, they accused each other. Higgins had been heard to say that she had 'done' the robbery. She told a woman that a man named Gallagher, with whom she cohabited, had undergone an operation at the London Hospital, where they had given him some stuff to send him to sleep, and that he had contrived to bring some of it away with him. The jury returned a verdict of 'Guilty', and the prisoners were sentenced to be transported for fifteen years. It is doubtful whether the unfortunate gentleman will ever recover from the effects of the treatment he suffered. (1850)

🕱 *February 9th* 🕱

A horrible affair has occurred near Bantry. Mrs. Sullivan, wife of a farmer in the vicinity, from some cause had fallen helpless in a field, and a Number of Starving Dogs Devoured Her. Her remains were found in the field, the bones of the limbs stripped of the flesh.

A child, fifteen months old, has died in Dublin from an Attack by Rats. They got into the cradle at night, bit the child in several places, and ate away half of the inside of one of the arms. (1854)

💀 *February 10th* 💀

William Smyth, a surgeon, in good practice, residing in Vauxhall Walk, was charged on the 10th, at Lambeth Police Court, with an Assault on Mary Ann Hall, a girl thirteen years of age. The evidence disclosed scenes of the most disgusting profligacy. It appeared that the prisoner, who is a married man and nearly 60 years of age, but separated from his wife, had in his confidence two strumpets, whom he induced to invite to his house a number of girls whose ages ranged from sixteen to eighteen years. Once within his reach, the prisoner commenced by plying his victims with spirits or wine; and the names of seven or eight were mentioned whom he thus succeeded to ruin. The magistrate exclaimed that in the whole course of many years' experience it had not been his misfortune to hear disclosed such a scene of abominable profligacy, which made one doubt whether we lived in a civilised or barbarous state of society. An application to be admitted to bail was indignantly refused. (1851)

💀 *February 11th* 💀

Edward Staggles, a youth of 18, was brought before the Southwark Police Court, on a charge of Attempting to Murder Mr. Barber, a manufacturing chemist at Bermondsey. He had formerly been in Mr. Barber's employ; one night Mr. Barber found him in his manufactory, and was almost blinded by a powerful acid solution which the young ruffian threw in his face. Mr. Barber locked the then unknown assailant in the place, and fetched a neighbour. Staggles had then got into an upper floor, and through a trap-door he fired two pistols at Mr. Barber; one bullet went through the hair and wounded a finger, the other passed along the back, but merely tore the clothing. Mr. Barber courageously mounted the ladder and seized him, and he made no further resistance. He was committed for trial at the Central Criminal Court. (1852)

💀 *February 12th* 💀

A case, curiously illustrative of the Profits of Mendicancy, has occurred at the Isle of Wight Borough Court. A vagrant, named David Brooks, pretending to be deaf and dumb, was brought up in custody, having been found lying drunk on the pavement on Sunday evening. He wrote on his slate, in a good firm hand, that the landlords and landladies of the town had behaved in a shameful way to him, by refusing him a bed, but that if he was liberated for this time he would leave the town directly. On searching his pockets, the constable turned out a Prayer-book, and some written prayers and cards, which he offered to the notice of the humane and benevolent; and amongst the collection appeared several memorandum books, by which it was clearly proved that he kept a daily entry of his collections and expenditure, as well as the 'Beggar's Directory', containing the names and residences of the charitable throughout the kingdom, with the roosting-places for the night. Some idea may be formed of the amount of money collected by these vagabonds, when it appears from this man's cash-book, that the islands of Jersey and Guernsey furnished him with the sum of 10*l*. 3*s*. for twelve days' trouble in collecting it. Ryde contributed 20*s*. during the previous week, and in several other towns the sums varied from 5*s*. to 34*s*. the day. Cirencester is marked down 'Not charitable', no sum being entered opposite the name. To other places where little cash was given or to be expected, it was marked 'No go'; and several fourpenny beds were noted down as 'small and uncomfortable'. (1851)

February 13th

A young fisherman, named Gee, sued a Mr. Elliff, an opulent farmer, residing in Holbeach Marsh, for 50*l*., as compensation for injuries sustained from being purposely shot by the defendant [at Lincolnshire, on the 13th]. On the 7th of December, the plaintiff went upon some land belonging to a Mr. Wooley, and killed a hare. He was about going away from the spot, when he saw the defendant (Mr. Elliff) in an adjoining field. The defendant followed him, and on nearing him, he pointed a double-barrelled gun close to Gee's head, and vowed he would mark him. He kept walking up with the plaintiff, when he suddenly lingered behind, and the plaintiff distinctly heard a percussion-cap explode, and the contents of one of the barrels lodged in the ground. The plaintiff then addressed Elliff, and said, 'Surely you don't mean to shoot me in this lonely place?' He replied, 'I do mean to shoot you.' After accompanying him about a quarter of a mile, he stopped, and having taken a deliberate aim, fired, and the shot of the second barrel struck him in the right hand and arm, inflicting serious wounds. The defendant then exclaimed, 'Now I can take you; I have marked you, so I shall know you again, and I will go back and look for the hare.' The plaintiff then contrived to crawl on to Holbeach, enduring the most excruciating agony, when he was taken into custody for trespassing in pursuit of game, and was committed to Spalding gaol for one month. Mr. Wilkinson, a surgeon, attended the wounded man in prison. There were from thirty to forty shot wounds on his right arm and hand; and great fears were entertained of lock-jaw setting in. The injuries he had sustained had entirely prevented him doing any work since. The Revd Mr. Morton, a magistrate, before whom the case was first brought, stated that he asked defendant why he committed so rash an act as to shoot Gee, when he replied that he had merely done so to 'mark him'. The judge (Mr. J.D. Burnaby) said, the act of the defendant in firing at Gee was wholly unjustifiable. In calculating damages he did not consider the loss of time for the month's imprisonment, because plaintiff had rendered himself liable to that by trespassing in pursuit of game, but considered the acute pain endured in gaol, and the probable loss of time to come; and he gave a verdict for plaintiff for 38*l.* and costs. (1851)

February 14th

The Revd James Commeline, rector of Redmarley, in Gloucestershire, has Lost his Life from Reading in Bed. The book had been placed on a reading-stand at his bedside, and it is supposed he had dozed off for a few minutes, as the inmates of the house were suddenly alarmed by hearing his screams, and on rushing into the room they found the bed in flames and the room filled with smoke. He was found to be badly burned, and died two days afterwards. (1853)

February 15th

Garotte Robberies have been renewed at Leeds. On the 15th inst., two men, named Lockwood and Murphy, the one a nut hawker, the other a hawker of oysters, were charged at the Leeds Court-house with 'garrotting' and robbing a person named Goodall, while on his way home, a few nights before. Goodall had been at the Horse and Jockey, public-house, Hunslet-lane, where the prisoners went to hawk their wares. They saw that he had money, and dogged his footsteps until he arrived at a lonely place called Leatherley-lane, where Murphy seized him by the throat from behind, and while nearly strangled, Goodall saw

Lockwood come in front of him, and rifle his pockets of their contents, amounting to some 15*s.* in silver. Both men were subsequently captured by detective officers, and are positively sworn to by the prosecutor. They are committed for trial at York Assizes. (1853)

February 16th

John Baguley, aged 70, who died at Chilwell, near Nottingham, on the 16th, Confessed on his death-bed that 23 years ago he Murdered a Hawker, and robbed him of shawls, blankets, &c., and disposed of the body. At the period of his sudden disappearance, the murdered man professed to be courting one of Baguley's daughters and, as he was known to be in possession of a considerable sum of money he was looked upon as being a rather desirable suitor, especially as the Baguleys were very poor. The hawker had not been missing more than twelve months before their circumstances began to improve, and from the poverty-stricken labourer Baguley became suddenly a comfortable cottager, with a number of pigs in his sty. Baguley's first wife, whenever she quarrelled with her husband, was in the habit of putting a stop to the violence of his temper by saying, 'Be quiet, John; you know I have your coat of arms upstairs,' alluding to some bloody clothes that were supposed to be kept in a lodging-room. This first Mrs. Baguley died five or six years ago, and said, a short time previously, that she had something on her mind which she should like to reveal; but this coming to her husband's knowledge, he never afterwards would allow a stranger to go to her room. The present Mrs. Baguley was married to him three years, and since which time she says his conduct has been very strange. In his sleep frequently he would jump up in a state of great excitement and exclaim that some one was about to seize him.

The day before he died he said to her, 'The pick that I did it with is in the dyke;' and other revelations followed. It is singular that the cottage in which the murder was committed has never since been occupied for any length of time, and in it periodically strange nocturnal noises are said to be heard. 'The Chilwell Ghost,' and tales respecting 'the haunted house at Chilwell,' have during the last twenty years dismayed many thousands of persons residing within a circle of 150 miles of the locality. (1850)

🕱 *February 17th* 🕱

Binstead, the seat of Lord Downes, near Ryde, in the Isle of Wight, was totally Consumed by Fire on the 17th. His lordship and family were crossing from Portsmouth, and saw the conflagration from the deck of the steamer: they were going to Binstead for a short time, the house having been prepared for their reception. (1851)

🕱 *February 18th* 🕱

At the Worship-street Police Court, on the 18th, William Edwards, a bird fancier, was charged with a most aggravated Assault upon his Wife, an emaciated and sickly looking woman. She stated that the defendant, who resided at Hoxton, had been married to her two years. She had borne him one child, yet living, but his treatment since their unfortunate acquaintance had been most cruel and unfeeling. For the last month she had absented herself from his dwelling, and supported nature as best she could; but last night, having failed in procuring relief from the parish, she was compelled to seek her husband at his father's, and there begged him to give her some bread. With the foulest language he refused, and threatening to rip her up and murder her, struck her heavily to the ground with his clenched fist. On rising he renewed the attack, beating her about the neck; 'indeed,' she said, 'I am bruised all over; my head is covered with lumps from the blows he gave me, and my body with bruises from kicks; besides this when he got me on the ground he attempted to strangle me with his hands round my throat.' The woman's features were swelled and blackened, while the impress of the fingers was distinctly visible on her throat. In defence the brute endeavoured to justify the outrage by declaring that his wife pledged their things, and on such occasions it was that he struck her. The magistrate said it was no wonder that she had recourse to that step, to procure the bread that her unmanly husband withheld from her. It was manifest that the defendant's cruelty towards her was systematic. For the present brutal outrage he should send him to the House of Correction with hard labour for six months. (1854)

February 19th

An action was brought in the County Court of Cornwall, on the 19th, on behalf of a boy named Robins, against William Brabyn, a schoolmaster of Withiel, arising out of a Savage Punishment. The master beat the boy on the head with a stick; the brain was afflicted, and blindness and deafness resulted. The jury gave a verdict of 20*l*. damages. (1850)

February 20th

A Fire broke out at Trinity Hall, Cambridge, on the 20th, about six o'clock in the morning, which very nearly destroyed the whole building; that part in which it raged was gutted by nine o'clock, but all danger of its extension was then over. The cause is not yet known, but is believed to have been either a spark from a candle left as a light on the staircase, or a beam running into a flue. The college is insured. Mr. Nunn, who was sleeping in an adjoining room to that in which the fire broke out, had a narrow escape. (1852)

February 21st

At the High Court of Justiciary, Edinburgh, on the 21st inst., John Williams, an American, was charged with the Murder of Andrew Mather, toll-keeper, on the 4th or 5th of December last, on the turnpike-road between Cleikumin Inn and Toll, parish of Lauder, Berwickshire. The deceased not returning home on the night of Saturday, the 4th of December, his daughters went out in search of him, and found him lying on the road-side, and the prisoner beside him. The clothes of the deceased were all torn, and he was nearly naked above the breast. There was a great deal of blood on his head and neck which were disfigured with wounds. When they went to seek for assistance, the accused ran away. He was apprehended two days after; and, on being questioned, he said he had killed the man, and that the devil had tempted him. He said he did not think they would hang him; but, if they transported him, it was just what he wanted, as he could not get back to his own country any other way. The jury found the prisoner guilty, and the court expressed concurrence in the verdict. He was sentenced to be executed at Greenlaw, the county town of Berwickshire, on Monday, the 14th of March. (1853)

February 22nd

A fearful Murder has been committed at Wakefield. The victim is a girl named Catherine Sheardon, a prostitute, living in the house of Ann Clough; and the person who committed the horrid crime is a man named Henry Dobson, a cabinet-maker, about twenty-four years of age. The murdered girl was found in a room by the woman of the house, lying across the room, on her side; a wound, two or three inches deep, had been inflicted on the left side of the neck, severing the jugular vein entirely, and giving evidence that death had been instantaneous. A razor, covered with blood, was found on the floor; and in one of her hands was found the street-door key. It is supposed that Dobson, having entered the house, had caught the girl in his arms, and using, perhaps, some expressions of endearment towards her, for she appears to have made no struggle, had suddenly cut her throat. He at once made his escape from the house, and on the entry of Clough she found deceased on the floor, quite dead, no one else being in the house at the time. The tragedy must have taken place within a very short time, as Clough asserts she was not absent from her house more than twenty minutes in all. Information of the affair was at once given to the police, and within an hour Dobson was apprehended. While on the way to the station-house, he asked repeatedly if the girl was dead, and on being told she was, he replied, 'And I have done it – what more do you want?' He added, 'You are a pretty set of devils, you police; I have been within twenty yards of the place all the time.' He was much excited, and appeared to have been drinking; he was not, however, at all drunk. An inquest has been held on the body, and a verdict of 'Wilful Murder' having been returned, Dobson has been committed to York Castle for trial. (1853)

February 23rd

A Melancholy Suicide has been committed by a poor woman named Stone, in Dean-street, Westminster. About seven years ago, her husband, an engineer, died, and was buried in the Broadway churchyard. The widow was left unprovided for, and left London to take a situation in Kent, where she was not successful. At the beginning of the present month, she took lodgings in Dean-street. Nothing having been seen of her, her door was broken open, and she was found lying dead on the floor. Mr Heath, the surgeon of Bridge-street, was of the opinion that she had been dead seven or eight days. He found on the mantelpiece two bottles labelled 'poison';

and upon a post-mortem examination, he discovered about an ounce of laudanum in the stomach. She had been in the habit for two years of going to the churchyard and weeping over the grave of her husband. In her room the following letter was found:

> To save trouble, Mrs. Ann Stone came by her death by a draught of laudanum, no one knowing that she did take it, as she is a total stranger in the house she is in. Every effort she has made to obtain an honest living failed her. She has the presumption to throw her soul in the presence of the Almighty and she fervently prays that God will have mercy on her soul. Good Christians, do not allow a number of persons to look on my unfortunate body. I have performed all the offices that are requisite; the body is quite ready for the coffin.

She then begs that she may be buried in the same grave with her husband, and expressed a fear that the New Victoria-street might destroy it. She concludes – 'If I could have died on my husband's grave-stone, I would have done so.' (1852)

February 24th

Major Charles Colville Young, a distinguished officer of the Royal Horse Artillery, who had just returned from the Crimea where he has wounded, has been Killed by a lamentable accident at Portsmouth. His wife and children reside at Ryde; on his way to join them, he arrived in the evening at the Fountain Hotel. On retiring to his bedroom, he told the boots to call him at seven next morning. When the boots left him, he had partially undressed himself. The bedroom was at the top of the hotel, facing the street. About two in the morning Major Young hailed a policeman from the window. He said he did not feel well, and wished to get quietly out of the house to a chemist's shop opposite, without disturbing the people, as it was so late. The policeman went to the inspector, to see what assistance he could give; and when he returned the major was lying bleeding on the pavement. He was fully dressed, and had his hat, great coat, and umbrella. When found he was unconscious; he never rallied, and died in less than two hours, apparently from the rupture of a blood-vessel. Major Young was a tall man; the height of the window-sill from the floor was only two feet four inches: it is supposed that the major was seized with vertigo while leaning out of window, and fell over this low sill. The verdict of the coroner's jury was 'killed by accidentally falling from a window.' (1855)

🕷 *February 25th* 🕷

John Drury, a painter in Carey Street, was Killed by a Fall on the 25th. He lived with his wife in a garret. They had had a quarrel and a fight, which was put an end to by a fellow-lodger, and the wife went down stairs. Drury said he would not meet his wife again by descending the stairs, but would go down by the waterspout on the outside of the house, as he had often done before. He made the attempt, fell into the yard, and died on the spot. (1850)

🕷 *February 26th* 🕷

An inquest on the body of Mr. James Gibbs, of Bristol, one of the Directors of the Great Western Railway, who was Killed by an accident on that railway, was held on the 26th. Mr. Gibbs was a vitriol-manufacturer at Bristol; he was sixty-one years of age. It was said that recently he had a presentiment that he should meet with some mishap on the railway; and he wished to resign his seat as a Director for the Bristol interest, but was induced by his colleagues and friends to remain in office. A few weeks before the accident he insured his life in the Railway Passengers' Insurance Company for 1000*l*. On his right temple there was a small incised wound, and the surrounding parts were suffused with blood; the right fore-arm was fractured; and there was a dislocation of the vertebrae of the neck – the latter alone sufficient to cause instant death … It is a remarkable fact, that when persons travelling in a railway carriage become alarmed, the first thing they do is to look out of window: nothing could be more dangerous, for if an accident happened, they receive injuries from their head knocking from one side of the window to the other. From the appearance of the right temple, he had no doubt that such was the case with the unfortunate deceased gentleman. The jury gave a verdict of 'Accidental death'. (1853)

🕷 *February 27th* 🕷

At Marylebone Police Office, on the 27th, Elizabeth Higgins, wife of a wheelwright, was committed to Newgate for trial, charged with Attempting to Murder her Three Children, respectively of the ages of seven years, five years, and seven months. Anne West, in passing along the Bloomfield Road on the 18th, saw the accused on the towing-path of the Regent's Canal; she had the three children with her; she lowered the baby into the water, put another child in, and then walked in herself with the third child. West saw this through a paling; she raised an alarm, and two men came up. One of these, John Rollins, a painter, plunged into the canal, and successively rescued all four. The mother was taken to the Paddington workhouse. To the inquiries of a police inspector there, she alleged her husband's cruelty and ill-usage as the cause of the act. She said: 'He earns 21s. a week, and out of that he gives me the odd 1s. to keep house and find everything: the 20s. he spends entirely upon himself. He comes home drunk, pulls me out of bed, and beats me, saying that he will be the death of me, and that it shall not be a sudden but a lingering death. I have also been afraid that he would poison me, and I thought that I and my children might as well have died at once as not.' The magistrate warmly applauded the conduct of Rollins and Mrs. West for their exertions in this distressing case. (1850)

February 28th

On the 28th, Frederick Drew, a solicitor's clerk who applied cancelled stamps to deeds in Chancery with a view to Defraud the Revenue, was convicted. The case was peculiar. Drew was defendant in a Chancery suit; he was very poor; he was compelled to put in certain documents, stamped; to save expense, or probably as the only way to meet it, he took stamps from old deeds and applied them to his papers. The jury recommended him to mercy on account of his previous good character, and because he had 'the misfortune to be defendant in a Chancery suit.' (1855)

February 29th

A whole family, with some friends, numbering altogether sixteen persons, were Poisoned lately at Bishop's Sutton, in Somersetshire, by eating some pancakes which had accidentally been mixed up with an ounce of white arsenic, sold by mistake for carbonate of soda, which was to have been used for lightening the pancakes. Medical assistance was obtained before it was too late, and fortunately no lives were lost. (1851)

March

March 1st

At the Central Criminal Court, on the 1st inst., William Anderson, formerly a merchant, was convicted of Forging and Uttering Bills of Exchange, amounting in all to 7,888*l.*, with intent to defraud Messrs. Overend, Gurney, & Co., and sentenced to eight years' penal servitude. The prisoner, upon hearing his sentence pronounced, suddenly drew himself up to his full height and opened his eyes to a fearful extent, his jaw dropped, his colour fled, and he became a livid blue, and making one or two convulsive efforts to hold the dock, he fell quite stiff into the arms of the gaoler. The Chief Baron added, that if there was any ground for mitigation it might be taken elsewhere. Hearing this, he tried to raise his hands over his head, and indistinctly ejaculating 'There is, there is,' fell quite senseless across the gaoler, and was carried out of the dock. (1854)

At the Clare Assizes an old man named Quinlivan was found guilty of the Murder of a poor woman, who had been left the sum of two shillings by her husband to support her during his absence in search of work. The prisoner, who was a neighbour, was aware of this circumstance, and, it appears, committed the crime for the sake of that wretched amount. (1850)

☠ *March 2nd* ☠

Edwin Harris was tried, on the 2nd, at the Winchester Assizes, for Stabbing his Wife, with intent to murder her. It appeared that these persons, who seemed decent people, had been married twenty years. Differences at last arose between them, which ended in a separation; but they had so far become reconciled as to meet and walk together; and shortly before Christmas-day they arranged to dine together on that day … They met again on the 27th of December. She went to his lodging, and made his tea. He cried, and kissed her. They saw his landlord, who said he wondered he would be seen with his wife after what he had called her. His countenance instantly changed. She said he dared not repeat the words in her presence, and she became angry, and said if he repeated it she would slap his face; she had always been a faithful and virtuous wife to him, and had supported herself by staymaking during the time she lived separately from him. After the words had passed in the public-house, they left, and walked together some distance without speaking a word. At length the prisoner said, 'What did he say?' alluding to what the landlord had said. He then said, 'There's no knowing the heart of any man;' and he began to push his wife. She told him not to do so. He laid hold of her, and she thought he was going to kiss her. She remonstrated with him, and she then saw him draw a knife from his pocket, and he attempted to cut her throat. She screamed, and they fell; he was still endeavouring to cut her throat. The cuts went through her shawl, bonnet, and ribands, and five wounds were inflicted on her face and neck. At the instant a young woman came up and seized the hand in which was the knife, and pulled his head back. She contrived to hold his hand and the knife for some time, till he got his hand away, and again cut at his wife, who screamed 'Murder!' and said, 'My dear, don't cut my throat!'

The other woman said, 'You bad man, you've killed the woman,' and she ran and procured assistance. She returned, and took the prisoner by the collar. He said, 'I'm not going to run away.' She said, 'I'll take care you don't, you bad man;' and she gave him into the custody of two policemen. The wife was confined to her bed for some time. When the prisoner was sober he was very kind to his wife; but he was given to drink, and was then very excitable; he would change in a moment. It was urged for the defence that the prisoner's act arose from an uncontrollable jealous impulse. The jury returned a verdict of Guilty, with intent to do grievous bodily harm; and the prisoner was sentenced to be transported for life. Mr. Justice Talfourd told the young woman who had tendered such assistance, that he could not let her go without saying how much they were all indebted to her for the great courage she had displayed; he had never heard of any one acting so well, he had the power of awarding a small sum to a person for apprehending a felon; and he should, therefore, in this case award her 5*l*., and he hoped she would purchase some trifle that might be kept by her and her family in remembrance of her courageous act. (1851)

🕱 *March 3rd* 🕱

A frightful Explosion of Naphtha, by which two persons lost their lives, viz., Mr. Chas. Blackford Mansfield, M.A., Cambridge, and a law student of the Middle Temple, aged 35, lately residing at Weybridge, and George Coppin, a practised chemist's assistant, aged 18, came under investigation on the 3d inst. at the Middlesex Hospital, before the coroner, Mr. Mansfield, who had studied at the College of Chemistry was, on the day of the catastrophe, trying experiments with a small model naphtha apparatus which he had invented himself and patented, in an old detached building, situated in Agar Town, and abutting on the Regent's Canal, when, about one o'clock at noon, a loud explosion was heard, followed by the falling of the building. The unfortunate men were observed directly afterwards escaping from the ruins, and making towards the canal, their clothes all on fire. Assistance promptly arrived, when, by rolling them on the ground, the fire was extinguished, but not before they had been so fearfully burnt as to resemble more the appearance of shrivelled mummies than living human beings. (1855)

🕱 *March 4th* 🕱

At Oxford Assizes, on the 4th, John Lambourne, a middle-aged labourer, was tried for the Murder of his Wife. The woman was found dead in the garden of the cottage, her husband giving the first alarm; death had been caused by a wound on the head, apparently inflicted with a pair of tongs which were found in the house. The couple had often quarrelled, and Lambourne had sometimes beaten his wife – a poor diseased creature; he had often wished she was dead, and dropped suspicious expressions respecting her. On the other hand, there was no direct evidence against him, and no blood was found upon him, though that evidence of the murder had been scattered in all directions round the body. His counsel urged that robbers might have been the murderers. After deliberating for an hour the jury gave a verdict of acquittal. (1851)

💀 *March 5th* 💀

A Fatal Railway Accident happened on the morning of the 5th, on the London and North-Western Railway, near Kilburn-gate. While some 200 or 300 men were engaged in gangs in carrying out some alterations in the sleepers, a down coal train was heard approaching, which led a gang of five men incautiously to step aside on to the up-line. At the same moment the up-train was coming up; it had entered the curve, and was travelling at the rate of perhaps 35 miles an hour. Unhappily the men were unconscious of the close approach of the mail, and they coolly enough awaited the passing of the coal trucks. The driver of the mail engine sounded the steam whistle, but the unhappy men continued on the line, the noise of the coal train no doubt preventing them hearing the whistle. The next moment or so the train was upon them. By some extraordinary effort two of the men contrived to escape, but the other three met with a horrible and instantaneous death. The train went over their bodies, and they were found frightfully mutilated. Their limbs were severely mangled, and the head of one was picked up some twenty or thirty yards from the body. The mutilated remains were afterwards removed to the Kilburn station. An inquest was held on the bodies, when the jury returned a verdict of 'Accidental death', adding to their verdict a recommendation to the directors to take precautions to prevent the recurrence of the accident in future, by the men being more effectually warned on the approach of trains. (1852)

🕱 *March 6th* 🕱

Sarah Chesham, a masculine-looking woman, was tried at Chelmsford, on the 6th, for the crime of administering to Richard Chesham, her husband, a quantity of Arsenic, with intent to murder him. This case created much interest on account of the terrible celebrity gained by the prisoner. She was tried in 1847 at these assizes upon a charge of poisoning two of her children; but although the evidence was most cogent, and left very little doubt of her guilt, she obtained a verdict of acquittal. She was implicated in another charge of poisoning, when she again escaped justice; and in 1849, a woman named May, who was convicted of poisoning her husband, and who was executed for that offence, admitted, after her conviction, that she had been instigated by the prisoner to the commission of the dreadful act for which she suffered. The evidence fully brought home the charge to the prisoner. She administered arsenic in rice puddings to her husband, who, after many weeks' lingering, died in May, 1849. The jury returned a verdict of Guilty; and sentence of Death was passed by the judge. The woman heard her doom without the slightest apparent emotion. (1851)

🕱 *March 7th* 🕱

A young woman, Mary Donnellan, of Rinana, left the Ennis Fever Hospital on the 7th, and endeavoured to crawl home, faint and fasting, a distance of 10 miles; she got into some kind of a wretched old hovel, where she was found next day, Dead of Hunger and Exhaustion, and her face eaten away by rats. (1850)

🕱 *March 8th* 🕱

A case was tried at the Middlesex Sessions on the 8th inst., which excited much attention in consequence of the judge having Altered the Sentence on the Prisoner in consequence of her deportment after it was pronounced. Mary Hill, a woman of the town, was indicted for stealing a gold watch, the property of T. Unwin, from his person … The Assistant-judge, Mr. Sergeant Adams, asked if anything was known of her previous character, for if there was, it was a proper case for transportation, as this system of robbery with the aid of bullies was a very serious thing. The police-officer in this case said she was the associate of reputed thieves and bad characters, and she was with a regular gang when she was taken into custody. The Assistant-judge then sentenced her to seven years' transportation. The prisoner, who had gone down on her knees imploring mercy, on hearing this rose up, and screamed out to the policeman, 'You —— pig! Oh, you pig! You perjured thief.' The Assistant-judge: The sentence upon you now is, that you be transported for ten years. The prisoner repeated her exclamations, and was so violent that she had to be removed by two officers. [This case having been brought before the House of Commons by Sir De Lacy Evans, Lord Palmerston stated that the original sentence only was to be carried into effect.] (1853)

🕱 *March 9th* 🕱

A young man met a dreadful Death by Machinery on the 9th inst. His name was Charles Brookfield. He worked in the Hoyland Corn Mill, near Sheffield, and was employed in cleaning some part of the machinery with an old sack, when the sack got entangled with the spindles, and before he could disengage his hands he was caught up and whirled round a shaft at the rate of one hundred and twenty evolutions per minute. His lifeless body was found in a shockingly mangled condition. (1852)

🕱 *March 10th* 🕱

W. Smith, apprentice to Mr. Pope, tea-dealer, Finsbury-pavement, and John McNay, errand-lad, were charged at Guildhall, on the 10th, with Absconding from their Master's Service. A constable of the Detective Force had brought them in from Biggleswade, where they had been detained on suspicion of having committed some offence, as they were each armed with a pistol and a dirk, and had a greater supply of cash than might be expected from persons of their appearance. Mr. Pope accounted for the possession of the implements of death, by stating that the mind of his apprentice had been poisoned by reading novels of which robbers were the heroes, and he had no doubt from the purchases they had made that they had resolved to become villains of that class. He had run away for a few days on a former occasion, when he lurked about on the country roads; but upon voluntarily returning, and begging forgiveness, the complainant received him again into his house. Mr. Pope said he did not mean to press any charge against the errand-boy, and as to the apprentice he was willing to receive him again if he would solemnly pledge himself to the magistrate that he would never offend again. On obstinately refusing to do this, he was committed to work on the cranks at Bridewell, for three months. (1850)

💀 *March 11th* 💀

At the Bedford Assizes, on the 11th, Abel Burrows was indicted for the Wilful Murder of Charity Glenister, on the 25th of November last, and when called upon to plead 'guilty or not guilty,' he said, 'I don't know. If I am guilty, I was insane at the time.' This was treated as a plea of not guilty. The evidence showed that the prisoner, who lives in a wild district near Leighton Buzzard, called Heath and Reach, had, shortly before the 24th of November, exhibited such signs of violence that on that day his wife sent for his father and begged the old man to sleep with him on that night. The father complied. During the night the prisoner was very violent, and early in the morning of the 25th, after his father had gone to work, he got up, seized a stonebreaker's hammer, and threatened to take the life of Charity Glenister, an old woman of seventy, who lived with him and his wife. The deceased escaped from the house, and was followed by the prisoner, still holding the hammer. She escaped into the house of a neighbour, and he, mistaking that into which she had gone, rushed in and inquired for her and his wife, saying that he smelt them, that they had ruined his mother, that he would kill them both; that they would cause him to be hung. He then rushed out and went to the house where the deceased was, broke open the door with the hammer – for at the request of the old woman it had been closed against him – and made for her as she was trying to get up the stairs from him. Before she could get quite up, he felled her with a blow of the hammer, and then dealt her two more blows which completely smashed her head, and so extinguished life. Thereupon the prisoner exhibited signs of religious triumph, singing out, 'Glory, glory to the Lord. Hallelujah! Hallelujah!' The prisoner said nothing in his defence, but the governor of the gaol handed in a paper, which set forth that one of his aunts had died insane, and that it was well known that at times he was also insane. The statement as to the aunt was made out by a surgeon. It was also shown that the prisoner was at times of weak mind; that he often complained of his head, and that sometimes he was very violent. The learned judge placed these circumstances before the jury, but, after deliberating for about half an hour, they returned a verdict of wilful murder. The prisoner: 'The Lord's will be done.' The Chief Baron then passed sentence of death in the usual form, and the prisoner was removed from the dock, apparently quite insensible to the perilous position in which he stood. (1854)

🕱 *March 12th* 🕱

A melancholy Suicide has taken place at Woolwich. About six months ago, a publican residing there, in a respectable way of business, together with his son, a promising young man, about 24 years of age, were charged with carting and removing several cart loads of bricks belonging to the railway company, and depositing them on the premises of the father; and after an examination before the magistrate, they were sentenced, the father to undergo an imprisonment with hard labour for eighteen months, and the son to six months' and hard labour. The son's imprisonment expired on the 8th, whereupon he immediately returned to the inn kept by his father, and resumed his avocation of waiting upon the customers as usual, and whilst so doing on the 12th one of them incautiously made use of the expression, 'How about the bricks!' which appeared to have such an effect upon the mind of the young man, that he immediately repaired to a shed at the back part of the building, and hanged himself. He continued hanging, until his family, missing him, made a search, when he was found. He was immediately cut down, and medical assistance promptly procured, but life had been extinct for some time. (1850)

🕱 *March 13th* 🕱

The Worship Street Court was crowded on the 13th by a large number of persons, amongst whom were many well dressed women, anxious to be present at the adjourned hearing of a summons against William Calcraft, the public executioner, issued by the parish officers of the Witham Union, in Essex, for Refusing to Support his aged Mother, an inmate of that workhouse …

The magistrate asked the defendant if he had any reasonable grounds to assign for refusing to contribute to his mother's maintenance? Defendant: Well, I should be very happy to support her if it was in my power, but it is not; … I can assure you that I have not earned a penny [making shoes, his other trade] for a great number of weeks. I admit that I receive a guinea a week from the City; but that is all we have to live upon; and when you deduct out of that 4s. 5d. for rent and the cost of a Sunday's dinner, you will find that there is not much left. Magistrate: Well, you are clearly liable for the support of your mother, and I feel it my duty to make an order upon you for the sum of 3s. per week …

The order was about to be made, when the turned round sharply upon the relieving officer, and said, 'Well, now, suppose I took my mother to keep myself, what would you allow me for her? Come, that's the point. Certainly, if you allow me something for her, I may be able to get on perhaps.' – The officer expressed his belief that the mother would prefer being in the union. – The mother: Oh dear, yes; I should not be alive a week in London, whereas I should be safe in the country if they even left me upon the common. I prefer being in the workhouse, for I am very comfortable there. – The defendant thereupon leant over to his mother, expressing his willingness to take care of her, and, with apparent feeling, told her that he was very sorry she should have to come there; and, upon the order being made, and one of the officers coming forward to raise her out of the chair, the defendant pushed him aside, and gently raising her, with his arm round her waist, supported her out of the court. (1850)

🕱 *March 14th* 🕱

Captain Hutchinson, of the Royal Engineers, superintendent of the Holyhead harbour works, was lately Killed by an extraordinary accident. A blast was fired containing two tons of powder; and though Captain Hutchinson had removed to a distance of at least half a mile, an immense block of stone fell upon him, striking him dead, in his wife's presence. A labourer suffered a fracture of his leg; while a lady's dress was torn to fragments by the concussion of the air. (1851)

🕱 *March 15th* 🕱

A fearful Explosion of Fire-damp took place in the Victoria Mine, at Nitshill, near Paisley, early in the morning of Saturday the 15th, while sixty-three men and boys were in the mine. Unfortunately, the shock was so great that the gearing of the shaft and the sides of it were destroyed, and the shaft was filled with rubbish. Only two men at a time could work in clearing the ruins away, and meanwhile the relatives of the miners assembled and caused a most distressing scene. At midnight, so much of the debris had been removed that voices could be heard at the foot of the shaft. But it was not till four o'clock on Sunday afternoon that actual communication could be established with two men who still lived. Provisions were conveyed to them; at midnight, one man was extricated, in an exhausted state, and half an hour after the second was got out alive. These men said they had been working with two others in a part of the pit where the explosion was not very severe; they hastened towards the shaft, where there would be an in-draught of fresh air; but two perished by the way from the choke-damp. On Monday morning, the corpses of these sufferers were got out of the pit; and at that time no hope existed that any of the fifty-nine people missing had survived. It is stated by all the accounts that the ventilation of this mine was good; but it is believed that the calamity arose from some great sinking of the roof, or the penetration of some great cavity full of explosive gas. (1851)

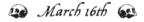

March 16th

At the village of Clayton-on-the-heights, near Halifax, on the 16th, a young man named Abraham Jessop Shot his Wife, to whom he had only recently been married, and afterwards Blew out his own Brains. Both were about twenty-five years of age, and though married but a few months, were living apart in consequence of domestic differences arising from Jessop's habits of intoxication. Jessop had latterly desired a reconciliation, but failing, sought an interview on the 16th, with a view to putting a period to all future strife, by murdering his wife, and afterwards destroying himself. After taking several glasses of ardent spirits at a public house to keep up his courage, he entered the house where his wife resided, and found her in the presence of her mother and sister. He asked her to accompany him to the door for a private conversation, but she declined. He attempted to induce her to listen to him in another room. This she also refused, and he then took from one of his coat pockets a pistol, and discharged it with the muzzle almost close to her person. The ball took effect in the left breast, but missed the heart. Before any attempt at interference could be made, he drew a second pistol, and placing the muzzle under his right ear, discharged the contents through his head. The unfortunate wife ran to the door, and sank upon the causeway in a state of insensibility. She was afterwards carried to bed, and surgical aid being procured and the wounds staunched, she still survives. It is feared, however, that the ball has passed through a portion of the lungs, and that she cannot ultimately recover. The wound which Jessop inflicted on himself was mortal. He fell upon the floor, and expired, his skull being fearfully shattered. (1850)

💀 *March 17th* 💀

Another frightful Explosion of a Railway Locomotive happened at Brighton on the 17th inst. On that morning the engine was about to be attached to a train which leaves Brighton at seven o'clock for Littlehampton; there were three people on the engine, driver, stoker, and engine-fitter; the locomotive was rent asunder with frightful force, and the metal fragments were hurled through the roof of the shed. The unfortunate men were torn to pieces, and some of the human fragments were found in a street three hundred yards from the station. The passengers were dreadfully alarmed, but not hurt. (1853)

💀 *March 18th* 💀

At Lincoln [in this month], Elizabeth Lownd, a girl of eighteen, was tried for the Murder of her Illegitimate Infant. She appears to have buried it alive – placed it on the ground, and covered it with earth and sods. She was in great distress when she committed the inhuman act. The jury gave a verdict for the lesser offence of 'manslaughter', Sentence, fifteen years' transportation. (1855)

💀 *March 19th* 💀

An alarming Fire broke out at Windsor Castle, on Saturday night, the 19th inst., a few hours after the arrival of the Royal Family from Buckingham Palace. The fire originated in the private apartments, which are situated in the Prince of Wales's Tower. On its ground floor stood the Gothic Dining-room, a very handsomely decorated apartment, and here Her Majesty and the Prince dined alone, as is their custom on the day of their arrival at the Castle. They had concluded their repast, and retired to an adjoining apartment, when dense volumes of smoke suddenly apprised the domestics that a fire had taken place behind the woodwork of the Dining-room. Every exertion was used to extinguish it, but the efforts were not successful until there had been a considerable destruction of property. The Prince of Wales's Tower is completely gutted, the roof even being destroyed, and the flames penetrated into portions of the Brunswick Tower, which adjoins, doing much injury there also. The apartments which have chiefly suffered are about a dozen bed-rooms and the Gothic Diningroom. The whole of the valuable furniture of the Red Drawing-room, which was placed in great jeopardy, was carefully removed by the soldiers and the Lord Chamberlain's men, and little damage is done to it, with the exception of the breaking of some of the glass of the magnificent chandeliers. In a very few minutes after the alarm was first given, the Fusileer Guards, 700 strong, were on the spot, and the 2nd Life Guards, under the command of Colonel Williams, followed with their barrack engine. The soldiers behaved manfully, some mounting the roof of the tower, some removing the furniture with the utmost care from the apartments contiguous to the conflagration, while others were using their utmost exertions at the engines. An express was despatched from the Castle to the London Fire Brigade, which arrived with two powerful engines, under the superintendence of Mr. Braidwood, at two o'clock in the morning. About this time the fire was partially got under, but it was not totally extinguished before four o'clock. Her Majesty remained during the whole time in the adjoining rooms, and happily has sustained no inconvenience from the alarm which such an event was likely to cause. The frost was so intense during the night as considerably to retard the action of the engines, while it favoured the action of the flames. The fire seems to have originated from a furnace-flue, situated at the basement of the Prince of Wales's Tower, for the purpose of heating the air which warms the Gothic Dining-room and many other apartments in this tower. (1853)

March 20th

At Exeter Assizes, on the 20th, Thomas King was found guilty of Attempting to Murder his aged Father and his housekeeper, with the object of effecting a robbery. On the 12th of February, he had gone to his father's, at Forder, and had supper; when he thought the old man was asleep, he went to his bedroom, cut him with a sharp instrument, beat him with the kitchen poker, and left him senseless. Then he went to the housekeeper's room, saying his father was ill; as soon as the woman opened the door, he felled her with the poker; and proceeded to rifle the house. He was taken at Plymouth next day, while attempting to sell his father's watch. The mangled victims subsequently revived a little; they were brought to the Sessions in a spring-van, quite helpless, and presented a pitiable spectacle. He was sentenced to transportation for life. (1850)

🕱 *March 21st* 🕱

In an action at Maidstone Assizes, on the 21st, brought by Miss Jane Emma Adams against Mr. Richard Gibbs, to recover damages for a Breach of Promise of Marriage, the defendant pleaded a special plea – that after making the promise of marriage to Miss Adams, he learned that she was suffering from an 'incurable disease called consumption', which would render her 'unable to perform the duties of a wife'. Mr. Gibbs was a neighbour of the plaintiff's father at Wateringbury, knew her from her infancy up, and made her a regular offer, with a full knowledge of her circumstances, in August, 1848, at which time she was twenty-four and he forty-eight. The licence was bought and the day fixed; but on the day of signing settlements the defendant disappeared, fled to America, and never reappeared till October, 1849, when he was found in London. It seems that two sisters of the plaintiff died young, of consumption, and that a brother went abroad to escape it. The medical attendant of the plaintiff admitted his having administered cod's-liver oil and other remedies very suitable for consumption, but said the plaintiff had not been ill of that disease. Several eminent London physicians, who had attended the plaintiff, were in court, attending the cause, but were not examined; neither plaintiff or defendant called for their evidence. The jury gave a verdict of 800*l*. (1850)

🕱 *March 22nd* 🕱

A lunatic, named Armsworth, has committed Suicide, near the Farnborough station. On Good Friday he was sent from the Union-house, to walk in the fields for the sake of his health, a person accompanying him as a guard though his quiet behaviour in the house had led to a belief that he was not at all disposed to suicide. When they were near the railway, an express-train was seen to approach; the lunatic darted away from his keeper, ran on to the rails, and advanced to meet the train; the people in charge of the train tried to stop it, but there was no time, and the madman was crushed to death. (1852)

March 23rd

The Danger of Stepping from a Railway Carriage while the Train is in Motion was fatally shown on the Midland Railway on the 23rd inst. A middle-aged well dressed man opened the carriage door, sprang out, and fell between the edge of the platform and the train. The wheels ran over his legs and mutilated them terribly. His body was then twisted into a posture more nearly parallel to the train, and the wheels of several carriages ran along his chest, literally opening the trunk from end to end. The accident was witnessed by a number of horrified officials and passengers, but no one was able to render the slightest assistance. (1853)

March 24th

A frightful Explosion of Gases took place on Saturday night the 24th inst., in Portsmouth Dockyard. A number of the dockyard police force were waiting in the large station-room at the entrance of the yard, to go on duty, when the smell of gas seemed to them to be stronger than usual. To ascertain where the escape came from, one of the men applied a light to different crevices in the flooring boards, &c, and at length doing so at the one from which the gas actually escaped into the room, a terrific explosion took place. The whole of the floor of the room was blown up, together with its furniture, and all the unfortunate men who were sitting in it. In addition to this, the roof of the building, only consisting of a ground-floor, was blown into the air. The sufferers were found to be Inspector Henry Stroud, both legs broken; Sergeant Thomas Ripley, leg broken; privates James Giles, arm and leg broken and internal injuries; George Lane, arm and leg broken; James Wassal, thigh broken; T. Sydenham, leg broken, D. Palmer, Henry Neville, W. Elmes, and W. Miller, seriously injured. With the exception of Miller, all the poor fellows required to be taken to hospital, and they were at once conveyed to Haslar. After enduring great suffering, private Giles died, next morning. Inspector Stroud is in a most dangerous state. Should he survive, he must undergo amputation of both legs. (1855)

🕱 *March 25th* 🕱

A poor man of colour, named John Clover, was charged at the Clerkenwell Police Court, on the 25th, with Begging. Two mendicity officers, having seen him, with a printed paper on his breast, craving charity, and some passengers give him alms, took him into custody. It appeared, from his account of himself, that he was a native of Africa, and had been a slave, but he ran away from his master to avoid his cruelty, and to save his life. He was flogged, kicked, and beaten by him, and on one occasion he inflicted several wounds upon him with a knife. The prisoner exhibited several wounds on his arm. His master was in the habit of putting hot chains on his legs, and other slaves were linked to him while they were at work. They had to work very hard and got very little to eat, but they dared not complain, or they would be ill-used and told they were lazy, and have their hands and legs tied together and beaten till their flesh was cut. One night their master went out, when he (the prisoner) and six other of the slaves, made their escape. They walked night after night, and in the day time stopped in the woods for fear of any one belonging to their master seeing them. At last they got to a country called Cilwa. They sailed from there to Calcutta, where they stopped twelve months, until they found a ship to bring them to England, where there were no slaves. He was willing to work, and he had no means of getting a living but by selling a few books. Mr. Corrie (the magistrate): Have you no friends? Prisoner (in broken English): I have no friend, only God. Mr. Corrie: Where were you born? Prisoner: I do not know. I never saw my father and mother. Mr. Corrie: Then what will you do if I discharge you? You will go and beg again? Prisoner: I must try and get a bit of bread. Mr. Corrie, under the circumstances, discharged him, with an advice to go to the workhouse, which he promised to do, and he was set at liberty. Mr. Deacon, the proprietor of the Sir Hugh Myddelton Tavern, near Sadler's Wells Theatre, who was present during the examination, humanely gave the poor man nourishment, and took him into his service. (1853)

🕱 *March 26th* 🕱

A Fatal Accident has occurred [this month] at the Kirkstall Station of the Leeds and Bradford Railway, from the incautiousness or error of two ladies. Mrs. Nichols and her sister Miss Leyland entered the station by a wrong gate, one which leads to the goods warehouse, and walked along the side of the warehouse towards the platform. While still on the roadway, an express-train approached, running upon the rails laid rather close to the warehouse wall. A guard and a porter called out to the ladies to warn them; but they considered themselves to be safe, as they were outside the rail, and continued to walk forward. Miss Leyland, who was nearest to the rails, was caught by the engine, whirled round, dragged forward twenty yards, and hurled upon the platform. The unfortunate lady was so dreadfully injured that she is not expected to recover. (1851)

🕱 *March 27th* 🕱

At the Mansion House, on the 27th, Rose Hunt, aged 19, was brought before Alderman Gibbs, on a charge of having attempted to commit Suicide. The unfortunate creature had been for four years living a wretched life of prostitution in the eastern parts of London. Her history presents a melancholy example of the way in which the streets of London are replenished with victims. – Rose Hunt is the daughter of a person who once kept a respectable inn in a country town, but who has become so reduced as to be now dependent upon parochial relief. About four years ago, when only 15 years of age, she met a young woman at a fair in Suffolk, who endeavoured to win her confidence. By means of this female she was introduced into a house of ill-fame, seduced, and eventually brought by her to London. She was taken to a low concert room in Tower-hill, and left to a course of prostitution amongst the lowest class of the waterside district. About nine months ago, as she wandered about one Sunday afternoon, she saw the door of a chapel open, and went in to rest. What she there heard of mercy for the vilest sinners, made such an impression as to render her most unhappy under the course of life she had been pursuing. At last, existence became intolerable, and she resolved to put an end to it. – Alderman: I have been told by the chaplain that you are truly penitent, and that you detest the life you have been leading. – The defendant: I would prefer death at this instant. – Alderman: Very well. You shall be protected. I shall refer you to the Ladies' Patronage Committee, with a view to your reception into the Elizabeth Fry refuge for the present. I trust it will be stated in the newspapers, that the wretch who was the cause of all this calamity is now at Norwich, engaged in the same dreadful traffic of seduction. – The defendant: May God bless you for saving me. (1850)

🕱 *March 28th* 🕱

At the Liverpool Assizes, on the 28th, Dr. Nolan, minister of a congregation of Independents at Manchester, appeared as plaintiff in An Action of Slander against one Pettigrew, for stating, in the presence of a person named Ford, that Dr. Nolan had seduced female members, and had given medicine to one to prevent the consequences. There had been strife in Dr. Nolan's congregation; he had resigned, and been re-elected minister; afterwards it had been found that the re-election was not legal in form, and a heated canvassing and contest arose. It was in the course of this agitation that the defendant made the statement complained of. The defendant was a respectable serious man, and had made his statement in good faith, privately, to Mr. Ford, as a person holding office in the congregation and having weight in the election. The defence was double: that the communication was privileged; and that it was true. The evidence was contradictory: some scandalous facts were sworn to on the one hand, and denied on the other. The judge ruled that the communication was privileged; and a verdict was given for the defendant. (1850)

🕱 *March 29th* 🕱

The beautiful parish church of St. Anne, Limehouse, was Totally Destroyed by Fire on the 29th. The fire originated in the chamber between the ceiling and the roof, where a heated flue-pipe emerged to the air. The two attendants who discovered it, about eight in the morning, alarmed the parishioners by an irregular tolling of all the bells, and in a short time a large multitude hastened to the spot. All endeavours to check the flames were futile, from the great height at which they raged; so efforts were confined to the saving of muniments, sacred paraphernalia, and valuable ornaments. The great central chandelier had scarcely been removed when the ceiling of the nave fell in. The organ stood a long time, apparently unattacked; at last its pipes were seen to give way, melted by the furnace heat of the air which rushed through them; suddenly the framework was enveloped in flame, and then in a short time the whole was destroyed. As the belfry was reached and the machinery consumed, the bells fell with a crash and shock that shook the earth. Ultimately, the bare walls, the steeple, and the calcined columns that once gracefully lifted the ceiling, were alone left standing. So completely is everything combustible destroyed, that the debris now covers the floor to a depth of some two or three feet. St. Anne's Church was one of Hawksmoor's most beautiful works; the date of its building was 1712, the cost about 35,000*l*. (1850)

🕱 *March 30th* 🕱

Three young women, the servants of a maltster named Miller, at March, in the Isle of Ely, having been detected in pilfering some flour, and threatened with dismissal if the offence was repeated, attempted to commit Suicide by taking laudanum. One of them accomplished her purpose, and was found dead under a hedge; the other two had taken more laudanum than the deceased, and voided it – hence they recovered. They have since been committed for trial for 'Wilful murder', on the charge of having incited their companion to commit suicide. (1851)

🕱 *March 31st* 🕱

Mr. Lowndes, judge of the Liverpool County Court, was accidentally Drowned on Sunday night, the 31st. He was awaiting with his son the arrival of the Seacombe steamer; and, as it neared the landing-stage, he moved as if to step on board, but missed his footing, and fell into the rapidly flowing tide. His son rushing forward, was seized by the skirts, but he tore away instantly and dived after his father, without success. The son was rescued a long distance down the stream. There is an insurance to the amount of about 5,000*l*. (1850)

At the Liverpool Assizes, on the 31st ult., Patrick Lyons and Bridget Lyons his wife, were tried for the Murder of Peggy Fahey, at Warrington, on the 4th of February. The prisoners, who are Irish, kept a lodging house, and Peggy Fahey, a travelling pedlar, was their lodger. It appears that the contents of her basket of wares had excited the cupidity of Lyons and his wife, and that they had murdered her early in the morning, when she was preparing to go out, by striking her on the head with a hatchet. Suspicion having arisen, the house was searched, and her dead body was found in a closet, together with her basket, and a butcher's cleaver with which the murder had been committed. The woman was immediately taken into custody, but the man had fled, and was traced to Dublin, where before he was apprehended, he had enlisted in the East India Company's service, and had been passed by the Surgeon. The prisoners were both convicted, and the judge pronounced sentence of death upon them. The woman has since received a reprieve. (1851)

April

April 1st

The *Emma*, bound from Dundee to Montreal, was wrecked on the morning of the 1st. At daybreak, amidst the fury of the gale, the ship was discovered adrift, off St. Margaret's, Orkneys. Those on board managed to make sail on her, and she stood to the eastward; then tacked and stood to the north, when she drove and struck on the point of the rocks with terrible force. It was utterly impossible to render any assistance to the crew from the shore. They took to the rigging, and their cries and gestures for help were truly heart-rending. Their sufferings were of but short duration; for within half-an-hour the masts were carried away, and with it the unfortunate men, every one of whom perished. The hull of the ship was shortly broken up into a thousand pieces. (1850)

April 2nd

On the 2nd, Thomas Denny was tried at Kingston-on-Thames for Murdering his Child. He was a farm-servant, and so poor that he lived in a hay-loft on his master's premises with his reputed wife. In August a child was born, and died immediately. Suspicions arose, and an investigation took place, which led to the prisoner's commitment charged with murdering the infant. On the trial the prisoner's son, an intelligent boy of eight years old, told the following graphic story of his father's guilt:– 'We all,' he said, 'lived together in the hay-loft at Ewell. When mother had a baby, I went to my father and told him to come home directly. When we got back, my father took up the baby in his arms. He then took up an awl. [Here the child became much affected and cried bitterly, and it was some time before he could proceed with his testimony. At length he went on.] My father took up the awl, and killed the baby with it. He struck the awl into its throat. The baby cried, and my father took the child to its mother, and asked her if he should make a coffin for it. Before he said this, he asked her if she would help to kill it, and gave her the awl. She tried to kill it also. My father gave her the child and the awl, and she did the same to it that he had done. I was very much frightened at what I saw, and ran away, and when I came back I found mother in bed.' The woman (Eliza Tarrant) had been charged as an accomplice, but the bill against her was ignored by the Grand Jury. On the trial, she was called as a witness; to which the prisoner's counsel objected, she being a presumed participator in the crime. The woman however was called, and partly corroborated her son's testimony; but denied that she took any share in killing her offspring. The prisoner was convicted, and Mr. Justice Maule passed sentence of death, informing him that there was no hope of respite. Subsequently however the objections of the prisoner's counsel proved more valid than the judge supposed, for the Secretary of State thought proper to commute the sentence. The unfortunate man received the respite with heartfelt gratitude. Since his conviction he appeared to be overcome with grief at his awful position. (1850)

April 3rd

A Dreadful Murder was committed in Lambeth on the morning of the 3rd. A son killed his mother, and then cut off her head. The murdered woman was Mrs. Elizabeth Wheeler, a widow, of about the age of forty-four, who resided in Durham Place, Kennington Road, facing Bethlem Hospital for lunatics.

The son who killed her was Thomas Cathie Wheeler, twenty-eight years of age, a young man who has been well educated and was a good linguist, who once filled a well-paid situation in the Brazils under a mercantile firm, but has been confined in a lunatic asylum twice, and lately has been unable to do anything at all for his own living. His mother was fondly attached to him, and wholly supported him. The landlord of Mrs. Wheeler was Mr. Toms, a carpet-bag manufacturer, who occupied the ground-floor of the house in which she lived; and in a floor above that occupied by her lodged Eliza Phillips, who has known her for nearly thirty years. In the examination of the criminal before the Lambeth Police-Court, Eliza Phillips said that, hearing a scuffling noise in Mrs. Wheeler's room, followed by a heavy fall, she ran up-stairs and tapped at the door, which was partly opened by the prisoner, and hastily closed again in her face. Fearing that something was the matter, she ran down-stairs, and called the landlord and landlady. Mrs. Elizabeth Toms, the landlady, stated that she ran upstairs, found Mrs. Wheeler on the floor, saw blood, ran down-stairs, and sent persons for a doctor and in pursuit of the prisoner.

Mr. Hutchinson, surgeon, stated that when he came into the room the body of the deceased was still warm; on the table, which was spread with a cloth for dinner, was the poor woman's head. On the floor was a pillow, bearing marks as if a person had knelt on it to be unstained by the blood on the floor. Mr. Toms stated that he followed and overtook the prisoner, and gave him into the custody of policeman Lockyer. Policeman Lockyer described what passed after the arrest. The witness: I said to him, he must consider himself in my custody, and go with me to the station. He said, 'They have not let me go far: I have been tormented for four or five years by them.' I said, 'Do you mean to say that you have killed your mother?' and he said, 'I have: I am sorry for it.' I said, 'How came you to do it?' 'Well,' he said, 'I have been tormented for four or five years.' I asked him how he did it, and he said, 'She was coming in at the door, and I knocked her down with the flat-iron, and I found that that was not sufficient, and I then took the carving-knife. She was very tough, and I then struck her head off with the hatchet.' (1852)

🕱 *April 4th* 🕱

A Miss Downie met, on the 4th, with an Extraordinary Death at Traquair-on-the-Tweed. She had suffered, since childhood, from severe pains in the head and deafness; her health had been gradually declining for the last three years, and in August last she was seized with most painful inflammation in the left ear, accompanied by occasional bleedings also from the ear. On the 20th of March an ordinary-sized metallic pin was extracted from the left ear, which was enveloped in a firm substance with numerous fibres attached to it; several hard bodies, in shape resembling the grains of buck-wheat, but of various colours, were also taken out of the right ear. The poor girl endured the most intense pain, which she bore with Christian fortitude till death terminated her sufferings. It is believed the pin must have lodged in the head for nearly twenty years, as she never recollected of having put one in her ear, but she had a distinct remembrance of having, when a child, had a pin in her mouth, which she thought she had swallowed. (1850)

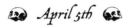

April 5th

At the Liverpool Assizes on the 5th, Charles Williams, a young sailor, was indicted for the Wilful Murder of John Marshall, at Liverpool, on the 23d of March. It appeared that the prisoner and two other men were standing in the street near a public-house, when the prisoner, on learning that the deceased was in the public house, said he should 'knife' him, and proceeded to sharpen on the flags of the gutter a knife, which he pulled from a sheath. Shortly afterwards the deceased and two other men came out of the house, when one of the men who was with the prisoner proceeded across the street to the deceased, and said, 'You Dutch son of a ——, what did you insult me in that concert-room for last night?' To which the deceased replied, 'I did not insult you.' Upon this the man struck deceased in the face, got hold of him by the hair of the head, and, pulling him down, tried to kick him in the face, and they wrestled together until they got back to the public-house door. While this was going on, the prisoner was standing behind them, and when they got to the public-house door he drew his knife and tried to stab the deceased in the breast. He then took hold of the deceased's right shoulder with his right hand, holding the knife in his left, and drove it into his thigh, saying, 'Take that for lick,' and then put the knife into the sheath again. Blood flowed from the deceased, and he staggered into the public-house. The prisoner ran down the street, but was afterwards apprehended. The deceased afterwards died in consequence of the wound. The prisoner, in his defence, said that the other men drew their knives, and he was compelled to draw his also, and in the crush his knife went into the deceased's thigh. Upon being asked if he had any witnesses, he said they were all gone to sea. He was found guilty, and sentence of death was pronounced upon him. (1853)

April 6th

Colonel Gordon, of the Royal Artillery – a distinguished veteran, in his sixty-seventh year – Died Suddenly on the 15th March, in a Railway-carriage between Stafford and Crewe. After the interment, circumstances came to light which led to the exhumation of the body and a coroner's inquest. It appeared that Colonel Gordon left London for Aberdeen on the night of the 15th; he travelled in the mail-train, as a third class passenger. In the same carriage with him, but in another compartment, was a man drunk, who annoyed the other passengers by his bad behaviour. At Stafford, a passenger complained; whereupon Inspector Saunders took the offender out of the compartment in which he had so misbehaved, and wished to put him into that occupied by Colonel Gordon. The Colonel protested against the intrusion, and offered his card; the Inspector answered him insolently, seized him by the shoulders, and eventually the drunken man was admitted. Colonel Gordon intimated an intention of prosecuting the inspector for an assault, and asked the names of three fellow-passengers as witnesses, but he seemed as if he were going to sleep; presently his head began to droop, and when the train arrived at Crewe he was dead. Saunders and other officials denied that the man put into the compartment was drunk. He 'walked into the carriage with his hands in his pockets.' A guard said it was 'not unusual to find third-class passengers who had taken a few glasses of liquor.' Sir John Liddell, who made a post-mortem examination, ascribed the death to a longstanding disease of the heart: any sudden excitement would be likely to cause death. The jury returned a verdict of 'manslaughter' against Saunders. Saunders was put on his trial, at Chester Assizes, on the 6th inst. (1854)

April 7th

A Destructive Fire took place, on the evening of the 7th, at Stanwood Farm, in the New Forest. Mr. Chanwood, the farmer, noticed a light in the farm, and, opening the door, found the interior in a blaze. There was a fresh wind, which carried the flames to the stables and ricks. The whole of the stables, with eight horses and three fat oxen, were consumed; the barn, with sixty quarters of corn, five ricks of corn, ten pigs, nearly 200 head of poultry, a vast quantity of farming implements, &c. The granary, though in the midst of the flames, escaped, as did four ricks and the farm-house; but the furniture was much injured by removal. The labourers looked on with apathy; some, indeed, stole a barrel of beer, and cut slices from the burning bullocks. (1851)

💀 *April 8th* 💀

An inquest was held on the 8th, on the body of Mr. Charles Mayo, a young man of nineteen, who Drowned himself on the 20th of last month, by leaping from London Bridge. He had been paying his addresses to a young lady at Rotherhithe; a disagreement occurred, and the lady desired in a note that their correspondence should cease. Mr. Mayo left a note for her, declaring that 'she was all the world to him – it was too heavy for his brain to bear, and she would only now see the wreck.' Verdict, 'Temporary insanity.' (1851)

💀 *April 9th* 💀

A daring Garotte Robbery was committed in Lincoln on the night of the 9th inst. Mr. T. Winn, an opulent citizen, resides in a large mansion in Newland – the house being a short distance from the street, and approached by a carriage drive. Mr. Winn had been to his brewery premises, and walked down Newland to his private house. Several persons were passing up and down Newland at the time, as Saturday night is a busy market night. As soon as he had got within his own premises, and closed the gate, he was seized by three men, one of whom grasped his throat tightly and threw him upon his back on the ground. Several persons in the street heard faint screams of 'Murder!' but until the villains had effected their purpose and got off, the direction of the cry was not ascertained. Mr. Winn, who is advanced in years, was then found just inside the gate in a state of great exhaustion, and suffering much from the injury and fright. The robbers obtained five 10*l*. notes, a purse containing six sovereigns and several half sovereigns, with a gold watch. The robbers are not known, but 100 guineas reward has been offered for their detection. (1853)

💀 *April 10th* 💀

A Frightful Accident has taken place at Ravensdale corn-mill, in Cumberland. Young Mr. Anthony Dawson was left alone in the mill by his father at half-past three o'clock in the morning. While in the act of placing the belt upon one of the wheels to set more machinery to work, he was caught by the axle, and wound up by his clothes, and crushed in the most shocking manner. Some idea may be formed of the sufferings of the unfortunate man, and the awful pressure upon him, from the fact that his body, thus entangled, stopped all the power and machinery of the mill, and that he was held in that painful position upwards of four hours. The accident was not discovered till eight o'clock, when the sufferer was released. Two surgeons were immediately in attendance, but could render him no assistance, and he only lingered until one o'clock. He was quite sensible all the time, and gave a full account of the accident. (1852)

🕱 *April 11th* 🕱

A shocking case of Starvation of a Child has occurred at Southampton. G. C. Elmes and Mary Ann Wake were indicted at the Southampton quarter session, on the 11th, for neglecting to give sufficient food for the support of Emily Lavinia Elmes, a child of the age of eleven years, and for beating her. The male prisoner, who is a compositor, was left a widower, with two female children, about three years since. Two years ago he went to lodge with Wake, who is a widow, with a grown-up family residing with her. The two children of the man were properly treated for a time, the father taking his meals with them. After a time he took his meals with the woman, and thenceforward regularly cohabited with her. The two children were then much ill-treated; one of them escaped, and is now the inmate of a local charitable institution. The other girl, the younger of the two, was from that period subjected to a system of close confinement and ill-treatment. She was not allowed to have the slightest intercourse with children of her own age, but was confined in a room, the blind of which was always kept close drawn, her father taking her a scanty allowance of dry bread only, and positively denying her any drink whatever. In the recent winter months the treatment was rendered much worse. She was then placed, during the day, in a cold, damp, dirty washhouse, opening upon the yard, with a brick floor, and without any article of furniture upon which she could rest herself. When unobserved she stole out into the yard, and drank some water kept in a bucket there; and when Wake saw her she beat and drove the child back again into the cold kitchen. The consequence of this inhuman treatment was, that the child became a mere skeleton, broke out in sores, had chilblains upon her feet, and an ulcer upon one of her legs. The neighbours heard her continually beaten, and were disturbed by her cries and entreaties for mercy. This continued until the Rev. Mr. Norton, the curate of the parish, heard of the matter;

he went to the house of the prisoners and found the child, whom he could scarcely recognise, so altered was her appearance from the fine healthy child who had formerly attended his school. Information was given to the Board of Guardians, who procured a justices' warrant, obtained possession of the child, and had the prisoners apprehended. The medical officers could not discover the slightest trace of organic disease; on the contrary, under humane treatment, she rapidly gained strength, and is now in a fair way of perfect recovery. The jury found Elmes guilty of neglect and assault, and convicted Wake of an assault. The Recorder sentenced Elmes to be imprisoned one year, and Wake six months. (1854)

🕱 *April 12th* 🕱

An Unfortunate Accident happened in Her Majesty's Theatre, during the performance of 'Masaniello,' on Saturday evening, the 12th. A young man, named Deuwell, was firing off some guns behind the scenes, when one of them rebounded and discharged its contents in his left leg, which was dreadfully shattered. He was conveyed to Charing Cross Hospital, and amputation was performed. When the accident happened, the Queen, with several of the royal family, and a crowded audience, were witnessing the performance. (1851)

🕱 *April 13th* 🕱

Elias Lucas and Mary Reeder were Executed at Cambridge on the 13th. Lucas was the husband of the female convict's sister, whom they had poisoned. Morbid curiosity had attracted from twenty to thirty thousand spectators. In the procession from the jail to the scaffold there was a great parade of county magistrates. (1850)

A Waterspout, a phenomenon seldom seen in these latitudes, happened on the 13th in the Bristol Channel. As the *Fanny and Jane* brig from London to Bristol was proceeding up channel, she had her masts, bowsprit, and everything above deck carried away by a waterspout. She was taken in tow by the *Alert of Bridport*, and brought into Bristol Harbour. Vessels distant from the brig at the time of the occurrence only half a mile escaped uninjured. (1850)

🕱 *April 14th* 🕱

At Liverpool Assizes, on the 14th, Mr. Peter Petrie sued Mr. Ellis, a London underwriter, for his proportion of 3200*l.* Insured by a Policy of Insurance on a Box of Gold-Dust. The case was singular. Mr. Petrie bought a small vessel in 1852 to make a speculative voyage to Australia; he made a good deal of money by selling goods and conveying passengers between Adelaide and Melbourne, and he also got something by a gold-digging trip; when about to return to England, he wrote over for insurances to be effected here on the ship, cargo, and treasure. In the British Channel the weather was bad at night, and there was much shipping about; to warn other vessels of his proximity, he burnt a blue light; by some means a blue light in a box of lights in Mr. Petrie's cabin took fire; a barrel of gunpowder was stowed there; he thought this would explode; he managed to hurl the burning light from the cabin, but other things had then caught fire; amid the flames, he seized a box of gold-dust, hurried on deck, and ordered all hands to the boats. In attempting to enter one of these, he stumbled, and the box of gold fell into the sea. It seems that the fire in the cabin was then put out, the box of blue lights thrown overboard, and the ship was brought safely to port. Mr. Petrie lost his eyesight by entering the cabin to save the gold. As the box had been thus lost on the voyage, he sought to recover its value from the insurers. Witnesses were called to support the story told by the plaintiff. For the defence, a scientific gentleman threw doubt on the probability of a blue light igniting spontaneously; and Sergeant Wilkins urged that Mr. Petrie had not satisfactorily made out that he possessed so much gold-dust. The jury returned a verdict for the amount claimed. (1855)

🕱 *April 15th* 🕱

A Fatal Railway Accident occurred on the Midland line, near Kegworth, on the 15th inst. A porter belonging to the company, named Lester, while the train was in motion, was attempting to throw some bags into the carriages, in doing which he approached too near the train, and his foot slipping, he got entangled among the wheels of the carriages, which passing over him, mutilated him in the most frightful manner, from the effects of which he died. (1853)

On the 15th inst. Catherine Savill, a married woman residing at Camberwell, Drowned her Infant while labouring under a fit of insanity. A girl who acted as servant to the child's parents found the body lying in a basin of water. The child, a baby of four months, had been dead at least three-quarters of an hour. In the meantime the wretched mother had proceeded to her husband's place of occupation in Finsbury square, and the moment he saw her he had a presentiment that something had occurred, and asked her what was the matter? She replied, 'George, prepare yourself for the worst – I have destroyed the baby.' He asked her how she had done it, and she said she had drowned it in a pail of water. The jury returned a verdict of 'Wilful Murder' against the woman. (1854)

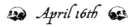

April 16th

Louisa Hartley was charged at the Southwark Police Court, on the 16th, with an Attempt to poison her Father, who is a fellowship-porter. On the previous morning she made the coffee for breakfast, on tasting it, it burnt Hartley's mouth, and he charged the girl with having put poison in his cup, which she denied; he then tasted her coffee, and found it had no unpleasant flavour. His daughter then snatched away his cup, and threw the contents into a wash-hand basin. But in spite of her tears and protestations of innocence, he took the basin to Guy's Hospital, where it was found that the coffee must have contained vitriol. The girl, who was said to be of weak intellect, and stood sobbing at the bar, being questioned, only shook her head and said she had nothing to say. At a subsequent hearing the magistrate decided that there was sufficient evidence for a committal. (1850)

Early on Sunday morning, the 16th inst., the house of a man named Fisher, at Millhouse, near Sheffield, was Blown up by an Infernal Machine. Fisher is a scythemaker, and lives in a very secluded place. He and his wife were alarmed, about one o'clock on Sunday morning, by an explosion which was afterwards found to have greatly shattered the house. The roof had been lifted bodily, the ceilings of two rooms brought down, the window of the back bed-room blown out, and the door carried away with the stanchions. The 'infernal machine' was a tin can, filled with gunpowder, the lid fastened down, and a fuse inserted in it. A ladder was found reared against the wall, near the back bed-room window, and by its aid some one had reached the window, broken a pane, and then thrown the machine into the room. A similar attempt was made the same morning at another house, but the damage done was not so serious. The refusal of the persons occupying the houses to join a trades' union is the conjectured cause of these diabolical outrages. (1854)

🕱 *April 17th* 🕱

The Inefficacy of the Poor-law in affording relief was exemplified at the Clerkenwell police court on the 17th inst. A sickly-looking youth, about 18 years old, applied to the court for relief. He wandered from his native place, Yorkshire, in search of employment, three months ago, but having been unable to obtain any, he had sold what few articles he possessed, and had now left only the tattered garments he was wearing. [A constable] said that he had been with the young man to the workhouses but could not move any of the parish authorities to take pity on his charge. The magistrate observed that, under all the circumstances, the applicant should be provided with a bed and proper nourishment in that neighbourhood, and the parish wherein that happened should take all the legal consequences afterwards if it refused to obey his order to relieve the young man, whose looks too plainly showed how much he had suffered. (1852)

🕱 *April 18th* 🕱

A man named Goodal, residing in the village of Milford near Derby, has Murdered one of his Children. He was living apart from his wife, they having separated about two years since, on account of his bad conduct. On the 18th inst. he went to his wife's house, after the two youngest children were in bed. While the woman was occupied with some work in the garden, she heard one of her children make a strange noise. She ran up stairs, and met her husband coming out of the bedroom. She said, 'My baby is crying'; to which he replied, 'Your baby is in heaven.' He went down stairs, and she went into the bedroom, and saw the child lying on the bed bleeding. She shrieked out 'Murder', and ran downstairs. An alarm was raised, and Goodall, who was found sitting on a sofa, was secured by a neighbour. The murdered child was a little girl, one year and a half old. On searching the prisoner's pockets two razors, 14*l*., and a quart bottle with some liquor in it, supposed to be poison, were found. (1854)

🕱 *April 19th* 🕱

Fresh Illustrations of Smithfield Cruelty were brought to light by Mr. Thomas, secretary to the Royal Society for the Prevention of Cruelty to Animals, at the Clerkenwell Police Court on the 19th, to complain of acts of gross cruelty on the part of drovers and others. It was stated that oxen were daily overdriven, until they became completely exhausted, and were obliged to lie down in the streets, when they were cruelly beaten and pricked in the hocks until the blood flowed from their flesh, and by being thus tormented they crawled along in pain to their destination, where they were tied up, and fresh and unnecessary cruelties were inflicted upon them prior to their being slaughtered. Numerous complaints had been made to the Society by humane persons, who were determined, if possible, to check or put down the intolerable nuisance. The magistrate highly commended them for their exertions, and intimated that he would grant warrants against offending parties who could be identified. (1850)

💀 *April 20th* 💀

A young man was charged on the 20th inst., before the Liverpool magistrates, with Shooting a Girl named Jane Riley. The hearing had been deferred, that the prosecutrix might recover sufficiently to give evidence. She was assisted into court, and gave the following statement:– 'About 12 o'clock on the morning of the 13th of March I went into a shooting-gallery in Murray street, Williamson-square. I wanted to see the master. As I went in I saw the prisoner standing on the steps. I heard him say to a friend, 'I will have another shot, and then I will go home.' He followed me into the gallery. I went into a small room, culled the snug, to see if the landlord was in. Whilst I was there, the prisoner came in and asked me to come to him. I did not speak to him. He smiled and took up a gun, and said he would shoot me. I thought he was joking, and said 'Oh, don't.' I then turned my back, and had hardly done so when the gun went off, and I felt a ball penetrate my shoulder. I believe I was afterwards taken to the infirmary. The prisoner appeared rather tipsy.' –When taken into custody the following morning, at his lodgings, the prisoner denied all knowledge of the affair. A surgeon pronounced the girl to be now out of danger, but had been unable to extract the ball, which was lodged in the dorsal muscles, near the spine. The prisoner was committed to take his trial at the assizes; the magistrates ordering him to find bail himself in 100*l*., and two resident securities in 50*l*. each. The prisoner's father offered bail, but was rejected. (1853)

🕱 *April 21st* 🕱

An Improvement in the Means for the Detection of Crime has been introduced by Mr. Gardener, governor of the Bristol City and County Gaol [this month]. The descriptions in the 'Hue and Cry', &c., of notorious prisoners in custody, with the view of learning their antecedents, &c., having been found most defective in practice, Mr Gardener has introduced the system of taking multiplied copies of daguerreotype likenesses of notorious offenders in custody, which, with written descriptions of the prisoners, are forwarded to the principal gaols and police-stations in the kingdom. As daguerreotype likenesses of the most accurate character can be now taken on paper, the only expense is the trifling cost of the apparatus. (1853)

🕱 *April 22nd* 🕱

A man named William Bennison, a workman in an iron-foundry, has been committed to prison at Leith on suspicion of having Poisoned his Wife.. Bennison and his wife occupied the second floor of a house in which also resides Alexander Milne, a cripple from his infancy, well known to the frequenters of Leith Walk, where he sits daily, in a small cart drawn by a dog. Mrs. Bennison, after, it is said, partaking of some gruel, became very ill, and died on Monday, the 22nd inst. The dog which drew the cripple's cart died about the same time: suspicion was drawn upon the husband, and he was apprehended, and the dog's body conveyed to Surgeon's Hall for examination. Some weeks before, Bennison had purchased arsenic from a neighbouring druggist, to kill rats, as he said. When suspected, he called on the druggist, and requested him and his wife not to mention that he had purchased the arsenic. He even pressed for a written denial of the fact, adding that there might he arsenic found in his wife's stomach, but he did not put it there. On the Monday previous to her death it is said he enrolled her name in a benefit society, by which on her death he was entitled to a sum of 6*l*. At the prisoner's examination before the sheriff the report of the chemists pronounced the content of the dog's stomach to have been metallic poison. The accused was eventually committed for trial. The deceased and her husband were members of the Wesleyan body, and bore an excellent character for piety. Bennison professed to be extremely zealous in behalf of religion, and was in the habit of administering its consolations to such as would accept of them. His 'gifts' of extempore prayer are said to be extensive. (1850)

💀 *April 23rd* 💀

On the night of the 23rd, Mr. Armstrong, of Sorbietrees, in Cumberland, through a lamentable mistake, was Shot by the Rev. Mr. Smith, the incumbent of Walton. In the middle of the night the rev. gentleman, alarmed by a noise at his window, fired a revolving pistol at random, with the view of frightening away the persons who, he apprehended, were attempting to break into his house. In the morning Mr. Armstrong was found lying near the door, shot through the heart. It does not appear how Mr. Armstrong came to Mr. Smith's door: he had dined at Bampton, it being market-day, and, when last seen, was riding homeward, slightly intoxicated. An inquest on the body has given a verdict of 'manslaughter' against Mr. Smith, who is said to be in a state bordering on insanity. [At his trial on the 6th August 1851, 'the jury retired, and after an absence of half an hour found the prisoner 'not guilty.' Mr. Smith immediately fell on his knees and raised his hands to Heaven, amid the deep silence of the crowded court.'] (1851)

💀 *April 24th* 💀

Professor Liebig, the celebrated chemist, has Narrowly Escaped a Fatal Accident at Munich. He was giving a lecture on chemistry at the Palace, before the Royal Family, when a bottle of oxygen gas being improperly handed to him by his assistant, who mistook it for another bottle, an explosion took place, and the bottle flew into a thousand pieces. Fortunately, the explosion occurred in an inner room, the door of which was open. Still some fragments of the glass passed through the door, and slightly wounded some members of the Royal party who were sitting in the front rank. Queen Theresa was cut in the cheek, and the blood flowed in abundance; Prince Leopold was slightly wounded in the forehead, Countess Luxburg in the chin, and Countess Sandizell in the head. The professor was also slightly injured, having escaped with his life by a sort of miracle. (1853)

💀 *April 25th* 💀

The Rev. M. Conway, Roman Catholic curate of Cahirconlish, has met with a Terrible Death near that village. He fell, it is supposed, upon the spikes of a gate, and was impaled by the neck, until the police patrol came up and extricated him, but he died before their arrival at the fatal spot.

He had been suddenly called out on a very urgent sick message, and in his anxiety to respond to the summons neglected ordinary precaution, striving in a dark stormy night to make his way to the bedside of a dying parishioner by the shortest route, and against all obstacles. With this view, struggling to surmount an iron gate, he sunk exhausted upon the spikes and there expired. (1853)

April 26th

At the Mansion House on the 26th April, Maria Biscomb was committed to prison for three months with hard labour for obtaining five shillings from a gentleman by the Feigned Death of a Child. This woman was well known as a notorious swindler, and had been continually in prison. On one occasion she applied to a lady for assistance, representing that she had a child lying dead, and was unable to bury it. The lady visited her house, and saw apparently the body of a child covered with a cloth. She gave the prisoner 10s, but on going to a window she heard a voice from beneath the cloth exclaim, 'Mother, how long am I to be dead?' (1855)

April 27th

An instance of the Punishment of Crime in the Act of its Perpetration occurred at Hove, near Brighton, on the 27th of April. On the previous day, a man entered the Ship Inn, ordered some refreshment, and engaged a bed for the night. Early next morning he was found lying in the street, under the inn windows, bleeding and insensible; and died in a few hours, never having spoken. A bundle filled with the landlord's bedding was lying by his side, and it appeared that he had fallen while endeavouring to escape with his booty. An inquest was held on his body, but nothing was known of his name or residence. (1855)

April 28th

A Mysterious Death took place at Clapham on Sunday the 28th of April. Mr. Maddle, a gentleman residing in Claremont place, went to church in the morning, leaving his housekeeper, Sarah Snelling, an elderly woman, alone in the house, desiring her as usual to lock the doors and gates. On his return he could not obtain admittance by ringing, but found the back garden gate unfastened, and discovered the housekeeper lying dead on the floor of the kitchen, with her head resting on a piece of carpeting, one foot without a shoe, and a coil of rope lying by her. The body presented no sign of violence. The house had been robbed, drawers and boxes forced open, and a number of articles carried off. The Coroner's inquest threw no light upon the affair. The examination of the body discovered no injury, either external or internal, to which death could be ascribed. Some suspicious-looking persons were observed in the neighbourhood of the house, but the police have been unable to trace them. It was supposed that the woman might have died from chloroform administered by the housebreakers; but, as the body exhibited no signs of the action of that drug, it seems more probable that she died from the effect of sudden terror. (1850)

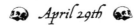

April 29th

Mrs. Robertson, of Ladykirk, in Berwickshire, has had a Narrow Escape from Death by a singular accident. While riding with Lord Elcho's hounds, in order to avoid a bridge at the head of a reservoir near Chatton, in Northumberland, she attempted to cross it where some one had gone before, at what seemed a shallow place; but her horse refusing, plunged into the middle of this large body of water – supposed fifteen feet deep – and threw her. Fortunately, Mr. Robertson, who is an excellent swimmer, was near, and got instantly off his horse and into the water, swam some distance, caught hold of his wife after she had been twice under water and was quite insensible,– a hold he happily never let go until she was safely landed. (1853)

April 30th

A young girl, named Catherine Morris, the daughter of a farmer at Clapham, threw herself into one of the basins in Trafalgar Square, on the night of the 30th of April; a passer-by saw the act, and managed to get her out when life was almost gone. The young woman was found to be Insane from Religious Fanaticism; she said she had been baptizing herself in the pool. (1850)

May

💀 *May 1st* 💀

Mr. Gunning Sutton, a commander in the Royal Navy, brother of Sir Robert Gunning, has been Accidentally Killed at Knightsbridge. He was riding on Saturday evening, the 1st inst., with his daughter; as they left Hyde Park by Albert Gate, it was necessary to draw up in the road to allow an omnibus to pass; Mr. Sutton's horse reared, threw his rider, and ran away. It was found that Mr. Sutton had been hurt in the abdomen; he gradually sank, and died on Tuesday morning. From an outward examination of the body, the surgeons had no doubt that the pelvis had been fractured behind the wound, most probably by a kick from the horse. The horse was a hired one: it had run away for some distance just before the accident. An inquest resulted in a verdict of 'Accidental death.' In running away, after having thrown Mr. Sutton, the horse knocked down a crossing-sweeper, and hurt him so badly, that it was necessary to take him to the hospital. (1852)

May 2nd

One of the diminutive African savages, called Bosjemans, now exhibiting in the provinces, terrified the people assembled to see them in the Town Hall at Devizes on the 2nd of May, by a sudden outbreak of ferocity. Taking offence at some imaginary affront, he discharged an arrow at the head of the offender, which pierced his hat. He then sprang among the company with a terrific yell, and his companions were preparing to follow, when the keepers rushed forward and secured them, amid the screams of the women and a scene of general consternation. They had once before made a similar exhibition of fierceness. (1850)

May 3rd

Mr. Louis Beecher, managing clerk to Messrs. Schwabe and Co. of Bradford, committed Suicide on the 3rd inst. Mr. Beecher was unmarried; a housekeeper lived in the house, and a young man attended during part of the day. This young man went into Mr. Beecher's bed-room on Tuesday morning, and found Mr. Beecher partly dressed, and, to all appearance, in good health and spirits. He had retired but a short time, when the noise of a pistol was heard. The housekeeper was alarmed, and, on entering the room she found her master lying on the bed – quite dead. He had applied a pistol to each side of his head, and discharged them simultaneously, death of course being instantaneous. He was a native of Saxony, and about thirty-two years of age. (1853)

A man named Steel, possessed of property, met with a Frightful Death at Bolsover, on the night of the 3rd. inst. He went to the Swan Inn, where he had a quantity of drink, and, as he had done several times before, refused to go home. He was therefore left asleep in a chair. There was a fire in the room, which had a guard before it two or three feet high. On the landlord coming down stairs, about 4 o'clock in the morning, he found the poor man leaning over the bar and burning. All his clothes which the fire could reach were destroyed, and a hole, which exposed the intestines, had also been burnt in his side next to the grate. The family were not disturbed in the slightest manner during the night, and he was quite dead when discovered. (1853)

💀 *May 4th* 💀

A dreadful Murder has been committed near Conway, in North Wales. A man of bad character, named William Williams, enticed a young man named Jesse Williams, teacher in the British School, Conway, into a public house, and, over a glass of ale, proposed that they should ascend an adjacent mountain to kill rabbits. The young man said he had not a gun, on which the prisoner said he had, alluding to one which he had just before surreptitiously conveyed from the inn, to which it belonged, and hidden behind a wall. He then sent for some gunpowder, and the two proceeded up the mountain. When about halfway up, the prisoner, it would appear, loaded his gun, deliberately shot Jesse Williams, and rifled the body of a valuable watch and some money. He then returned to the inn, and quietly restored the gun to its place. When questioned about his companion, he said he had gone further up the mountain, where he expected better sport. Some hours after a man with a dog was crossing the mountain, when he discovered a large pool of blood. Occasional droppings of blood appearing, he tracked them a considerable distance, and eventually arrived at a precipice, down which the body had been thrown. Having reached the spot, he found the unfortunate young man shot through the back. Meanwhile the murderer proceeded to a watchmaker who had sold the watch to the young man, and said he had been sent by the latter to obtain some useful articles, instead of the watch. The watchmaker, after expressing surprise, gave in return an old watch, an American clock, teaspoons, and other articles. Hearing soon after that the body of Jesse Williams had been discovered, he informed the police that his watch had been exchanged by the prisoner. They the same night took the prisoner into custody when in bed. Hundreds of people assembled to see him finally secured, and were loud in their execrations. (1853)

💀 *May 5th* 💀

Eight Irishmen, labourers at the Vauxhall gas works, were charged at the Lambeth Police Court, on the 5th and 7th, with the Murder of Henry Chaplin, a Police constable. Police Constable Newton stated, that at one o'clock on Monday morning, he found the prisoners making a great disturbance in Vauxhall Walk, and Chaplin trying to get them home. As they continued disorderly, Chaplin threatened to lock some of them up. Five or six of them then went away, but presently returned armed with sharp metallic clinker-stones, which they had taken from the border of a neighbouring garden. One of them, John Heckey, threw his clinker at Chaplin, and struck him on the mouth: Chaplin staggered, but recovered himself, and struck Heckey with his staff. Patrick Cane and the others then rushed in, and shortly laid Chaplin on the ground insensible, from blows on the head inflicted with the heavy and sharp clinkers. He died shortly afterwards, in Guy's Hospital. Newton grappled with some of the men, but they knocked him down, and all escaped for the time. When arrested at their several places of resort, Heckey and Cane were still bleeding from wounds given by the staves of the constables. Mr. Rhys, surgeon of the Hospital, proved that Chaplin died from the wounds which Newton saw inflicted by Cane and others. The prisoners were remanded for examination of further witnesses. (1851)

🕱 *May 6th* 🕱

Charlecote Lucy, near Stratford-upon-Avon, celebrated as the seat of Shakspeare's Justice Shallow, was Broken into and Robbed on the night of the 6th. The property stolen consisted chiefly of articles of jewellery and other property, to the value of several hundred pounds. One of the burglars was taken in Birmingham at his lodgings, and a great portion of the property was found upon him. (1850)

A Child was Killed by a Bear at Portsmouth on the 6th inst.. The bear belonged to the 38th regiment. It was kept in a yard in Nicholas Street, and the child, aged five years, son of Mr. Martin Curley, landlord of the Rose and Crown, Nicholas Street, was in the habit of feeding the bear with bits of bun and such matters. It is supposed when the accident occurred that he was teazing the bear, when the bear seized him by the back of the neck and broke his windpipe, causing his instant death. The officers immediately ordered some poison to be given to the bear, and it died in twenty minutes. (1853)

🕱 *May 7th* 🕱

Two little children, whose heads scarcely reached the top of the dock, were charged at Bow Street on the 7th with Stealing a Loaf out of a baker's shop. They said, in defence, that they were starving, and their appearance showed that they spoke the truth. They were sentenced to be whipped in the House of Correction. (1850)

💀 *May 8th* 💀

A brutal Murder was perpetrated on the morning of Sunday the 8th inst., at Bacton, a secluded village, near Stowmarket, in Suffolk. The rectory house is in the occupation of the Rev. Mr. Barker, a gentleman upwards of eighty years of age. His establishment consisted of a housekeeper, named Maria Steggall, upwards of seventy, and a housemaid. Mr. Barker left home about half-past ten o'clock to proceed to church, and was shortly after followed by Susan Clarke, his housemaid, leaving the housekeeper at home in charge of the house. Mr. Barker on his return from church, not finding his housekeeper in the hall as she was wont to be, called out loudly for her, but, receiving no answer, went into the kitchen, where he was horror-stricken at seeing her lying upon her back on the floor in a pool of blood. His cries and those of the housemaid brought three countrymen to her assistance, who, upon entering the kitchen, discovered that, although the skull of the housekeeper had been broken in three places, she still breathed. Her clothes were much disordered, showing evidently that she had struggled much with her murderer. Surgeons were soon in attendance, but their assistance was of no avail, as she died in about an hour after she was discovered by her master. An inquest was held, and the jury returned a verdict of 'Wilful murder against some person or persons unknown.' A man has since been apprehended on suspicion. (1853)

💀 *May 9th* 💀

A frightful case of Murder and Suicide has occurred [this month] in Cheshire. At the village of Wheelock, near Sandbach, Mr. James Sproston, joiner and cabinet-maker, killed his wife with a sword, and afterwards blew out his own brains with a pistol. The cause appears to have been jealousy on the part of the husband, for which it appears there was no foundation. The husband was 46 years of age; the wife, Ann Sproston, 42. They had been married fifteen or sixteen years, were without children, and enjoyed a competence. With them lived a widowed sister of the wretched man, named Gill, and her son, a young man working as a joiner. For some weeks Sproston had made the suspicions of his wife's conduct the subject of frequent conversation with every one he knew. This had greatly affected her health. After breakfast on the morning of the murder they were left in the house alone. The last that was seen of them alive was at half-past seven o'clock. Mrs. Gill having been on an errand to Sandbach, returned about half-past nine. In the kitchen she found

Mrs. Sproston kneeling in a pool of blood, with her head frightfully disfigured, there being a sword beside her. In her own parlour Mrs. Gill found Mr. Sproston seated on a chair, with his dreadfully shattered head hanging forward, and a pistol lying between his feet on the floor. She obtained immediate assistance; but Mr. Sproston was quite dead, and his wife did not live half an hour. An inquest was held, and the jury found that Mr. Sproston had killed his wife and then committed suicide, being at the time in a state of insanity. The details of the evidence were very shocking. It appeared that both the deceased were very tall persons, the husband being full six feet and the wife not much less. They were proportionally powerful, and the struggle must have been terrific, as the kitchen presented the appearance of a slaughterhouse. There was blood even on the ceiling. The blows had been dealt with immense force, and had cloven the skull; but the wound which had been the immediate cause of death was a frightful gash at the back of the neck, severing the vertebral column. Sproston had made a will, excluding his wife from all benefit or interest in his property; but this was the less remarked as she had a private income settled in her own right, and sufficient to maintain her in comfort. (1855)

🕱 *May 10th* 🕱

Several fatal Colliery Accidents have taken place this month. A most frightful explosion occurred on the 10th at the Duffryn pit, in the valley of Aberdare, in Glamorganshire, and was attended with the loss of sixty-four lives. At four o'clock on the morning of the explosion, a careful investigation appears to have taken place, and the mine was reported free from gas. A few hours afterwards another fireman was sent down, who discovered symptoms of an approaching fall in a certain section of the mine. When the intelligence was conveyed to the agent above, orders were immediately given to a party to descend and use the necessary means to prevent the anticipated fall. This was about seven o'clock, and two hours afterwards a report was heard which gave token of the terrible tragedy which had occurred below. Mr. Skipley, the agent, descended by the winding shaft, and passed some poor wretches who had just escaped from the terrors of the explosion. At the bottom of the shaft eight of the men who had been despatched to prop up the roof were found dead. As he proceeded to grope his way, he next encountered a few half-suffocated men who were staggering to the mouth of the pit, if it might be found. He then found a heap of dead bodies, the one piled upon the other, scarcely at a hundred yards' distance from the pit. In trying to escape, it would seem the people had fallen upon each other and blocked up the passage. A little further on – about fifty yards – Mr. Skipley and his companions came upon just such another pile as the first. The two together contained the bodies of about sixty men and children. A father and his two sons were found among one of the heaps of the dead. The poor man in his frantic eagerness and anxiety to save himself and his two sons, had clutched one under each arm, and thus had in vain sought to escape. Sixty-four persons have perished altogether, and twenty-eight were brought out alive, making the total number who were in the pit at time of the explosion ninety-two. It appears that no blame can attach to any of the officials of the colliery. The coal worked here, however, is of a highly gaseous quality, insomuch that numerous cargoes which have recently gone from the shipping port (Cardiff) have exploded, and destroyed the vessels bearing them. (1853)

💀 *May 11th* 💀

The body of a young man was Discovered on the morning of the 11th inst. in a small copse near the Crystal Palace at Sydenham with his head blown to pieces, and a pistol lying by his side. An inquest was held, when it appeared he was a lad of seventeen, named Mason, in the employment of a butcher in Camberwell. He had left his master's service, in consequence of his disapproving of a correspondence the young man was carrying on with a young woman of fourteen. Two letters, which were found on his person, were then read, the first of which was addressed to his master, and was as follows:– 'Sir,– I have been in your service upwards of four years, and I must say I have met with every encouragement I have wished for, until lately. I have noticed, that you did not seem satisfied with what I have done, which has made me answer you at times very sharp, which you have noticed; and as I am to be separated from the sole object of my affections, there is no more comfort for me in this world; my heart is ready to burst with grief. In fact my agonies at the present time is more than I can bear, and therefore I am determined to ease myself of them by taking my own life. No doubt by the time you receive this I shall have breathed my last. I hope you will forward my box and all that belong to me to my afflicted parents. I cannot say any more, so farewell for ever.' The second was addressed to the young woman, and ran thus; 'These few lines come from your broken-hearted lover, whose happiness is going never to return again. I hope you will accept this as a last token of my love, and keep it in remembrance of me. I have now left the world, never to see you more, so farewell, for ever. No doubt you will hear some sad news from your father after you have received this note.' The jury returned a verdict of 'Temporary insanity.' (1853)

☠ *May 12th* ☠

Mrs. Chitty, the wife of a shopkeeper at Guildford, has, under the influence of a lunatic frenzy, Murdered two of her young Children. A grown-up son, hearing an alarming noise, ran into his mother's room, and found her battering the children's heads with a wooden mallet. It appeared at the inquest, that the poor woman's husband had become insane, and the misfortune had deranged her mind also. After she was arrested she attempted to strangle herself with a handkerchief; and she asked a man who was watching her, to 'make away with her by striking her on the head with anything he could get at.' The jury, as a matter of form, returned a verdict of wilful murder, and she was conveyed to prison. (1852)

A dreadful Murder was perpetrated at the village of Kate's-hill, near Dudley, on Saturday morning, the 12th inst. A young man, named Meadows, had been paying court to a young woman named Mason, but, becoming jealous, he determined that she should die. He borrowed a carbine, and having loaded it proceeded to the public-house where the girl lived as a servant, and where she was engaged in cleaning. He called for something to drink, and, watching his opportunity, he deliberately discharged the contents of the deadly weapon. The principal portion of the charge lodged directly under the left ear. She only lived a few minutes after. The murderer made no attempt to escape. He said, 'Revenge is sweet; I have had mine, and the law must take its own.' (1854)

☠ *May 13th* ☠

A melancholy Suicide has been committed by a young lady at Glasgow. She had resided for several days at a fashionable hotel, and on Saturday evening, the 13th inst., she was found suspended from a cord fixed in the window shutter of her room. Some letters found in a French ornamented fruit box led to her being identified as Jessie Lauder, whose family resides in Edinburgh. The act appears to have been the result of disappointed love, and to have been deliberately premeditated. She must have been engaged for the last day or two in writing parting letters to relatives and friends, all couched in the most affectionate and endearing terms. A letter to her sister reminds the latter of a stroll they had together in the cemetery at Edinburgh three weeks before, in which 'I told you where to lay my head. You thought I was joking with you, but now you know how deeply I was in earnest. I kissed my little brothers as they lay asleep in bed the morning I left home. Alas, it was to me a painful kissing, knowing that I never should see them more.' She further advises her sister, 'Never let intoxicating liquor enter the threshold of your door – it is the cause of my death; not that I ever drank myself – nobody on earth can ever say I did.' She appears to have written to her lover a few days previously, and the letter which the servant girl took up to her room when she found her dead was an answer to it. He apologises for delay in writing to her, ascribes this delay to her letter having been missent to a town three miles distant from his proper address, in proof of which he encloses the envelope marked 'missent to G.' The melancholy event was immediately intimated to her father, and to the young man, to whom she seems to have been so deeply attached. (1854)

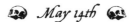 *May 14th*

A frightful Railway Accident happened on Sunday night the 14th inst., on the London and South Western Line. Between Richmond and Mortlake, a crash was heard, and the passengers experienced a sensation as if the carriages were being lifted off the metals. Being unable to communicate with the driver, the train went on, and on reaching the Mortlake station, the stationmaster missed the guard, whose name was Day, from his accustomed place. Lamps were procured, and the wheels of the carriage examined, when it was found that blood, hair, and brains were adhering to them. A porter named Forrester, belonging to the Mortlake station, was despatched to look for the poor man, and found him lying across the outer rails quite dead, the wheels of the engine or carriages having passed over him. His cap was found six or seven yards this side of the body. It seems that he must have been standing on the steps of the carriage, and have slipped down, as his boots were found about five yards between his body and his cap. (1854)

🕱 *May 15th* 🕱

An extraordinary case of hydrophobia has occurred in Lincolnshire. In January last, a girl named Taylor, 12 years of age, was bitten in the hand by a mad dog, in a field at Fillingham. She was taken to a surgeon, who not only cauterized the wound, but applied the cupping-glasses. She was subsequently removed to the village of Brocklesby, where she took a quantity of medicine, supposed to be a certain preventive or cure. After returning home, she remained in apparently good health until the 16th inst., when she was attacked by spasms and great thirst. She was perfectly sensible when free from the spasmodic attacks, but when they returned the paroxysms were distressing, and she ultimately died from their effects. The wound was small, and had healed. (1853)

🕱 *May 16th* 🕱

Between one and two in the morning of the 16th, the house of Mr. Richbell, at Wickham St. Paul's, in Essex, was Broken into by Thieves, who forced open the front door, and the door of the parlour where Mrs. Richbell, who is infirm, was sleeping. One man broke open a bureau, while another endeavoured to stifle Mrs. Richbell's cries by holding his hand on her mouth. A servant girl who slept at the back of the house jumped out of the window, ran to a neighbouring cottage for help, and brought with her a labourer armed with a poker. Mr. Richbell, who slept up stairs, got up at the same time, and the robbers, finding themselves discovered, made off after a short scuffle, and escaped. The window from which the courageous girl jumped is more than twelve feet from the ground. (1850)

The Great Western steamer, one of the royal West India Mail Company's ships, brought to Southampton a large amount of Gold dust from California, consigned to the Bank of England. On the 16th inst., 157 boxes were unshipped, and packed upon four trucks to be conveyed to London: the average weight of the boxes was nearly half a hundredweight. When the train arrived at Nine Elms early next morning, it was found that three boxes were missing from one of the trucks. The same afternoon, a boy, the son of a publican living near the Winchester station, while searching for bird's nests on the railway bank, found one of the missing boxes: it had not been opened. A watch was set at the spot; and at half-past eleven o'clock at night a man came to the place. He was arrested. When taken before the mayor and magistrates of Winchester, he said his name was William Plankin, and that he was a tailor of Earl Street, Soho: which was subsequently found to be true. He accounted for his presence at Winchester, and for his going to the bank, in a way by no means satisfactory; and he was remanded. A reward of 250*l.* has been offered for the apprehension of the thieves and the recovery of the other two boxes of gold: one weighed fifty-three pounds, and the other forty pounds. The value of the three was 7,000*l.*

🕱 *May 17th* 🕱

A dreadful Murder and Suicide were committed on board the Countess of Wilton, of Liverpool, on her homeward voyage from China. On the 17th of May, when the ship was near the Indian coast, the late captain, Mr. James Crangle, ordered all hands on deck. The chiefmate, William M'Fillen, did not seem inclined to perform his duty, and the master sent two men to look for him. He was found in the storeroom under the cabin, and the captain despatched the second-mate to bring him up for disobeying orders. M'Fillen was met approaching the cabin, and the master ordered the seamen away in order that he might have some conversation with him privately. A cutlass was lying on the table in the cabin at the time. Angry words were passing between them. Soon afterwards the second mate, hearing a noise and some heavy groans, looked through the skylight, but could not observe anything. He called the crew, and, arming himself with wood, went down to the cabin, where to his horror he saw the lifeless body of the captain stretched upon the floor, and M'Fillen thrusting at him with the cutlass. The murderer made an attempt to escape by running up the rigging, but he was pursued, secured, and chained down in his cabin. About a week afterwards, while he was being conducted to the water-closet, duly guarded, he made a sudden spring, bounded overboard, and was drowned. The catastrophe is attributed to the free use of ardent spirits on board. The master is said to have been often in liquor, and while in that condition treated the chief-mate with excessive severity. The second-mate took command of the ship, and brought her safe home. (1853)

🕱 *May 18th* 🕱

A distressing case of Poisoning through Carelessness with Drugs has occurred [this month] at Leeds. A woman, named Stancliffe, went to Mr. Exley's (druggist) shop, in Hunslet-lane, and purchased a pennyworth of bichromate of potash and vitriol for colouring, which, though of a very poisonous nature, was supplied to her without being labelled, and she took it home, and being ignorant of its nature, laid it on the table. Whilst occupied in putting some water upon the fire, one of her children, a little boy two years old, took hold of the parcel, went with it to the door, and after eating a portion of the contents scattered the rest on the floor. Very shortly afterwards he was seized with vomiting, and was conveyed first to the druggist's and thence to the Leeds Infirmary; yet, notwithstanding every effort to counteract the effects of the poison, he died during the afternoon. At the inquest on the body a verdict of 'Accidentally poisoned' was returned, and the jury specially urged upon chemists the importance of labelling all poisons disposed of by them. (1854)

🕱 *May 19th* 🕱

Edwin Hucker, a boy not ten years old, has been committed [this month] on a Coroner's warrant for the Murder of another boy, William Saunders, by pushing him into the river Avon, at Keynsham, near Bristol. A playmate, three days after the boy was found drowned; said that Hucker pushed Saunders into the water, after Saunders had jumped upon Hucker's neck as he was lying on the grass. The extreme youth of Hucker has raised a question as to the legal responsibility of one of such tender years in a case of 'murder.' It appear that a boy of ten was convicted at Bury, in 1748: he killed a girl five years of age, cut up the body, and buried it in a heap of dung; he was sentenced to be hanged, but punishment was respited till the opinion of all the judges could be taken, and they held that he was an object for capital punishment. But subsequently he was pardoned by the Crown, on condition of entering the Navy. (1853)

🕱 *May 20th* 🕱

Captain Henry Whittingham was Run Over by a Timber-Waggon on the 20th, after having escaped the varied dangers of the deep for nearly half a century. He had been for many years in the service of the General Steam Navigation Company, and previously Commander of the Sir William Carter, a cutter, belonging to the late Mr. Rothschild, and used for the conveyance of specie to and from the continent. Captain Whittingham was passing Thornton-street, Bermondsey, when he fell under the hind wheel of a heavily laden timber-waggon, and before the horses could be stopped, the wheel rested on his breast. (1850)

💀 *May 21st* 💀

A dreadful Murder was committed at Hull in the night of the 21st. The body of a respectable young man named Maplethorpe, a clerk in the house of Messrs. Thomas and Co., merchants, was found lying on the edge of a ditch adjoining a piece of waste ground near his father's residence. Marks of a scuffle on the pavement, and the dragging of a body across the road, were perceivable, showing that the poor youth had been attacked within a few feet of his own threshold. The external appearances of the body indicated that death had been occasioned by suffocation, no marks of violence being observed, but some scratches, as of human nails, upon each cheek. A gold watch which the deceased carried had been torn from his waistcoat pocket, and his money to the amount of about 11*l.* had also been taken from his person. Two men, named John Snape and James Smith, were apprehended on suspicion and brought before the magistrates, by whom, after an examination, they have been remanded. (1852)"

💀 *May 22nd* 💀

Mr. Daniel Barnett, head of the firm of Neustadt & Barnett, general merchants in Birmingham, was Killed on the North Western Railway, on the 22nd inst. He had left Birmingham by the mail train for London about midnight. He occupied alone a compartment of a first-class carriage, and very soon after the train had entered the Beechwood tunnel, near Coventry, the guard felt a slight concussion; he looked out, and saw a carriage door open. He signalled the driver to stop, and presently the body of Mr. Barnett was found lying across the rails, his legs nearly severed from his body and his carpet bag a little distance off. He had fallen from the carriage and been jerked from the wall of the tunnel to beneath the rails, and the train had passed over him. He was alive when picked up, and he uttered a sentence or two: but he had scarcely reached Coventry before he expired. It seems probable that he was laying down the cushions and making his bed comfortable for the night, and that the door of the carriage not being fastened he fell backward on to it, and was cast beneath the rails. (1854)

💀 *May 23rd* 💀

Mr. Robert Lindsay Mauleverer, a magistrate in the county of Londonderry, and an agent over extensive estates in the North of Ireland, was Murdered on the 23rd. He was travelling on an outside car to meet the train on the Dundalk and Enniskillen railway, when he was shot through the head and killed on the spot. He had been engaged of late in serving ejectment notices on a very extensive scale. Two persons have been arrested on suspicion. (1850)

💀 *May 24th* 💀

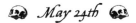

A fatal Experiment in Aerostation was made on Friday evening, the 24th. A monster balloon, fifty feet long, twenty-two in diameter, and capable of containing 15,000 cubic feet of gas, ascended from the Phoenix Gasworks, under the direction of Mr. Monro, the superintendent, and descended safely in the parish of High Laver, Essex; but a poor labourer, named Frederick Clark, while assisting to secure the balloon in its descent, was so dreadfully injured by the grapnel, that he died a few hours afterwards. (1850)

💀 *May 25th* 💀

The proverb 'Murder will out,' has just been strikingly illustrated. Stephen Carlin, beast-jobber, residing near Skipton, in Yorkshire, was last seen alive at Pateley-bridge, in company with his partner (a cousin), eleven or twelve years ago. His cousin said that he had gone to America, but foul play was always suspected; and on Saturday the 25th of May, a digger of peat on Roggin-moor, near Pateley-bridge, found the body of the missing man, a few feet below the surface in such a state of preservation (owing to the antiseptic nature of the soil) that it was readily identified. A tailor, too, knew the clothes to be Carlin's; and a married woman, whom he had wooed in her maidenhood, recognised as her property a handkerchief and comb that were found in the pockets. The cousin, Jonathan Bland, was apprehended at Skipton two days afterwards. (1854)

🕱 *May 26th* 🕱

A fatal Boiler Explosion took place on boat the *Times* steamer, as she was leaving Dublin, on the 26th of May, with a large number of passengers. A number of poor deck-passengers had gathered on the waist of the ship for the sake of the warmth, and these were all dreadfully scalded. Two children died directly after, and ten more of the unfortunate people afterwards died in the Dublin hospitals. At an inquest on one of the bodies, the jury found 'that the cause of the bursting of the boiler is to be attributed to the gross neglect of James Haig. Government Engineer Surveyor, in not making a proper inspection of the boiler of the said steamer in April last; and we consider him highly culpable in not giving up the key of the parliamentary safety valve to the captain of the vessel at time of his last inspection in April last.' The Coroner deemed this verdict tantamount to one of 'manslaughter,' and he issued his warrant for the arrest of Mr. Haig. (1853)

🕱 *May 27th* 🕱

A Soldier was Rolled to Death on the 27th, at Portsmouth. A party belonging to the 28th Regt., while doing fatigue-duty on Southsea Common, were returning to quarters, drawing after them a very large iron roller, charged with iron shot, when, in descending the road to the centre of the glacis at a rapid pace to escape the rain which was falling, one of the men fell. In an instant, the ponderous machine passed over him, and his head and body were so fearfully crushed that instantaneous death resulted. (1850)

🕱 *May 28th* 🕱

A Serious Riot, caused by a Protectionist Meeting, took place at Tamworth on the 28th of May. The protectionists dined in the town-hall. A cold collation was sent from Birmingham, the use of the principal Tamworth hotel having been denied, through the influence of the present Sir Robert Peel ... About nine o'clock, Mr. Newdegate rose to propose the chairman's health. He had no sooner done so than an enormous paving-stone was thrown through the windows into the middle of the hall, and immediately volleys of large stones were thrown at the hall windows, till every window and every chandelier was smashed. The company had made a hasty flight into the lobbies, where they armed themselves with chair-legs, pokers, knives, and all such weapons as were within reach, and to the number of three hundred made a sally into the street. A hand-to-hand fight took place; many persons were seriously injured; and the protectionists and their friends took refuge in the King's Arms Inn, every window of which was broken to atoms. As the daring of the populace increased, it was deemed expedient to swear in special constables. This was, however, unsuccessful at first: when the constables made a sally from the hotel, the populace drove them back, and the most savage beating took place on both sides. For two hours the town was in possession of the mob; and amongst the acts of daring committed was the taking of the farmers' vehicles from the inn-yards and casting them over the bridge into the river. Towards midnight the populace cleared off, and the constables paraded the streets. About a dozen persons were taken into custody. At one o'clock on the following morning, the disturbance had so far subsided that the order for the military was countermanded. At noon on that day, however, matters looked so threatening that a detachment of dragoons was obtained from Birmingham; and in the evening all was again quiet. Not more than twenty of the Peel tenantry were present at the dinner. (1851)

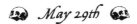 *May 29th*

An accident occurred on the Shropshire Union Railway, on the 29th ult., from the negligence of a fireman. At Shrewsbury station, a man lighted a fire in a locomotive which was presently to be used; without shutting off the steam or throwing the machinery out of gear, he left the engine untended in a shed. When the steam got up, the locomotive slowly left the shed, and moved down the rails upon which a train for Stafford was then proceeding. The engine gradually increased its speed, till on descending an incline near Wellington it is supposed that it went at the rate of seventy miles an hour. Three miles farther on, at Donnington, the Stafford train had stopped. The runaway engine dashed into it, and the two hindmost carriages were smashed to pieces. Thirteen persons were hurt, three of them so badly that they could not be removed from the place. A coroner's inquest has found a verdict of 'manslaughter' against Joseph Thompson, the man who had negligently left the engine untended in the shed. (1852)

💀 *May 30th* 💀

Mr. Robert Dundas Jones, a solicitor, Poisoned Himself with prussic acid on the evening of the 30th of May. It appeared, at the inquest, that he had several bills of exchange unpaid, and that one, of considerable amount, had been presented for payment on the morning of his death. The jury found that he had died from the effects of poison, but that there was not sufficient evidence to prove the state of his mind. (1850)

💀 *May 31st* 💀

A case of Brutal Assault by a military officer on his mistress was tried in the Court of Common Pleas on the 31st ult. Ellen Walsh was the plaintiff, and John Hatton Keane the defendant. The declaration contained two counts, one for assault and the other for detaining the plaintiff's clothes. The defendant pleaded not guilty to the first count, and to the second that he had not detained the clothes. Mr. Serjeant Shee said that his client in this case was a beautiful girl, only sixteen years of age, but although so young he was sorry to say that she had led an immoral life, she having been seduced at the early age of fifteen years ... The defendant, Captain Keane, was a man of fortune, about twenty-five years of age, and he resided at Loughton, in Essex. In August, last year, he met the plaintiff at a place in the neighbourhood of Leicester-square, which was a cigar shop, and he apprehended was a house of ill-fame as well. He stayed there all night, and he induced the plaintiff to go with him to Loughton; but in a few days she returned again to London. The defendant, however, again induced her to live with him, and she remained at his house at Loughton until the 7th February last, when she was taken by a child, who was the daughter of the defendant's gardener, to a cottage in the neighbourhood. She had been beaten in a frightful manner, and was bruised and bleeding in various parts of her body, as the witnesses would more particularly detail ... She was in a very bad condition, and appeared as if she had been dragged about by the hair of her head. There was a wound in her left cheek, her face was bloody, her left ear was quite discoloured, her face was all bruised, there was a mark as if of a whip half round her neck, and witness thought her left shoulder was bleeding. There was a great bruise on her knee, her teeth seemed to be loose, and she could not take anything while she was with witness. She stayed from ten o'clock in the morning until the evening next day, when her mother came in consequence of having been sent for.

The plaintiff's ankles were cut as with a whip, and her night clothes were saturated with blood. Mrs. Welsh and a surgeon deposed to the condition the girl was in after the assault, and the jury almost immediately found a verdict for the plaintiff – damages 100*l.* for the assault, and 1*s.* upon the other count. (1854)

June

June 1st

In October 1848, a small deal box, labelled 'Mr. Watson, passenger, Exeter,' was found on the railway platform at Slough. No one applied for it, and after a time it was sent to London to the 'lost property' department. On the 1st inst. the box was opened, and was found to contain the Mummy of a Child, supposed to be a girl, about eighteen months old. The corpse was quite shrivelled up; round the neck was tied a cambric handkerchief; attempts had been made to separate the limbs, and there were other mutilations. No arsenic was detected by analysis. A coroner's jury has returned a verdict of wilful murder against some person or persons unknown. (1850)

On the 1st inst. a labouring man of the name of Taylor, living at the village of Tushingham in Cheshire, Murdered his own Son, a boy of seven years old. Some of the man's younger children complained to the neighbours that their brother was ill, and that they were shut out and could not get to him. On looking through a window one of the neighbours discovered the boy lying on the floor weltering in his blood. An entrance was forced into the house, and it was ascertained that the skull of the child had been split with an axe. Taylor was found upstairs in bed, and immediately accused of the murder. He was sullen, but after a coroner's inquest was held, he confessed himself guilty, and was committed for trial. Although in very poor circumstances, it does not appear that absolute want drove him to commit the crime, nor did he assign any motive for it. His wife stated that he had for some time past carried a rope in his pocket for the declared purpose of hanging himself. (1850)

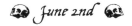

June 2nd

A young man named James Smith, residing at Keighley, has met with an Appalling Death [this month]. He had been an apprentice with Messrs. Hattersley, machinemakers of Keighley, but had latterly been leading an idle life and wandering about the country. Being destitute and without lodgings, he lay down to sleep between two limekilns. One of them was partly empty, but still emitted a sulphurous stench and smoke, and the other was burning and red. At two o'clock a person passing by saw the youth near the empty pit, and having warned him of his danger passed on. Another person, named Wakefield, approached the kiln about half-past six o'clock, and found the body on the top of the burning lime. He immediately aroused a workman who resided hard by, and the remains were drawn off with an iron drag. The legs and bowels were entirely consumed, the flesh burnt from the ribs, the eyes from their sockets, the hair and scalp from the skull, and the arm upon which he had fallen was entirely gone. A mass of charred and blackened matter alone remained, scarcely distinguishable as the vestiges of a human being. It is supposed that he had been partly suffocated by the fumes issuing from the nearly empty kiln, and that when rolling over in half-unconscious agony he had dropped into the one adjoining. His cap lay upon the brink, and from that alone his name and occupation have been traced. (1854)

💀 June 3rd 💀

The proceedings of a coroner's inquest, held on the 3rd, at University College hospital, on the body of Ann Truscott, a young woman who had poisoned herself, were disturbed by the Disgraceful Conduct of a number of Medical Students. During the examination of the witnesses, they entered the inquest room in a body, and behaved so rudely that the coroner had to send for the police to clear the apartment. The students again forced their way into the room, and a repetition of the former scene took place. The coroner adjourned the inquest till the evening. When the jury reassembled there were about twenty students present, who, on the coroner's desiring strangers to leave the room, took their departure, but only to recommence a new course of annoyance, by constantly ringing a large bell in the room which communicated with the front door of the hospital. The jury added to their verdict an expression of their great disapprobation of 'the gross conduct of a number of the students of University College hospital,' and their wish that the fact should be made known to the heads of the institution. (1850)

💀 June 4th 💀

A man of the name of Reynolds, who lived in Yarmouth, had been for some time separated from his wife. He met her accidentally on the 4th, and after some abusive words, attacked her savagely with a clasp-knife, cutting her on the neck, hands, and arms. She contrived to escape with her life, on which he Cut his Throat with the knife, and threw himself into the sea. An inquest on the body returned a verdict of *felo de se*, and the corpse was buried by torchlight. (1850)

💀 June 5th 💀

An atrocious Murder has been committed at Glasgow [this month]. Boyd and Law, ship-carpenters, were drinking together at night; two loose women enticed them into a den in the New Vennel; there the men were plied with drugged drink until nearly insensible; then the women and a man who lived with one of them began to strip the carpenters of their clothes. Boyd had sufficient consciousness to know what was going on, and he resisted; but the wretches succeeded in stripping him.

He threatened to call the police, upon which they dragged him to the window on the third story, and tossed him head foremost into the street. He fell on the back of his head, the skull was fractured, and he died on the spot. The murderers fled, leaving Law insensible from the drugged drink. But there had been witnesses of the crime: two destitute boys were lying under a bedstead in the room, doubtless forgotten by the murderers; some women living in the house had also peeped through a chink in the door, and witnessed the scenes. The police were quickly informed of the murder, and the wretches were arrested before they could escape from the city. (1853)

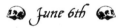

June 6th

On the 6th inst. the small town of Crowland, in Lincolnshire, was the scene of a Dreadful Murder. Mr. Hickling, a farmer residing in South street, has been twice married, and a daughter by his first wife was married to a tradesman of the town, named Joseph Baines, tailor and draper. On the above morning, about ten o'clock, a woman named Rowlett, who lived opposite the Hicklings' residence, saw Baines go in alone, opening the street door himself, and shutting it after his entrance. In the course of a few minutes, Mrs. Hickling rushed out screaming 'Murder!' closely followed by Baines, with a poker in his hand. A few yards from the door of the house she fell to the ground; and while thus prostrate, with her face downwards, she was struck a violent blow on the head by Baines, who seemed much excited, holding the poker with both hands, and striking blow upon blow, apparently with all his force. The woman Rowlett immediately cried out, 'Oh! Mr. Baines, what are you going to do?' and a shoemaker, named Ringrose, hurried to Mrs. Hickling's assistance; the latter was then quite senseless, and, indeed, never spoke after the assault. On Ringrose's interference, Baines threw down the poker, and ran away, but when he had gone a few yards he returned, took up the poker, and made another blow at the deceased. After this he ran off a second time, and was followed by Ringrose, who, however, was afraid to seize him, as he looked very wild. He did not speak a word during or after the murderous attack, and no evidence was adduced before the coroner explanatory of the motives impelling him to the dreadful deed. The woman had her arms broken in two places, and her skull was completely fractured, several portions of bone being driven also into the brain. The above facts were deposed to by various witnesses at the inquest. The evidence of one of

97

the constables who arrested Baines showed that he was alternately much excited and depressed at the time and after his arrest. He cried, said he 'could not rest night or day,' wished the constable to 'pray for him,' and often put his hand to his head, saying, 'Oh, my poor head! Oh, my poor mind!' Presently he began walking sharply round the room, and then, complaining that the air was oppressive, he went to the window with the intention of opening it, and, but for the constable, would, it is believed, have thrown himself out. He seemed very unwilling to be left alone in his cell. The coroner said the evidence was clear; and the jury immediately returned a verdict of wilful murder against Joseph Baines. (1854)

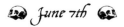

June 7th

A frightful Boiler Explosion occurred on the 7th, at Mr. Braine's colliery, at Kingswood, near Bristol. The Starveall pit, together with several others, is worked by means of a steam engine. The old boiler having fully done its work, a new one was to have been erected, and while a number of men were in the act of removing the masonry in which the old boiler was fixed, without waiting for the steam to blow off, suddenly the boiler burst with a terrific explosion, by which it was completely blown out of its bed, and huge fragments of it, together with the surrounding stone and brickwork, hurled to a great height in the air. The boiling water and red-hot cinders were scattered around in all directions, falling on the persons of several of the men, and scalding them in the most fearful manner. Mr. Braine himself was thrown down by the violence of the explosion, and his hat knocked off by a portion of the flying debris, but fortunately he escaped without serious injury. Medical assistance having shortly arrived some of the poor fellows were laid on beds, and carried on carts to the Bristol Royal Infirmary, but in many instances the injuries were too desperate to warrant the removal of the sufferers. During the day four men died, and the deaths of four others were afterwards reported. At the inquest, it appeared from the evidence that the accident was produced by a want of sufficient water, and from there having been a considerable quantity of steam evaporated while the engine was standing. The jury returned as their verdict – 'That the deceased parties came by their deaths through the explosion of a steamboiler, which explosion was caused by the carelessness and inattention of the engineer, John Burchall.' Burchall was one of the men who had lost their lives. (1851)

🕸 June 8th 🕸

A dreadful attempt at Murder and Suicide was made in Westminster on the 8th inst. A Chelsea pensioner, named Martin White, having quarrelled some days ago with a woman, named Hurley, with whom he cohabited, left her and went into lodgings at Devonshire-place, Broadway. On the above evening the woman came there, and hearing he was there waited for him. On his return, partially intoxicated, high words ensued, and on a policeman entering the room he found both the parties lying exhausted on the floor, bleeding profusely, the woman from very severe gashes about the face, neck, and arms, and the man White from a dreadful wound in the throat. A razor covered with blood was lying on the floor, and had evidently been the instrument with which the wounds were inflicted. They were immediately removed to the hospital. White has affirmed that the woman cut his throat. (1852)

🕸 June 9th 🕸

A Fire, attended with the Death of Three young Children, took place on Saturday morning, the 9th inst., in a house in the Hackney-road, occupied by a man named Graham. About nine o'clock flames were observed issuing from the first-floor windows of the house, and loud shrieks of children were heard by some of the neighbours. Assistance was obtained immediately, but all attempts to get to the first floor were unavailing, the fire having taken such a firm hold of the interior. The flames were not extinguished until the upper part of the house was nearly burned out. A shocking sight then presented itself. Under the remains of a bedstead, in one of the upper rooms, were discovered the bodies of the three children of Graham, one fine girl seven years of age, and two younger children, boys. They were crouched together in a heap, burned dreadfully. It is presumed that one of them had been playing with Lucifer matches, and had set fire to the bed. There was no escape for the poor little creatures. The mother, who had gone on an errand, had, in order to keep them out of the streets, locked the room door. The anguish of the parents, on becoming acquainted with the melancholy fate of their children, was very great. (1855)

A Frightful Tragedy occurred at Wilnot, Annapolis County, in the United States, on the 9th ult., when a Mrs. Miller, of Handley, after her husband had gone to church, walked out with her four youngest children, and having tied them to her dress, plunged with them from a cliff, and all were drowned. Her mind has been slightly deranged, but on that day she appeared unusually well. She left nine other children. (1850)

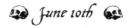

June 10th

Richard McAllister, a man of rather shabby appearance, was charged at the Marylebone Police Court on the 10th, with having been near the house of Miss Bellew, Primrose-hill road, for an Unlawful Purpose. The man had been Miss Bellew's footman, and was in the habit of saying to his fellow-servants and others that his mistress was in love with him. This coming to her ears, she discharged him, and since then he has persecuted her with importunities and threats of violence, pretending she owes him money, and that she had encouraged his passion. During the investigation, Miss Bellew, who told her own story, was in a state of great excitement, while McAllister insisted that the lady had promised to marry him and none but him, with more to the same purpose. He was held to bail to keep the peace to Miss Bellow and her household for a month and sent to prison in default of sureties. On hearing the decision, Miss Bellew exclaimed with great agitation, 'I am surprised, sir, that you have only secured this man for a month – at the end of that time we shall all be shot!' (1850)

June 11th

Miss Seymour, of Bath, daughter of Lady Seymour, who had come to Oxford with a party of friends to be present at the commemoration, was Killed by a Fall from her Horse, while taking an airing, on the afternoon of the 11th, with several ladies and gentlemen. The horse stumbled, and threw Miss Seymour on her head. She was taken up insensible, and remained in that situation till the 14th, when she expired.

On the 11th, an inquest was held at Chiswick upon the body of Mr. Samuel Thorrington, a coal merchant and bargemaster, late residing at Hill Cottage, who had committed Suicide by discharging a rifle pistol at the back part of his head. It appeared from the evidence of the wife of the deceased that on Monday evening he came into her bed-room with a pistol in his hand, and exclaimed 'Here old girl, the time has come.' She, fearing he was going to shoot her, rushed out into the garden, and called to the police, when the report of a pistol was heard, and on her re-entering the house, the deceased was found in the agonies of death, and weltering in his blood. He was considered by his medical man to have been decidedly insane. His wife had lived separately from him on account of some unhappy difference, and had come on that occasion to see his mother. A verdict was found to the effect that the deceased destroyed himself while in an insane state of mind. (1851)

🕱 *June 12th* 🕱

On the 12th, a young servant-girl was cleaning the attic windows of a house in Blackman Street, Borough, and, as usual, had placed herself on the window sill, when she lost her balance, and, falling into the street, was Killed on the Spot, her head being shattered to pieces. (1850)

🕱 *June 13th* 🕱

At the High Court of Justiciary at Edinburgh, on the 13th, Mr. David Robertson Williamson, of Lawers, Perthshire, formerly an officer in the Coldstream Guards, pleaded guilty to a charge of Assaulting the Reverend William Robertson, minister of Monzievaird and Strowan. Mr. Williamson got admittance to the clergyman's house during his absence, waited for him in the study, and when he entered, violently beat him with a stick. The motive for the attack did not transpire. Sentence, nine months imprisonment. The culprit had been originally indicted for 'hamesüken' – seeking after a person in his own domicile with the intention of using violence towards him; the extreme penalty for which ancient Scotch offence is death. The Solicitor-General withdrew this charge: the Court intimated that had Mr. Williamson been convicted of it, he would have been transported. (1852)

🕱 *June 14th* 🕱

Colonel Craigie, a retired officer of the Bengal army, committed Suicide on the 14th at his house in Exeter. Not appearing in the morning to breakfast, and not answering when called by Mrs. Craigie, his bedroom door was forced open, and he was found lying on the floor in a pool of blood, his throat cut, and with frightful wounds in his belly and both his legs. He was breathing when found, but died in less than an hour. No cause is assigned for this dreadful deed. (1850)

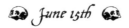 *June 15th*

On the 10th, while several men were engaged in laying down what arc called 'turn-tables', or great cast iron tubes weighing five tons each, on the Brighton Railway, the tackle employed in lifting one of them to the top of one of the arches, suddenly gave way, and the mass fell, bringing with it a quantity of the brickwork. One poor man, named George Rowe, was Instantly Crushed to Death, and two others, John Hackett and George Howison, were injured, the former so dreadfully that he was not expected to survive. (1850)

June 16th

A serious Balloon Accident occurred on the evening of the 16th. Mr. and Mrs. Graham ascended from Batty's Hippodrome, near Kensington. The balloon rose slowly, but had not ascended above fifty or sixty feet when it again sank, and in doing so the silken envelope came in contact with a pole or flag-staff, sustaining a considerable rent, by which the gas began to escape. The balloon again ascended, and by a succession of alternate risings and sinkings at length got clear of the enclosure, and floated away in the direction of the Crystal Palace. When over the building the aeronauts discharged their ballast, which they had been compelled to carry, greatly to their own disadvantage, while moving over the heads of the crowd. After clearing the building with some difficulty, and damaging a flag-staff, the balloon drifted towards the Green Park, and skimmed the surface of the reservoir, whence it again suddenly rose to the altitude of the houses in Piccadilly. A breeze at this time carried the balloon towards the roof of Col. North's house in Arlington street, which looks into the park. In its passage over that dwelling the car became fixed between the sloping roof and a stack of chimneys rising from it. A gust of wind now gave a new impetus to the machine, which dragged heavily, and carried away the chimney stack. Its buoyant force seemed to have been exhausted by this effort, and as the gas was fast escaping, it offered no resistance to the wind sufficient to permit any further progress before the arrival of aid.

As all the windows in the upper story of Col. North's house were barred, no assistance could be rendered from the interior; but the inmates of the house adjoining found a way to the roof, and conveyed the voyagers, much injured, by the skylight into a place of safety. They were immediately attended by a surgeon of the neighbourhood. Mr. Graham had a severe scalp wound, his chest bone broken, his collar bone fractured, and several other injuries very serious to a man of sixty-six years of age. Mrs. Graham had a very severe scalp wound, and also a few incised wounds on the face. She has written a letter to say that the accident was entirely owing to the violence of the wind, and that no part of the Crystal Palace was touched by the balloon. (1851)

June 17th

Mr. Samuel Adcock, a young farmer of Ashby Shrubs, near Leicester, has been Robbed and Murdered. He went to Leicester market on Saturday the 17th inst.; very early next morning his corpse was found in a ditch by the roadside, at a lonely place, three miles from Leicester. From the appearances observed, the farmer, a tall man, had been shot in the base of the skull, at the back of the right ear, by a shorter man; the assassination had occurred in the middle of the road, and the body had been dragged into the ditch. One of the victim's pockets had been turned inside out, and all the money was gone. The neckerchief and hat were missing, but the hat has been since found behind a hedge. A post-mortem examination has detected a bullet between the scalp and the skull, where it had lodged after passing through the brain. (1854)

June 18th

Two children of Mr. Lewen, a visitor to Brighton, were playing on the beach on the 18th, when a bathing machine, on the wheels of which they had climbed, was suddenly put in motion, and threw them down. The one, a boy of seven, escaped with slight injury; the other, a girl of nine, was Killed on the Spot, the wheel having passed over her head. (1850)

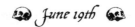

June 19th

On the 19th, William Jones, a labourer in Messrs. J. Whitbread & Co.'s brewery, was Suffocated by Foul Air, in a vat into which he had descended for the purpose of cleaning its bottom. The coroner's jury found that no blame was attached to the firm, as it appeared that he had been frequently cautioned against entering the vats to clean them without first allowing the carbonic acid gas, generated from the grounds, to escape. (1850)

June 20th

On the 20th, a Fire broke out in the warehouses belonging to Alderman Humphery, on the Surrey side of London Bridge; an immense pile of buildings six stories high, and 300 feet in length. The fire was discovered about three in the afternoon, when Alderman Humphery was at the House of Commons engaged on a committee; he heard the rumbling of engines in the street, and enquiring the cause, learned that his own property was on fire. Notwithstanding every exertion, the warehouses were almost wholly destroyed; and the loss of property is supposed to amount to 150,000*l.*; but happily there has been no loss of life. The fire is ascribed to spontaneous combustion. (1851)

June 21st

An extraordinary case of Murder has taken place in Belgium. The Count and Countess de Bocarmé have been tried at Mons, on the charge of having poisoned the Countess's brother Gustave Fougnies, in order to obtain his fortune. The Count, whose affairs were much embarrassed, invited his brother-in-law to dinner. Gustave dined in company with the Count and Countess, and died immediately after dinner, while they were both present. It was proved, by the appearance of the body and other circumstances, that a corrosive fluid had been forcibly poured down his throat. On the trial the Count endeavoured to represent the circumstance as accidental, while his wife charged him with the deliberate murder of her brother, admitting her own previous knowledge of her husband's intention, but denying any participation in the deed. After a protracted trial, which terminated on the 21st inst., the Count was convicted, and condemned to death; while the Countess was acquitted. (1851)

💀 *June 22nd* 💀

A deliberate Suicide was committed on the 22nd, by a Child Seven Years Old, the son of John Hanson, a waterman, residing at Newark. The boy having been beaten by his mother, had threatened that if she did so again he would drown himself, and carried his threat into execution, by walking resolutely into the Trent till the stream carried him away. (1850)

💀 *June 23rd* 💀

On Sunday the 23rd, early in the morning, a respectable-looking middle-aged man was observed to throw himself from the centre arch of Southwark bridge. In his fall his head was seen to strike against one of the abutments with a force which must have shattered his skull. His body has not been found. (1850)

On the 23rd inst., a person named Bosworth, alias Elliot, a printseller in Holywell-street, in the Strand, was tried in the Court of Queen's Bench, on the charge of selling Disgusting and Indecent Prints. The defendant did not appear, but the charge was proved by two witnesses, agents for the Society for the Suppression of Vice, who prosecuted. He was convicted, and sentenced to three years' imprisonment, with hard labour. (1854)

💀 *June 24th* 💀

Mr. J. Smith, of Sheffield, a young man of 21, lost his life on the 24th from the Incautious Use of Chloroform. He was found dead in his bed in the morning, with a handkerchief in his hand firmly pressed to his mouth and nostrils; and a bottle which had contained chloroform was found by him. He had been in the habit of inhaling chloroform to allay the pain of toothache. (1850)

💀 *June 25th* 💀

A Workshop suddenly Fell on the premises lately occupied by the Philanthropic Society in St. George's Fields, on the 25th, while a number of French polishers were at work in it. One man named Wilson was crushed to death, and several others so much injured that they were conveyed to the hospital. (1850)

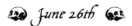

June 26th

During a Thunder-Storm, which lately passed over Ipswich, a young woman named Stevens was struck by the electric fluid. She had retired to rest, and noticed nothing during the storm, beyond being greatly heated; but upon rising on the following morning she discovered that the whole of her hair on the right side and part on the back of the head had been burnt off by the lightning, the other portion being much singed. The left side was uninjured. The hair removed is about a foot long. (1852)

June 27th

An Atrocious Attack on Her Majesty was made shortly after six o'clock on the evening of the 27th. The Queen, accompanied by a lady in waiting and the royal children, had been to inquire respecting the health of the Duke of Cambridge, at his residence, in Piccadilly. A man was observed loitering about for some time, keeping his eye directed towards the entrance at which the royal carriage would come out, when on reaching the end of the road from the house, the villain deliberately aimed a blow at Her Majesty with a light cane, which he held in his hand, striking her on the cheek, and crushing her bonnet over her forehead, which caused a great sensation to the bystanders. The fellow was instantly seized by the persons on the spot, and the weapon wrested from him. Her Majesty then immediately proceeded to Buckingham Palace. The police were quickly on the spot, and took him in charge, and conveyed him to the Vine Street station. Upon being placed before Inspector Whall, he gave his name as Robert Pate, 27, Duke Street, St. James's. He assigned no reason for the act; said he had been a lieutenant in the Tenth Hussars. The charge was then entered as follows: – 'Charged with assaulting Her Majesty on leaving Cambridge House.' He was then locked up. Her Majesty arrived at the palace perfectly safe, and apparently little alarmed at the outrageous assault that had been committed on her. In a short time, however, the news had spread to the various club-houses, and the noblemen and others there assembled instantly hastened to the royal residence to ascertain, if possible, whether Her Majesty had sustained injury. However, she appeared at the Royal Italian Opera in the evening, and presented herself in the front of her box perfectly unharmed. Her reception by the audience was something more than enthusiastic; it was affecting – many shed tears. (1850)

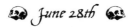

June 28th

At the Thames Police Court, on the 28th June, Mrs. Acock, wife of a timber-merchant at Stepney, was fined 5s. for an Assault on Catherine Tiernay, her servant. On the following day, Mr. Acock accused the girl of stealing four gold pins. Mr. Acock asserted that the girl had secreted a little box containing the pins in her clothes-box; the girl's solicitor endeavoured to show that this was a conspiracy to ruin her, to revenge the fine for assault and a threatened summons from the County Court for wages. A policeman was called in to search the prisoner's box; the contents were turned out; when they were nearly all returned, Mr. Acock picked the pin-box off the floor, and accused Catherine Tiernay of stealing it. The policeman gave very unsatisfactory evidence with regard to this box. It was wrapped in a piece of paper, and he first said that Mr. Acock had declared it was a box containing pins 'before the paper was removed'; subsequently he retracted this, and said Mr. Acock made the remark 'after' the paper was removed. Mrs. Mary Ann Curd stated that Mrs. Acock, after she was fined, exclaimed to the prisoner, 'I'll have you before to-morrow! I have not done with you yet; I'll have you up hard and fast.' Mrs. Curd went with the girl for her box. Mrs. Acock was abusive. When she talked of searching the box, the girl said a policeman should be sent for. The box was emptied of its contents, and the things turned over four times; and while they were putting the things in the box, Mrs. Acock stooped down and picked up, or pretended to pick up, something. The witness had emptied the prisoner's box, and shaken it, and turned it upside down, and was certain the red case did not fall out of it. The magistrate decided, with such conflicting evidence before him, to send the case to a jury; but he offered to take bail – on surety for 20l. A gentleman who had heard the investigation, though quite unacquainted with the prisoner, kindly gave bail for the amount. (1852)

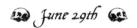

June 29th

On Saturday night, the 29th of June, a skiff containing six gentlemen, proceeding up the river, was run down by a steamer, near Westminster bridge, and two of them – Mr. W. Hawtrey and Mr. Needham – were Drowned. One swam ashore, and the others were saved by a boat that was passing.

On Saturday evening, the 29th of June, Mr. Green, the aeronaut, ascended with a friend from Vauxhall Gardens, and the balloon fell into the Thames, near the Nore. Their lives were saved by the people in a revenue cutter that was passing, but Mr. Green was hurt on the head and face. The balloon was secured with difficulty, the gas being liberated by volleys of musketry from the cutter. (1850)

June 30th

The Duchess of St. Albans and Lady Beauclerk met with a Dangerous Accident on the 30th June. The Duchess had visited the exhibition of the Botanical Society in the Regent's Park, and was crossing the ornamental basin in her carriage by the bridge: suddenly the box on which the coachman and footman were sitting gave way. The footman managed to gain his legs, but the coachman fell. The horses, being unchecked, plunged violently, and started off. Before they passed through the gates, the coachman, fortunately, got extricated; he had apparently received no hurt, for he got up directly, and ran after the carriage, followed by the footman. The horses went at their utmost speed towards Marylebone Church; where they came in collision with the iron railings in front of the portico, two bars of which were snapped; both the horses fell, and it was found afterwards that one of them had its neck broken. The ladies were taken from the carriage unhurt. (1852)

July

July 1st

A Shocking Railway Accident took place on the London and North-western line, near Coventry, on the 1st inst.. A young man named Ross was employed in removing some hay cut on the embankment of the railway. He had occasion to cross the permanent way, and was standing between the metals of the up line, watching the progress of a down luggage train, when the express for town came up at its usual speed of thirty-five or forty miles an hour, and caught the unhappy lad. In an instant almost the whole of the carriages had passed over him, when his body was found to be most shockingly mutilated. His head, neck, arms, legs, and other portions of his remains, were smashed and almost cut to pieces. It being shown that the catastrophe was not the result of any neglect on the part of any of the company's servants, a verdict of accidental death was returned. (1853)

🕸 *July 2nd* 🕸

An extraordinary case of Attempted Abduction has occurred in Tipperary. For some time Miss E. Arbuthnot, daughter of the late Mr. George Arbuthnot, of Elderslie in Surrey, has been on a visit to her sister, the wife of Captain Gough, son of Lord Gough, at Rathronan house, two miles from Clonmel. She is an heiress possessing 50,000*l*., and of course had many suitors. Among them was Mr. Carden of Barnane, a justice of the peace, and a deputy-lieutenant of the county. On the 2nd inst., Mrs. Gough and her sister were present at Rathronan church; and Mr. Carden, apparently absorbed in his devotions, was there also. But during the service, a groom leading two horses, a carriage and pair of thoroughbreds, and five or six men, arrived outside. The ladies had driven to church in an outside car; but as rain fell slightly, the coachman drove home to fetch a covered car. As soon as Mrs. Gough's car appeared, one of Carden's band stopped it: Carden attempted to seize Miss Arbuthnot, but her screams rapidly drew a number of defenders to the rescue. Carden and his band were armed with revolvers and bludgeons, but no shot was fired. A conflict, however, ensued; the defenders freely using sticks and stones; and while Carden held Miss Arbuthnot, M'Grath, one of the rescuers, struck him down with a stone. The assault having failed, Carden's men covered his retreat to his carriage, and the whole party dashed off. As soon as the ladies were driven to Rathronan house, and assistance obtained from the nearest police station, a pursuit began, and was continued for twenty miles. Not far from Farney Castle, the flying carriage was overtaken and overturned into a ditch by the police; and Carden and his men were carried prisoners to Cashel. One of the carriage-horses, an animal of great value, dropped down dead immediately after the capture. The magistrates committed Carden with his associates on the charge of attempting the forcible abduction of Miss Arbuthnot; and he was sent to Clonmel prison. An application for his liberation on bail has been refused. (1854)

🕸 *July 3rd* 🕸

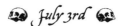

A respectably dressed young man, who refused to give his name, was charged at Guildhall, on the 3rd, with uttering seditious language in a public-house. Several papers were found upon him. One consisted of hints to those who thought of suicide, urging that they might as well be hanged – or take the chance of it with the alternative of a comfortable provision for life – as drown themselves; and that they might manage this by killing a policeman, a duchess, or a countess, and then pleading insanity. Another paper said the writer would like to kill five hundred of the aristocracy, and a third contained a plan of setting fire to ladies' dresses in Kensington Gardens, at a time 'when the aristocracy are congregated to hear the band play.' Before the alderman the prisoner admitted that these writings were by him, and said that merely to explain how an unlawful act might be committed, was no offence. He was remanded that inquiries might be made. He was brought up again on the 10th, when Mr. Maule, the solicitor of the Home Office, was in attendance, who requested the alderman to deal summarily with the case by binding the prisoner over to keep the peace. He seemed much disappointed that he was not to have a regular trial, and made a nonsensical speech about his plan for thinning the numbers of the aristocracy. The alderman cut short his oratory: – 'You are one of three things, insane, mischievous, or seeking notoriety; I believe you are the two latter.' He was ordered to find bail and removed in custody. (1850)

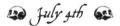

July 4th

A lady named Martin lost her life, on the 4th, by Walking on the York and Scarborough Railway. A train was approaching, and the engine-driver gave the alarm by his whistle. Seeing her danger she attempted to escape by running back; but she was struck down in a moment, and the whole train, of seventeen carriages, passed over her body, which was literally torn in pieces. This should be a lesson against an imprudence often committed. (1850)

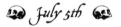

July 5th

A case of Death through the use of Chloroform at Guy's Hospital was investigated by a Coroner's Inquest on the 5th. The patient was Alexander Scott, a policeman, aged thirty-four, and the operation was the removal of a part of his hand, which had been bitten by a man about a year before. The bone and nerves were diseased, producing great pain in the arm and side; otherwise the man was strong and healthy. He desired that chloroform should be administered, though Mr. Cock, the operator, endeavoured to dissuade him. The operation did not last above a minute and a half, but by the time it was finished, it was found that the patient had expired. Mr. Cock said that he always objected to the use of chloroform, for it never could be given without some degree of danger. In this instance a very small quantity had been used, not a tenth part of what had been administered in other cases. He could not account for the deceased dying, and was certain there was no disease about him. So strong and powerful an agent was chloroform, that it could not be administered without some amount of risk and danger, and the penalty the public must pay for the alleviation from pain would be a death occasionally. A similar death occurred about twelve months since at St. Thomas's Hospital, and many other deaths might be recorded. It might be used one or two thousand times or more, successfully, and was of great assistance to the operator. The public ought to know the danger attending its administration. (1850)

July 6th

A case of Revolting Cruelty has come to light at Salford. The police heard that Esther Swinnerton, a girl of seventeen, was badly treated by her step-mother. The officers went to the house, and found her in a damp cellar, in a shocking condition. She was taken to the workhouse, and died a few days after. At the inquest, the surgeon of the workhouse stated that the deceased was a cripple from curvature of the spine; she was in an advanced stage of consumption, but death had been hastened by diarrhoea and inflammation, the result of neglect, want of nourishment, and confinement in a damp cellar. Several witnesses described the treatment of the girl by her father and step mother. The man is a collier, and the woman kept a small-ware shop: the husband, though he did not sufficiently protect his daughter, does not appear to have ill-treated her himself; in fact, his wife was 'master;' he once talked of destroying himself, from domestic unhappiness. With regard to the step-mother, the disclosures showed most atrocious conduct towards the 'cripple'. The coroner pointed out, that if the stepmother wilfully accelerated the girl's death, she was guilty of murder. Twelve out of the thirteen jurymen found a verdict of 'Wilful murder against Elizabeth Swinnerton.' (1851)

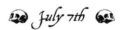

July 7th

An Irishman named Fahy attempted to Rob the House of Mr. Swetenham, near Congleton, on the afternoon of Sunday the 7th, while the family was at church, but was prevented by the intrepidity of Ann Tranter, the maid servant. The man pretended to be deaf and dumb, and begged for alms; the servant gave him some bread; then he attempted to push past her into the house; on the girl resisting his entrance, he assailed her with a stick; she took it from him; then he beat her with his fists; the girl grappled with him, and being tall and stout, managed to throw him on the ground, and kept him there for some time. When the man succeeded in overpowering her, and rose, she ran to a bell and pulled it to give an alarm. Again she baffled Fahy's attempts to enter the house, pushed him into the stable-yard, and locked him out. The bell had attracted a gamekeeper's notice, and he hurried to the house; where he found the courageous girl in a fainting state. The keeper seized Fahy on the road a short distance from the place, and had him committed on a charge of assault with intent to rob. The Congleton magistrates highly commended Ann Tranter for her conduct. (1850)

July 8th

On the evening of the 8th, Lieutenant Gale ascended in a Balloon from Shoreham, was carried across the channel, and landed on the beach near Dieppe. He was at first arrested by a gendarme as a suspicious person, but, on explanation, he was kindly treated and his balloon secured for him. (1850)

July 9th

At the Westminster Police Court on the 9th, Eliza Medland was charged with endeavouring to Obtain Money by Fake Pretences, from Prince Albert. She had written to the Prince as 'M.A. Purkess', setting forth that she had a child suffering from a disease of the spine, for which sea-bathing was ordered, and soliciting 5l., on the score of having been wet nurse to the Princess Alice Maude. The name of the wet nurse was Perkins, not Purkess, and Col. Phipps, the Prince's Secretary, detected the applicant as an impostor. She was remanded, there being other charges against her, and brought up again on the 13th, when it was proved that she had endeavoured to extract money from the Marchioness of Londonderry, by representing herself as Mrs. Macbride, a poor woman with a husband out of work, a dead child, and no means to bury it. She tried to get off by promising amendment for the future, but the magistrate sent her to the House of Correction for three months, remarking, 'if you have formed any resolution of amendment, you can carry it into effect when you come out.' (1850)

💀 *July 10th* 💀

A singular and Fatal Accident occurred at Woolwich about four o'clock on the 10th inst., when a very respectably-dressed woman, who was standing on Roff's pier waiting for a steam-boat, had her parasol taught by a gust of wind, and was herself blown into the river and drowned. No person present was acquainted with her, or knew her name or address. (1851)

💀 *July 11th* 💀

The Dangers of the Serpentine were shown at an inquest held on the body of a young man named Corner, an excellent swimmer, who was drowned in that river on Sunday the 11th inst. The testimony of the witnesses went to prove that he had swum half way across and suddenly called for help, when he turned over head foremost and went down into the deep mud beneath. It was nearly 20 minutes before he could be got up by the Royal Humane Society's men after the time he went down. Mr. Williams, the superintendent of the society, stated that observing the drags were out he instantly got a hot bath in readiness, and when the body was brought in it was black with the mud over the head to the waist where he had been fixed. He was quite dead, but still every means were used to restore him, and Dr. Woolley attended. In answer to a juror, Mr. Williams said that three boats were on the river, but there were a great number of persons in the water. – The juror: Then three boats are not sufficient? – Mr. Williams: No; nor would six be. It is impossible for the boatmen to see what is going on. – The Coroner: The Serpentine, I have understood, is a most dangerous place to bathe in. Mr. Williams replied it was the most dangerous in the world. There were holes thirty feet deep, and then twelve feet of mud, out of which the best swimmer could never get. There were cold springs too in all parts. – The Coroner observed that it had been suggested in consequence, as he understood, that the bed of the river should be levelled. As this had not been done there seemed no alternative but to prevent bathing altogether there. – The jury returned a verdict of 'Accidentally Drowned.'

💀 *July 12th* 💀

Daniel Donovan, a smith, was tried on the 12th at the Central Criminal Court, for Throwing his Wife out of a Window, with intent to murder her. They were both intoxicated, and having quarrelled, the husband, after beating the woman savagely, opened the window and threw her into the yard. From the injuries she received her life was long in danger. The charge was proved by the evidence of the woman and the prisoner's two children, who were present. Judgment of death was recorded, the judge saying that he would recommend the prisoner's life to be spared, but no more. He was re-conveyed to gaol and placed in the cell allotted to prisoners after trial; about three o'clock it was discovered that he had hanged himself, and was quite dead. (1850)

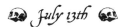 *July 13th*

Dreadful Election Riots have taken place in Ireland. At Belfast, on the 13th, there was a desperate affray between the Protestants and Romanists ... They began to wreck the houses on either side of the street, each party assailing those in which the families of the opposite party resided. Fire arms were now in requisition; and many of the combatants, some from the street and others from the houses, kept up a continual volley from muskets and large pistols, which gave the spectator the idea of a town being sacked. A lad of sixteen years of age, named Henderson, received one ball through his breast and another through his wrist. He was taken to the hospital in a dying state. Respectably dressed women were seen supplying the combatants with huge paving-stones and brickbats, which they carried from the rear of their houses in baskets, in their aprons, and in crocks, to the street front; and while the stones were flying and balls whizzing above their heads, young girls were breaking the larger brickbats into more handy missiles for the use of the rioters. One woman was seen at a window signalling to the Romanist party beneath when to advance or when to retire, as she perceived the motions of the police ... In consequence of an application forwarded to the barracks, a troop of Dragoons, and two companies of the Forty-sixth Foot made their appearance on the ground, and rapidly cleared the streets in every direction. (1852)

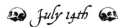 *July 14th*

Another Railway Accident happened on the 14th. While the mail train of the Bristol and Exeter Railway was on its way towards Bristol, and had arrived within a mile or two of the terminus, it was discovered, to the consternation of the passengers, that one of the carriages was on fire. Efforts were made to signal the engine driver, for a time ineffectually, as the train was carried fully a mile before it was pulled up. Fortunately, it was nearing the city, and had to pass through a densely populated district, and the inhabitants of the houses skirting the line gave the alarm as it passed them, which drew attention to the accident, when the train was stopped in sufficient time to prevent any very serious consequences. (1851)

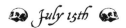

July 15th

On the 15th, while the two daughters of Mrs. Stoner, of Ringrone House, and nieces of Lord Camoys, were walking among the rocks of the seashore at Salcombe, they were overtaken by the flowing tide, when one of them was Drowned. Her sister held on by the rocks and was saved by the coast guard, whose services are described as being highly commendable. (1850)

A terrible Boiler Explosion took place at Rochdale on the 10th inst. at Mr. Williamson's calico factory. On the previous night the engineer got drunk, and was taken into custody by the police. In his absence, next morning, William Taylor, and Howarth, the manager of the mill, proceeded to get up steam; and if the explosion occurred by any mismanagement on their part they paid dearly for it, for both perished. Soon after the workers had all entered the mill – a one storey shed – the boiler was torn to pieces, with a frightful noise; part of the factory was destroyed; a neighbouring cottage was demolished; a house was damaged; and a shower of masses of iron, bricks, and other articles descended for a long distance round. Across a road, a short distance off, was another cotton-mill, belonging to Mr Bottomley. A broadside of bricks and iron entered the windows at one end of this mill, traversed the rooms, and shattered the machinery: a young woman was struck on the head by a brick and killed; near her was found the head of another young woman – the remainder of the poor creature was buried in the ruins of Williamson's factory. When those ruins were removed, the corpses of six other men and women were found, and one young woman who was taken out alive died the same day. Besides these, thirteen of the workpeople sustained fractures, bruises, cuts, and other hurts, and the cases of several were pronounced dangerous. Mrs. Howarth, who occupied the cottage which was destroyed, was killed; her father and two of her children were in bed at the time – bed and mattress and occupants were blown into a river which flows by the spot, and the old man and his grandchildren were seen floating on the water – they were rescued unhurt. (1854)

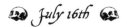

July 16th

At the Oxford Assizes, on the 16th, Elijah Noon, a plasterer, was indicted for the Murder of his wife. The circumstances of the case were very painful. The principal witness for the prosecution was the prisoner's daughter, a little girl twelve years of age. She stated that she lived with her parents in Oxford. In consequence of her father not returning home on Saturday night, her mother went to look for him soon after midnight. They returned together in a few minutes; he was not sober. Her mother upbraided him with staying out late. He took some money out and counted it. She said he could treat other persons and not her. He then took down a sword from the shelf, pulled it out of the sheath, and struck the deceased, who was sitting down, on the back with the flat part of the sword. The child ran to the door and got outside; the mother got up and attempted to follow her, and her daughter took hold of her hand to pull her through. The father was standing in the room, and according to the child's first account he went to his wife at the door with the sword, and ran it into her left side. It appeared, however, that the witness could not see the actual thrust; but her mother screaming out, the child pulled her out of the room into the street, where she fell down. She was then led to a neighbour's, and was taken back to her own house. On examination, a wound was found in her left side, of which she died in about 24 hours. The prisoner paid every attention to her during her last hours. On being brought back to the house he took hold of her hand, and helped her up stairs. She said to him, 'Elijah, I freely forgive you, as I hope the Lord will forgive me; but always avoid passion.' In defence it was contended, that the facts proved were consistent with the supposition that the deceased, in resisting the effort of her daughter to remove her from the room, fell back on the sword, which the prisoner was too much intoxicated to know was unsheathed. A number of witnesses deposed to the prisoner's good character. The jury, after considerable deliberation, returned a verdict of guilty of manslaughter, and he was sentenced to two years' imprisonment. (1852)

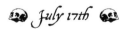

July 17th

A frightful Railway Accident occurred on Saturday evening, the 17th, to an engine-driver named Stanley at Gobowen, on the Shrewsbury and Chester line. The unfortunate man had got off the engine at a siding, and was examining the machinery to see that it was in proper working order and not over-heated, and at the same time the stoker was engaged in filling the boiler with water, when three or four waggons which were moving down on an inclined plane towards the engine were allowed to proceed too rapidly by the person who had the charge of them, and who, it is supposed, did not apply the break so vigorously as he ought to have done. The consequence was that the waggons dashed with great velocity against the engine which Stanley was engaged in examining, and the unfortunate man's arm was caught in the machinery, and he was thrown down and the engine went over him, tearing his arm out of the socket and mangling him so frightfully that he expired immediately. (1852)

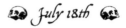

July 18th

Lately, at the works of Messrs. Cummings, machinists, Belmont, near Bolton, a man met with a melancholy Accident whilst oiling some machinery in motion. His arm was caught by a wheel making about 100 revolutions per minute, and he was carried round with it bodily, two of his limbs being literally torn off, his head smashed to pieces, and his body shockingly mutilated.

Miss Wetherby, a young lady residing with her family at Broadstairs, has lost her life by Falling from the Cliff between that place and Ramsgate. She was walking and reading on the verge of the precipice when this lamentable accident happened. (1855)

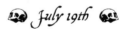

July 19th

A Child of Eight years old, named Willis, was brought before the sitting magistrate at the Mansion House, on the 19th, charged with having attempted to stab a boy of his own age with a knife, and with having wounded another boy so seriously in the eye that he was likely to lose it. It appeared that the prisoner had been brought up in utter ignorance of moral responsibility, and that his father, on hearing of his apprehension, had said that he had a good right to use a knife in his own defence. The magistrate said he could not commit a child of such tender years to Newgate, but would require security for his good behaviour for a year. He was then locked up in the cage, uttering screams and curses. (1850)

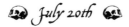

July 20th

A melancholy accident from the Incautious use of Firearms, occurred at Standen-house, near Hungerford, Berks, the seat of the Rev. J. P. Michell on the 20th. His youngest son had been rabbit shooting, and returning home about 9 o'clock in the evening was called by his two youngest sisters from the nursery window, and in turning round to answer them, the gun, which happened to be loaded, went off, and unhappily lodged the contents in the forehead of the youngest, a fine little girl between nine and ten years of age, who survived only a few minutes. The children at the time of the melancholy occurrence had their arms round each others' neck, but strange to say, not a shot touched the other. (1852)

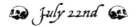

July 21st

Mr. John Dewdney, a respectable gentleman of sixty, Died while playing at Cricket on the 21st inst. During a match in Copenhagen fields, he was in the act of making a run when he suddenly fell down, and in a few minutes expired. He had only just taken the bat, scoring one for his first hit, so that it is quite evident that the fatal result was not the effect of fatigue. He had complained of ill health, and said that during the last week he had suffered from sun-stroke, but declined standing out of the match, though advised to do so by several friends. (1852)

July 22nd

A calamitous Steamboat Explosion took place at Bristol on the 22nd. The Red Rover steamer left the Hotwells about eight in the evening, and was about to proceed to Bristol, full of passengers, when she suddenly blew up with a noise which shook the neighbourhood, and was heard at the distance of miles. The engines and machinery were torn to pieces; her funnel, the plates of her boiler, and the other portions of her machinery being hurled into the air. The bodies of some of the passengers were thrown by the shock high above the houses; others were cast into the water; and almost every passenger was more or less injured. The vessel almost immediately sank, going down by the head, her stern fortunately remaining long enough above the water to enable some of the passengers to be taken out of the aft-cabin windows. Such was the force of the explosion, that some of the plates of the boiler of the steamer were thrown with considerable violence on to the roofs of the houses in Avon Crescent and Rawlings's Yard, more than one hundred yards from the spot where the explosion took place; and one piece, upwards of one and a half hundred weight, was thrown into Messrs. Hennett's timber-yard, at fully as great a distance. A little girl, named Jefferies, was hurled by the explosion with such violence as to be thrown completely across the lock to the road on the opposite side, where her brains were dashed out against the wall. The most prompt assistance was given, and a number of persons, alive and dead, were picked up. Six dead bodies were found, and many, carried to the hospital, were so dreadfully injured, that their recovery could hardly be expected. On the following day an inquiry into the cause of the accident commenced before the coroner. (1850)

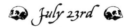

July 23rd

At the Lewes Assizes, on the 23rd, Mary Hardwick, a miserable-looking creature, was indicted for attempting to Murder her Child. On the Saturday preceding she was seen standing with a child in her arms near the custom-house at Brighton, when she suddenly ran down to the sea, threw the child into the water, and then jumped in herself. The woman and child were dragged out in a state of insensibility, but both recovered. A man was on the spot, who appeared to be the woman's husband, who, after she was recovered, abused her violently, and expressed a wish that she had drowned herself. The poor woman, during the trial, seemed hardly aware of what she had done. She was convicted, but recommended to mercy, and judgment was deferred. (1850)

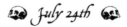

July 24th

In December last, a milkman named George Bush, a quiet, inoffensive man, residing near Bath, was Murdered. He had attended an auction-sale at a neighbouring village, and, after having spent part of the evening at the village public-house, left it to go home, and next morning was found dead in a field, with his throat cut, and his pockets rifled. Several persons were apprehended on suspicion, but discharged. But an Irish pedlar, named Christopher Smith, while imprisoned in Dorchester jail as a vagrant, told a fellow prisoner that he had committed a murder in

Somersetshire. This led to his apprehension on suspicion of the murder of Bush; and the prisoner made the following confession to the chief of the Bath police: – 'I was at the public house, and at the time selling lucifers and other little things. I had half a pint of beer, and I saw the man I murdered pull out his purse, which tempted me. I followed him from the public-house until he went two or three fields over a stile, and when he got 70 or 80 yards I tripped him up with my foot. He fell on the back of his head and called out 'Murder' very loudly, and said to me, 'Do you want to murder me?' I replied to him, 'Yes.' The prisoner, then looking at his arms, said, 'I was then much stronger and more active than I am now, and I held him a few minutes and drew my knife across his throat two or three times, and he never moved afterwards. There was not much struggling, as it was soon over. I knelt on him, and when I was on him the blood came over me, and I tore up some grass and stuffed it into the cut. I then took his purse, but did not get more than seven or eight shillings. I thought he had more, or it would not have happened. I am sorry for it. It was a cold-blooded deed, and one of the worst murders that ever was done. I slept in a cart-house that night, and in barns and under haystacks ever since; but wherever I was I could not rest, as I saw the man. It was a dreadful thing to have on the mind, and I am perfectly prepared to die for it.' On the 24th inst. Smith was brought before the county magistrates at Bath. A number of witnesses were examined, whose evidence corroborated the prisoner's confession. When the magistrates were considering the propriety of calling further witnesses, he said, 'Gentlemen, there's enough of evidence to hang twenty, without any more.' He was committed for trial at the next assizes. (1852)

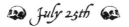

July 25th

The East India trader *Randolph*, of London, was Wrecked on the coast of the Mauritius, on the night of the 25th of July, immediately after she had taken her departure from Port Louis for Calcutta. She had on board 250 steerage passengers, natives, consisting of men, women, and children, for Calcutta; also Lieut. Holland and Ensign Scott, of the 48th Regiment. Near midnight a cry was raised of 'Breakers ahead,' and the captain found that he was close to a dangerous reef of rocks, upon which the ship immediately struck, and fell over on her beam-ends. As the vessel went over the scramble for life amongst the crew became desperate. Men, women, and children were seen hanging to and crawling up the sides of the wreck. Some fell into the surf, and by clinging to floating spars preserved themselves, while others were swept away, and met with a watery grave, Ensign Scott being amongst those who perished. In the morning, daylight disclosed their actual position. Land was observed two miles distant, the space between the wreck and the beach being studded with small, steep, dangerous patches of rock. The boats happily remained whole; with great exertions, all the survivors were safely landed; and the chief officer, Mr. Scott, was despatched to Port Louis, about thirty miles distant, with intelligence of the calamity. The governor immediately forwarded a steamer to the spot, and on its arrival it was found that she could render little service; the ship was fast breaking up, and the cargo scattered in all directions. It was found that, besides Ensign Scott, who was a young man of one-and-twenty, between 29 and 30 of the passengers, and two of the crew, had perished. (Reported September 1851)

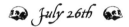

July 26th

Another Garotte Robbery has been committed at Leeds. On the 26th, four men, named George Wood, John Bone, John Hudson, and Robert Turner, were brought up before the Leeds sitting justices, charged with assaulting and robbing Michael Coleman, a carver and gilder, residing at Huddersfield. A police officer stated that about one o'clock on Sunday morning, while on duty at the west end of the town, he heard a loud cry of 'Murder,' and on going to the spot, he found Michael Coleman in Corporation-street, standing with his hat off, and bleeding profusely about the head and face. He complained of having been knocked down by some men, who, he said, had robbed and nearly killed him. After endeavouring but in vain to trace out the parties, he (the policeman) returned to Coleman and set him off towards Woodhouse, where he said his mother resided. About an hour later on, he (the policeman) heard another call of 'Watch.' This was on the Kirkstall road, not far from Corporation street, and on going to the place he met a man named John Broadbent, who complained of three or four men having assaulted and robbed him, and he further stated that the men who had assailed him had walked off towards a haystack, which he pointed out, and behind it they found the four prisoners covered over with hay. On two of them was found a hat, a shirt front, two tobacco boxes, and other articles belonging to Coleman, the man who was first robbed. Coleman himself was too ill to attend to give evidence against the prisoners, who were remanded. (1852)

☠ *July 27th* ☠

A Frightful Accident occurred to a labourer named Clarke, in the employment of Mr. Mechi at Tiptree Hall, Essex. He was feeding a chaff-cutting machine, worked by steam power. His hand was caught in the roller, and the limb was cut into pieces before the engine could be stopped. The screams of the poor sufferer all the time were heart-rending. Surgical assistance was immediately obtained, and the remaining portion of the arm was amputated; but the poor man died on the following day. (1853)

☠ *July 28th* ☠

An atrocious case of Murder was tried at the Exeter Assizes. Harvey, a sweep of Buckland Brewer, was accused of murdering Mary Richards, at Little Torrington. From the testimony of many witnesses, and from the dying declarations of the girl, the crime was clearly brought home to the prisoner. Mary Richards had been taking home some gloves to Torrington; on her return, Harvey got into conversation with her, and subsequently dogged her steps into a field, and offered her violence. She resisted; he took a hammer from his pocket, struck her on the head so as to fracture her skull, and thus compelled her submission. He then stole some currants and saffron from her basket, and left her in her helpless condition. She was found next morning, alive; and she lived for many days after, with intervals of consciousness which enabled her to indentify her murderer. The monster was found guilty, and sentenced to be hanged. The sentence has been executed, the criminal having confessed his guilt. (1854)

☠ *July 29th* ☠

A distressing Suicide was committed on the 29th of July, at Shipston-on-Stowe, by a lady named Elizabeth Rees, who had lately opened a seminary for young ladies with excellent recommendations. On the morning of the above day, a servant, going into an out-house, discovered her hanging, and quite dead. An inquest was held on her body, when it appeared that she had lost a considerable sum of money by unfortunate railway investments; and this, with some disappointments in regard to the opening of the school, had doubtless impelled her to commit the awful act. It also appeared that her friends had, in the course of Friday or Saturday, posted a letter addressed to her and calculated to ease her mind regarding her future prospects. This letter, however, owing to the stoppage of postal communication on Sunday, did not arrive in Shipston until late on Monday. Its timely arrival might have saved her life. (1850)

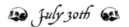

July 30th

A most painful case of Matricide has occurred at Birkenhead. Elizabeth Thomas was a widow, who lived at the village of Prenton with her three sons, William, Joseph, and Samuel. William was twenty-three years old, Joseph twenty, and Samuel nine. They all lived happily; the mother going out charing and to wash, and the elder sons working as labourers. Some months ago Mrs. Thomas called in Mr. Byerley, a surgeon, to attend William, who complained of headache and drowsiness. Mr. Byerley bled him and gave him medicine, and in about a fortnight he got well. Three weeks after, he again grew ill; but to the surgeon he always appeared rational. Blisters were applied, and he again improved. This lasted, however, only a short time; and his manner became sufficiently singular to be noticed by both his brothers and his mother. The symptoms increased; and on the morning of the 30th July Mr. Byerley again ordered him to be blistered on the back of the neck; and his mother spoke to the surgeon about sending him to a lunatic asylum. But she did not live to do it; for in the night of the next day William murdered her in her bed. The story is told by the evidence taken at the inquiry made by the magistrates at Birkenhead, before whom William Thomas was taken. William and Joseph went out on Saturday night, leaving behind their mother and Samuel. William returned first, and told his mother not to sit up, as he would wait for Joseph. Mrs. Thomas went to bed, where she slept with her youngest son. This part of the story was narrated by Samuel, crying bitterly. After he had been some time asleep, he was awoken by his mother 'knocking against' him. He saw his brother 'kneeling on his mother with a candle in one hand and a razor in another. William put the candle down, and laid hold of my mother's throat with one hand, and drew the razor across her throat.' She wrestled a little, but 'soon lay down quite still. After he had cut my mother's throat, he hauled her down.'

Samuel was then carried to William's bed; whence, looking out, he saw his mother's head on the top of the stairs being dragged down. By and by Joseph came home, and was frightened by seeing a light in the back-room window. 'I walked into the houseplace [a cottage sitting-room is so called in Lancashire], and William called out from the back-room, who was there? I said "It's me." He then came down. When at the foot of the stairs, he said to me, "Joe, I have killed my mother, and buried her in the garden, comfortable; and she will be a good deal better off. I have made her comfortable. Don't you go and say anything." I cried out, and asked him where Sam was, and he said, "He is up-stairs in bed." Joseph then carried Samuel to the house of a neighbour. [Just at this moment he was requested by one of the magistrates to speak more audibly; when the prisoner, at the top of his voice, and in a shrill tone, exclaimed, 'Speak up as they can hear thee, Joe: nobody can hear thee speak, man.']

Joseph called up the neighbours, and several came with him. 'We searched the premises and the garden. The first thing that we saw was the bed and bolsters lying on the ground. There was a good deal of blood upon them. We then saw a mound of new earth, and we commenced digging. About two feet under the soil we came to a hand sticking up. We then cleared away the earth, and found the body of my mother, Elizabeth Thomas. She had only her shift upon her. There was a blanket wrapped around her. It was very bloody. There was a rope tied round my mother's waist. The body was then taken out, and conveyed to the house. I became too much affected to observe more, and went into the house. William, all the time that we were searching for the body, was sitting in the house talking with a man from Prenton.' Both the brothers spoke as to the strange and excited manner of William during the past twelvemonth, and especially during the last week. Samuel said he was generally kind to his mother, and she to him. They never quarrelled; but he would sometimes sauce her. 'A few days ago, I heard him sauce her.' Joseph said, 'I considered him wrong about the head for a twelvemonth back: his oddness showed itself in getting foolish, and during the last week he got more excited.' The Magistrates committed William, and the coroner's jury found a verdict of 'Wilful murder' against him. He was tried at Chester Assizes, and acquitted on the ground of insanity. (1852)

🕱 *July 31st* 🕱

A determined act of Suicide was committed on the 31st ult. by a man in the employ of the Great Western Company, named Watts. In the morning he left home to see, as was his custom, where his or his men's services were needed, and about twelve o'clock was observed to be standing, apparently in a thoughtful mood, near the Wallingford station. Shortly after that hour an express train was seen coming up, and on its approach towards the station, the deceased ran forward and threw himself across the rails. By the engine he was struck and knocked forward at least 150 yards, and the whole of the carriages passed over him, mutilating him in a dreadful manner. (1851)

A most appalling Suicide occurred on Sunday morning, the 31st ult., at the house of Mrs. Burnes, fruiterer, London-street, Greenwich. The unfortunate deceased, Lavinia Mary Cuthbert, was a married woman, who, with her husband, for some time past, had been in the employ of Mr. Shove, corn-dealer, but had been lately discharged. It appears that she went to her bedroom, and, after a short time was discovered to have ripped open her stomach with her husband's razor, and before medical assistance could be brought to her aid, she had expired. An inquest was held next day, when the jury returned a verdict of 'Temporary derangement.' (1853)

August

🕱 *August 1st* 🕱

A Fire broke out at midnight, on the 1st inst., at the New Model Prison for juvenile offenders at Parkhurst, of a serious description. One of the principal wings, containing 200 cells, was totally destroyed, besides damage to other parts of the prison. It has been found that the prison was fired by some of the elder convicts, to enable them to effect their escape. (1850)

🕱 *August 2nd* 🕱

Two workmen met with a Fearful Death at Sunderland on the 2nd inst. Some time ago a tall chimney upon Messrs. Hartley & Co.'s Wear glasswork was struck with lightning. It has since been taken down to within 50 feet of its base, and built to the height of 185 feet. The scaffolding for conveying the labourers to the top was erected in the inside, and they ascended the summit by means of a bucket drawn by a gin. Two workmen named Vower and Rhodes, employed in Messrs. Hartley's works, resolved, notwithstanding express orders to the contrary, to go to the top of the chimney, and, though warned of the danger of their frolic, they induced the driver of the horse which turns the gin to send them up. They reached the top in safety and remained there ten or fifteen minutes, when they both got into the same bucket and prepared to descend. One of the men was much heavier than the other, and owing, it is supposed, to the bucket being unequally balanced, it struck in its descent against a piece of timber which runs across the chimney; the bucket was thus loosened, and fell to the bottom, when the men were left hanging by the rope. They maintained their hold firmly for some time, and repeated efforts were made to bring them to the top again, but they were in vain, and one after the other, the poor creatures were obliged to let go their hold, and were dashed to the bottom, a distance of 180 feet. They were killed upon the spot. They had been drinking, and had taken a bottle of porter to the workmen at the top of the chimney. (1854)

August 3rd

A shocking case of Premature Burial has taken place at Tipperary. Mary Neill, a young woman, apparently died on the 3rd inst. in the poor house, and was buried next day. On the morning of the 5th a man heard her cry as he passed close to her grave, and he ran as rapidly as possible to town, and gave the alarm. She was disinterred; and on opening her coffin, she was found lying on her right side, the shrouding torn, a cap which she wore on her head removed, and scratches and blood on her face, and other marks of recent violent exertion apparent, but she was quite dead. Her apparent death previously was sudden, but it is believed she was only sunk in a trance. She had been above twenty-four hours apparently dead previous to her interment. (1851)

August 4th

Another frightful Balloon Accident took place on the 4th inst, when Madame Garneron ascended from Batty's Hippodrome at Kensington.

Six o'clock was the time appointed for the ascent, but in consequence of some little difficulty about the inflation, it did not take place till near seven. The wind was rather strong, and blowing south-west, and the moment the machine was released from its moorings, it rose very heavily, and barely cleared the circus enclosure. Madame Garneron immediately emptied a bag of ballast among a crowd who were watching it in Victoria Road, but before she was able to discharge another, the car of the balloon struck a projecting garret window, and in an instant the poor lady was seen with her feet entangled in the netting at the side of the half-inverted car, and hanging out of it with her head downwards. A loud exclamation of horror burst from the frightened crowd, and just at the critical moment, when they expected to see the balloon rise with its occupant in that fearful situation, the netting caught in a stack of chimneys, the balloon at once collapsed with the shock, and in a few seconds it was hanging helplessly flapping over the house-side into the garden, while the unfortunate lady was left lying on the roof. But she had received no injury, and after she had recovered from her faintness, she stood up and feebly waved her acknowledgments to the spectators below, who had hailed her safety with loud cheers. (1854)

August 5th

A child has been Killed by Lightning in its mother's arms. On Sunday afternoon, the 5th inst., the wife of William Sprugg, a bricklayer, of Grimstone, Norfolk, was proceeding to church with her little boy, three and a half years old, along a road lined with trees, when a storm came on, and she took him up in her arms and went along with an umbrella over her head. Suddenly, when near a tree, the lightning struck her at the feet, and she felt, as she describes, as if her feet were suddenly taken off, her strength instantaneously gone, and she was immediately unconscious. She had not seen the light of the flash, nor heard any sound, although the electric fluid must have passed with a great crash down the tree, which it tore as it passed, proceeding thence along the ground to the poor woman's feet, tearing open her boots and ripping up the whole length of her stockings, then passing up her body as far as her breast, which as well as her legs are very much burnt; and making its way out through her dress over against her left breast into the child which was held there, killed it. (1855)

🕱 *August 6th* 🕱

At the Carlisle Assizes, on the 6th inst., Edward Wilson was tried on the charge of Forging and Uttering a Cheque for 539*l*. 12*s*. 8*d*. on the Cumberland and Carlisle Bank. The prisoner was formerly clerk to Mr. Mounsey, a solicitor at Carlisle, and had thus an opportunity of becoming acquainted with the signature of Messrs. Hodgson, another law firm. These gentlemen have an account at the bank. On Saturday the 3rd February, the bank received a letter from the 'Rev. Thomas Sanderson, Langford Vicarage, near Lancaster,' enclosing another purporting to be written by Messrs. Hodgson to the clergyman, containing an account of the sale of some property, and an order on the bank in Mr. Sanderson's favour for 539*l*. 12*s*. 8*d*. The clergyman wrote to the bank that he had applied too late at the office on Friday afternoon; he was obliged to leave for his parish; would the bank forward him a cheque for the money? The bank was deceived, and sent a cheque on Hankey's, in London. Wilson had written to the postmaster at Langford, requesting that a letter missent there for the Rev. Mr. Sanderson might be forwarded to Carlisle. By this means he got the cheque. He then hastened to Langford, and posted a letter to the bank in acknowledgment of the cheque, thus preventing suspicion. He next went to London, and obtained cash for the cheque. He received a bank-note for 500*l*., and four five-pound notes. The 500*l*. note was changed for sovereigns at the Bank of England, no doubt by Wilson. So far the rogue was safe. But with the five-pound notes he took some watches and chains out of pledge at Luxmoore's, in St. Martin's-lane; the shopman indorsed the notes 'Wilson,' and he knew the prisoner. It happened that some considerable time elapsed before Messrs. Hodgson discovered that a cheque for 539*l*. had been paid on their account. In the meanwhile, Wilson had taken his plunder to the Isle of Man, bought a house there, and was living in it with his mother. The police were set to work; the five-pound notes had not been returned to the Bank of England; they were 'stopped.' When presented they were traced to Luxmoore's; thence to Wilson; and step by step the whole fraud was made clear. Mr. Mounsey and a clerk proved that the letters purporting to be written by 'Mr. Sanderson' were in Wilson's writing. He was convicted, and sentenced to be transported for twenty years. (1853)

August 7th

A very melancholy Accident happened at Staleybridge, on the 7th inst. Four children, between the ages of ten and seven, were playing on a balk of timber, which had been thrown over the river Tame. The youngest fell into the river, dragging his three companions after him, and they were all immediately carried away by the strength of the stream. Immediately on the accident taking place, several persons promptly and courageously rushed into the river in various places. Three were saved, but the youngest, named David Armitage, was never seen after he fell into the river. (1855)

August 8th

Three men have Perished [this month] by being Carried over the Falls of Niagara. A boat, in which they were asleep, got adrift, and floated into the current, where it was upset. Two of the men were carried immediately over the Falls, and dashed to pieces on the rocks below. The third, named Joseph Avery, caught at a stump in his passage, and clung to it. He was discovered almost on the brink of the Falls. Several boats were launched in order to rescue him, but they were swamped the moment they touched the Rapids. A life-boat was then launched, but proved too light, was swamped immediately, and went over the Rapids. At length the man went over the Falls. He was swept from a raft which was floated to him, when he attempted to swim to a small island, but was eventually swept over the Rapids. He had remained for nearly four and twenty hours in his dreadful situation, in the view of thousands of spectators. (1853)

August 9th

A fearful Thunderstorm occurred near Ipswich on the 9th inst., when three children were Killed by Lightning, and twelve others injured. From the statement made by Mr. Alexander, school master to the National School, Capel St. Mary, it appears that about three o'clock in the afternoon, a class of thirty boys was standing near the windows of the school-room, and the master was standing in the middle of the room, when a heavy clap of thunder burst over his head, and the lightning entered at the west end of the gable, passing through the ceiling of the room just by the window, knocking the window-frame completely out, and splitting the end of the house from top to bottom. The school master was struck by the lightning and blinded for some seconds; he ran out of the room; and, fearing that some accident might have occurred in the girls' school-room adjoining, he ran there, but happily finding that no injury had been sustained, he hastened back to the boys' room, where a dreadful scene presented itself. All the children, amounting to about thirty, of from four to twelve years of age, were lying upon the floor, some of them screaming and others too frightened to speak or to move. It was not long before one or two of them saw their master amongst them, when they called out to him for assistance, clinging round his legs in a frantic state. By this time the school-room and the whole building was in flames. The master, however, and his wife were ignorant of the fact until made acquainted by a neighbour, who ran to their assistance and by whose aid the children were removed from the house. Three little boys, named J. Kettle, ten years of age; W. Scrivener, eight; and D. Cook, between seven and eight, were found lying upon the floor, dead, with scarcely any marks upon their countenances or bodies. The flames spread rapidly, and in a short time the house was a mass of ruins, together with the furniture belonging to the master. The poor children who were killed were standing not a yard from their master, and reading at the time they were struck. Almost all the children injured, but not killed, were scorched on the right side of their bodies. (1854)

💀 *August 10th* 💀

A singular case of Assault was tried at the Inverness Sheriffs Court, on the 10th. Donald Macdonald, of North Uist, was charged, with several others, with violently entering the house of J.R. Macdonald, of Harris, and putting the inmates in bodily fear. The prisoner's defence was that his object was to obtain the lady, now his wife, from whom he had been separated against their mutual wishes. It turned out that young gentleman and Miss Jessie Macdonald were lovers, but her father had provided another match for her, and they resolved to elope together. Accordingly, the young chieftain, with a party of friends and dependants, arrived at her father's house, on the sea-shore, at midnight, in a stormy night, made their way into the house, and even into the young lady's bed-room, and carried her off in triumph, as it was proved, with her full consent and concurrence. The jury returned a verdict of acquittal, and the young couple left the court-house amid the cheers of a great concourse of people. (1850)

August 11th

On the evening of the 11th inst., after the review of the fleet, a Singular and Fatal Accident occurred at the George Hotel in Portsmouth. Mr. Powell, a gentleman of Chichester, had recklessly deposited a loaded double-barrelled gun in a case, with percussion caps on the nipples. He dined at the George. Suddenly he ascertained that unless he made great haste he would be too late for the train: he seized the gun-case, and was hurrying away, when some person came into contact with him; the case – which hung down at one end – fell from his hand, and the loaded gun went off. William White, the head waiter, was shot dead, and several other persons were wounded. At the inquest, Mr. Powell stated that he had no idea there was any possibility of the gun exploding when locked in the case; if he had, he should not have exposed himself to danger by putting away the gun loaded. The jury pronounced the death 'Accidental', but censured Mr. Powell for carrying about a loaded and capped gun. (1853)

August 12th

At Clerkenwell Police Court, on the 23rd, Thomas Ledger, master of the national school in Agar Town, was charged with Assaulting one of his Pupils, 12 years of age, named Philip Wheaton. The boy's back was bared in court, and a number of black and blue marks were visible. It appeared in evidence that the schoolmaster first gave him two cuts across his hand, and afterwards caned him, no one else being present, at the same time holding him up with one hand until the weapon split. He then got another cane, and then held him with his face downwards, and, putting his foot upon him, flogged him for a considerable time, when a gentleman and some of the boys, who had heard his screams, came to the door, and he was permitted to crawl away. The schoolmaster said that the complainant was an obstinate and wicked boy, and he punished him for making a noise and snapping his fingers while the school was at prayers. He denied using two canes, and called two of the boys, who on oath corroborated his statement. The magistrate was of opinion that the case ought to end there, for no great harm had been done. He would repeat what he had often said, that he had seen punishments far more severe inflicted in the school where he was brought up upon some of the first noblemen now living, clergymen, naval and military officers, and others of very high standing, who never flinched from it, but took it manfully and in good part, knowing they had deserved it, and that it was necessary for the character and dignity of the establishment; that such a discipline was actually necessary; 'and without it,' emphatically exclaimed the worthy magistrate, 'what would have become of our army and navy? Why, instead of a brave and manly race, we should have had a set of cowards and runaways.' The father said that undue severity had been exercised, and he was desirous that defendant should be tried before a jury. The school-master was accordingly committed for trial at the next Middlesex sessions, and bail was taken for his appearance. (1851)

🕱 August 13th 🕱

A fête at Cremorne Gardens on the 13th inst., for the benefit of the Wellington College, was attended by a lamentable Accident. There was a representation of the storming of the Mamelon at Sebastopol. For this especial occasion some five hundred Grenadier Guards and other soldiers were permitted to appear on the scene. At the very climax of the mimic war, when the soldiers were rushing forward to the capture of the Mamelon with bayonets fixed, their ardour carried them away, and they sprang upon a slightly-built platform, not intended for their use; it gave way under their weight, and sixty men were precipitated a considerable distance. The consequences were serious: five cases of fracture, one soldier having both legs broken; and more than twenty men received wounds from bayonets or were otherwise hurt. (1855)

🕱 August 14th 🕱

A young girl, named Amelia Snoswell, Murdered the child of her sister, Mrs. Cooper, an infant of eighteen months old, at Gravesend, on the 14th. The infant had been put to bed along with another child, when the girl went into the room with a knife and cut its throat. She then returned to her sister and said, 'I have killed her now, and she is happy.' She had always been affectionate to the child, but had lately shown symptoms of mental derangement. She was committed for trial. (1850)

🕱 *August 15th* 🕱

A little boy was Killed on the 15th, in the belfry of St. Mary's Church, Monmouth, while the bells were ringing in honour of the judges opening the commission. One of the ringers, named Jones, found that something obstructed the machinery. He went up to ascertain the cause; when he was horrified to discover the mangled body of his younger brother under the bell. The upper portion of the face and skull was completely shattered in, and the back part of the head was cloven in two, and the brains bespattered the roof. The dreadful calamity which befell the poor little fellow was the consequence of his dangerous curiosity. He must have introduced his head into the bell, which he was doubtless viewing just at the moment his brother raised it, and his death immediately followed. (1851)

A collier, named William Loft, has committed Suicide at a place near Oldham, by throwing himself headlong down a coal-pit, 200 feet deep. It appeared, at the inquest on his body, that he had a wife and family, and lived on bad terms with the former, owing to inequality of temper, and committed the act in a fit of temporary insanity. The jury returned a verdict to that effect. (1851)

🕱 *August 16th* 🕱

Mr. Frank Hartland, who was for many years a great favourite on the London stage as a pantomimist, was Accidentally Killed on the 16th. A plank having been detached from a building scaffold in Mount Street, when he was passing, struck him with great violence on the side of the head, completely crushing in the skull. He died on his way to St. Thomas's Hospital. Mr. Hartland has left a large family, hitherto entirely dependent upon him, to deplore their untimely loss. (1852)

A gentleman committed Suicide by throwing himself from the top of Shakspeare's cliff at Dover, on the evening of the 16th inst. He was conversing with a man named Anderson, who has his station on the cliff as a vendor of fossils. Anderson warned him that as darkness was coming on, it would be dangerous to stay. He retired some short distance, immediately turned round, and, exclaiming that he came from 19, Waterloo Crescent, jumped over the boundary-stone. Anderson immediately gave an alarm, and some of the coastguard and boatmen, proceeding to the base of the cliff, found his remains mangled dreadfully, he having fallen between

300 and 400 feet. The unfortunate gentleman was staying at 19, Waterloo Crescent with his lady, who was anxiously waiting his return when the dreadful news arrived. His name is the Rev. Thomas Robinson, and he held a living in the Isle of Wight. (1854)

🕱 *August 17th* 🕱

William Bennison, who was committed to prison at Leith, in April last, [*see* April 22nd] on the charge of poisoning his wife, has been tried before the High Court of Justiciary and convicted of the crimes of Bigamy and Murder. It was a case of singular atrocity. Some years since, when resident in Ireland, he married an Irishwoman; but soon deserted her, and coming home to Scotland, married there a woman remarkable for her meek virtue and her devotion to himself: he left his second wife, returned to his first wife in Ireland, and soon after she died suddenly. He then once more returned to his second wife, and gave her the garments of his first wife as those of a deceased sister – 'a sister in the Lord.' He was distinguished for his gift in prayer, and at last was every evening at the prayer-meeting. Here his eye fell upon one whom he resolved to make his third wife. Six weeks after his acquaintance with this girl, his second wife died: it was proved that six weeks before her death he bought arsenic, and with that poison frequently administered he took the unfortunate woman's life. Her deathbed strikingly exemplified pious resignation and trusted attachment to her husband. With a climax of hypocrisy, immediately after her death, he exclaimed at her bedside, 'Thank God, she is gone to glory! I have seen many a deathbed, but never a pleasanter one than my wife's.' The wretch was found guilty on both charges. Sentence of death was passed, and he was removed protesting his innocence of the murder: but he afterwards confessed. He was executed on the 17th. (1850)

🕱 *August 18th* 🕱

A calamitous Colliery Explosion took place on the 18th, at Washington Colliery, near the Washington Station on the York, Newcastle, and Berwick Railway. In the afternoon of that day about 60 men went down into the pit on the night shift. A little before midnight the inhabitants of the neighbourhood were aroused by a loud explosion. Unfortunately the resident viewer, Mr. Cruddace, was absent, and no person being left to act for him in his absence, the scene became one of the greatest confusion. The head over-man was at length aroused, and he, in company with a few of the miners, descended the pit, and found several dead bodies very much burnt and mutilated near the cross-cut way, where it is supposed the pit was fired. They discovered that the explosion took place in the 'whole' workings, where about 40 men were employed, and that the other 20 men, who had been working in the 'brokings' were uninjured. No language can describe the intense grief and horror of those who, on the first report being given, rushed to the spot, and remained to witness the blackened and disfigured corpses of their husbands, children, and fathers. Three hours passed away before any of the bodies were brought up. Almost immediately after the explosion took place, two furnace-men, desirous of being instrumental in saving the lives of their comrades, went down to render assistance, but the afterdamp was so strong that they were brought up again almost dead, and both of them have since died. In the course of the following day the corpses of the people who had perished were brought up – thirty-five men and boys. A coroner's inquest on the bodies was commenced on the 20th, and adjourned for a week. From the evidence already reported, it appears that the pit was badly ventilated, and that Bell, the under-viewer, who had been left in charge of the pit during the absence of his superior, had been drinking on the evening of the accident. (1851)

🕱 *August 19th* 🕱

Alfred Waddington, a dissolute young man of Sheffield, has Murdered his Illegitimate Child, and attempted to kill its mother, Sarah Slater. The mother had taken out a summons because Waddington had not paid for the child's support; on the evening of the 19th inst. he got the infant from a girl who was nursing it, carried it to a wood, and cut its head off, leaving the remains in the wood; then he went to a place where the mother was, called her into the street, and with a large clasp-knife attempted to cut her throat; but she held up her hands and saved her neck at their expense, and Waddington ran away. After this he met Sarah Dobson, and when she questioned him, he cut her on the face with the knife, and again fled. He subsequently surrendered himself to the police, and has been committed for trial. (1852)

Early on the morning of the 19th inst., a man named William Hall was Found Dead on the Railway, near Netherton Station, Worcestershire. He was horribly mutilated, his head being completely severed from the body; both arms and legs were also cut off, one of the legs being found at some distance. He was recognised as guard to a coal train from Stoke. It appears that he came up with the train as usual on the previous evening. He got off at Brierly Hill, and left his under guard to take charge of the train. He remained behind himself, bargaining about some fowls, and the train went on about nine o'clock without him. He appears to have spent the remainder of the evening drinking. About one o'clock in the morning he was seen walking along the line toward Netherton. About two o'clock the driver of a goods train passed over the body. The driver noticed a jerk, and suspecting that something was wrong, went back from the Netherton station, accompanied by the watchman, and had not gone far when they came upon the frightful spectacle of the mangled body. (1854)

August 20th

A Female Aeronaut has been Killed in France. On the 20th inst., a young woman named Emma Verdier ascended by herself in a balloon at Mount-de-Marsan. The balloon rose most evenly, and, as the weather was perfectly calm, no apprehensions were entertained of any accident. The next day, however, it was ascertained that the young woman had fallen to the ground in about two hours and a half after the time of the ascent, at Montesquieu, a village sixty miles distant, and was killed on the spot. Some haymakers were startled at seeing a white body fall to the earth a short distance from them. They found it to be the body of a young woman dressed in white. She had fallen headforemost, and her skull was split open. At no great distance was to be seen the anchor of the balloon fixed in an oak, a long piece of rope being attached to the iron. The balloon was also seen rising rapidly and floating away. It is supposed that on the young woman attempting to effect her descent, the anchor caught in the tree and the rope then breaking, gave such a shock to the wickerwork basket in which she was sitting, that she lost her balance and fell out. (1853)

August 21st

At Guildhall on the 21st, Eliza Bently, a good-looking young woman, was charged with Attempting to commit Suicide. The prisoner was seen by a policeman rushing down the steps of Blackfriars bridge on the previous night; he followed her, and was just in time to prevent her from plunging into the water. He took her to the station, where she expressed a determination to destroy herself, and even attempted to hang herself with her shawl in the cell. She was drunk, and had been in custody on several occasions for similar attempts. Her husband attended, and complained of her drunken habits, and she complained of her husband's conduct towards her. He earned as much as 36s. per week, and spent it all in profligacy. It was that which first drove her to drinking. She earned money herself as a singer. She was married very young, and had had ten children. It was finally arranged that she should make herself chargeable to the parish, so as to enable them to compel her husband to support her. (1852)

August 22nd

A singular case of Assault was tried at the Chester Assizes [this month]. The plaintiff was Ralph Hulse, a small freeholder; the defendant, Mr. William Spence Tollemache, brother of the member for the county. Mr. Tollemache had horsewhipped Hulse, though without doing him much injury. But it appeared that Hulse had for a long time been annoying Miss Tomkinson, sister to Mr. Tollemache's wife: he persecuted her with letters offering love, waylaid her out of doors, planted himself opposite her at church in order to stare at her, make grimaces at her, and threw kisses to her. He received not the slightest encouragement, only evidences of fear and disgust. As the law gave no remedy, Mr. Tollemache was impelled to administer what he thought was preventive justice. The evidence was very laughable in some parts, and far from creditable to the plaintiff and his attorney. Mr. Justice Wightman left it to the jury to assess the damages for the assault upon a consideration of the circumstances provoking it. They gave one farthing, and requested the judge not to certify for costs. The decision was met with a burst of cheering. (1851)

August 23rd

At Guildhall, on the 23rd, Margaret Raymond was charged with Throwing her Son, a Child of six years old, from a third-floor window in Sun Court, Golden Lane. The charge was proved by several witnesses. The child fell on his head, which was much injured, but the skull was not fractured. Mary Ann Regan, an intelligent girl, aged 11, deposed that she lived in the house, and was looking through the second-floor window. She saw the prisoner holding the child out of the upper window. He exclaimed, 'Oh, mother, don't chuck me out!' The mother then took him by the heels and dropped him out of the window. At the same time a little girl in the mother's room exclaimed, 'Oh, mother, don't throw him out.' The prisoner was committed for trial. She subsequently admitted that she had wanted the boy's boots in order to sell them for gin. (1851)

🕱 *August 24th* 🕱

A young Austrian, named Francis Thopier, was charged at the Mansion-house, on the 21th, with having Attempted to destroy himself, by throwing himself from a boat into the Thames. The young man, whose wild look indicated great distress of mind, had been dragged out of the water by a waterman named Carpenter. A medical gentleman, who was acquainted with part of his history, said the unfortunate young man was acquainted with several languages, and had read with such intense application as to affect his intellect. His object in coming to this country was to avail himself of the opportunities of distinction which an education at Oxford would afford him, and he had separated himself from his nearest relatives because they were, according to his account, opposed to his desire to abandon the Jewish religion, and become a Christian. The Lord Mayor desired that particular inquiry should be made into the case, and remanded the defendant. (1852)

🕱 *August 25th* 🕱

A dreadful Agrarian Murder was committed in the Queen's County, on the 25th of August. The victim was Mr. Edward White, who had purchased, a short time since, a portion of the Portarlington estate in the neighbourhood of Abbeyleix, in which village he resided. A dispute arose with some persons in the locality about the right of turbary, and some summonses to petty sessions had been issued on both sides. On the morning of the day above-mentioned, whilst Mr. White was driving to his land, he was met on the road by a man, who stopped the gig, deliberately shot him through the heart, and then, having thrown the pistol into the vehicle, coolly walked away, when the pony proceeded on its journey, and conveyed the corpse of its master to the farm. The murder was committed within sight of hundreds of people reaping in the surrounding fields, but the slightest attempt was not made either to render assistance, or to apprehend the assassin. Mr. White had been an extensive trader in the town of Abbeyleix, for nearly forty years, and was generally esteemed and respected. (1851)

🕱 *August 26th* 🕱

The Irish papers contain many accounts of Affrays and Disturbances, caused by the 'evictions' which are daily taking place. On the 26th of August an affair of this kind took place near Ballinasloe. It is thus related by the Western Star: – 'On Wednesday last, Mr. John Kelly, poor-rate collector, proceeded with three assistants, named Murray, Gavan, and Kenny, to distrain for poor-rates due by a man named Turley – the amount 11*l*. 3*s*. After going on the lands of Ballymana, and seizing eleven head of cattle, several people collected and succeeded in rescuing the cattle, with the exception of one cow. Some blows were given on both sides, when Mr. Kelly and his men were attacked with stones. Murray was struck by a stone on the forehead, which forced the blood through his ears and nose; and Mr. Kelly was hit on the back of the head and some other parts of his body. He had a double-barrelled pistol in his hand, and when knocked down two or three of the 'rescuers' held him, wrested the pistol from his hand, searched his side-pocket for another pistol, which they got, and when taking it out also took 50*l*. in notes, either through mistake or design. So Mr. Kelly states. Mr. Kelly and his party, however, got away, and came into town, when Murray, who received such dreadful injuries, was put into hospital. He is the only support of a widowed mother. We understand that the lands on which the seizure was made were waste, and the cattle found there belonged to a number of poor farmers living in the neighbourhood.' (1855)

🕱 *August 27th* 🕱

A Shocking Death at Hastings Castle took place on the evening of the 27th of August. A party of young men and women were amusing themselves with the game of 'whoop-hide' within the walls. On the south side of the garden, within the old ruins, there is a fence about three feet high, and a hedge growing outside of it, which serves as a protection from the bow of the cliff, which rises perpendicularly above St. Mary's Chapel, in Pelham Crescent, about 200 feet. In the heat of the chase, and to avoid being caught, a young man named Joseph Beck leaped over the fence, believing that there was a footing on the outside, and fell upon the roof of the chapel, where his body was found frightfully mangled. He was a respectable young man, who supported his widowed mother. (1850)

🙂 *August 28th* 🙂

Mr. Feargus O'Connor has commenced legal proceedings for the purpose of Recovering Rents from the allottees at Snig's End, near Gloucester. On the 28th of August bailiff's proceeded from that city to serve fifty-two writs. The colonists, who had got intelligence of the coming storm, held a meeting on the preceding evening, and concerted their arrangements. On the appearance of the bailiffs they intimated that they would 'manure the land with their blood before it should be taken from them.' The bailiffs, therefore, retired. (1855)

🙂 *August 29th* 🙂

There has been another dreadful case of Murder in Tipperary. On the morning of the 29th August, as Thomas Batters, of Clashdrumsmith, was going along the road at Breansha, near Emly, he was fired at from behind a hedge, and was wounded in the wrist and thighs with large shot, making a dozen wounds. The assigned motive was that Batters was employed as caretaker on crops under seizure for rent, and also blamed for entertaining the keepers in his house. The unfortunate man lingered until the following day, when he died of his wounds at eight o'clock in the evening. (1855)

🙂 *August 30th* 🙂

A Scotchman, passing himself under the name of Robert James Webster, has Killed Himself, and Attempted to Murder a Girl in a house of ill fame in Dublin. He appeared to be about thirty-five years of age; his features indicated a life of hardship or dissipation. He went to the house on the 30th of last month, and remained there till the 18th inst., spending profusely, and drinking hard, night and day. At one time he pretended to be attached to the Queen's service in the veterinary department; at another, that he had just arrived from Australia. He attached himself to Emma Fawcett, one of the girls of the house. Last Sunday evening, he discharged a pistol at this girl, wounding her in the side with a number of shots, but not dangerously; he then fired a second pistol into his own breast, and he was found dead. The police have discovered a bag filled with sovereigns and five pistols in the room he occupied. Latterly, his behaviour indicated insanity; and the coroner's inquest has given a verdict of 'Temporary derangement.' (1853)

August 31st

A child has died from Foul Air in a Railway Carriage. An inquest was held on the 31st ult., touching the death of an infant of ten mouths old, named Carr, who died in a carriage on the London and North Western Railway. Mary Green, a nurse, stated that the child's parents resided at Edinburgh, from whence she arrived at the King's-cross terminus of the Great Northern Railway on the previous Sunday morning, having charge of deceased, whom she carried the whole journey on her lap with its face uncovered. During the journey the infant was slightly indisposed, but upon arriving at the terminus witness was horrified at finding it dead. The third-class carriage in which she travelled was not overcrowded, yet, through the windows having been kept shut during the whole 400 miles' journey, it was rather close. Mr. Superintendent Williams said that although the windows might have been kept closed, yet the ventilation over the window admitted air sufficient for the comfort and health of the passengers. Mr. G.F. Jones, surgeon, found that death resulted from suffocation produced by inhaling foul air in the carriage. The ventilation spoken of would not neutralise the effects of the poisonous gas, because the latter, being heavier than atmospheric air, would sink, and having no escape at the bottom of the carriage, would act fatally on an infant of deceased's tender age. The coroner suggested to Mr. Williams the propriety of directing the attention of the directors to the necessity of having at the bottom of the carriage a proper ventilation. The jury returned a verdict that the deceased was accidentally suffocated by impure air in a railway carriage. (1853)

September

💀 September 1st 💀

A case of Domestic Disagreement, which excited considerable interest, was brought before the sitting magistrate at the Mansion-House on the 1st inst. Mr. May, the Dutch consul, attended, accompanied by a father and two daughters, natives of Amsterdam. He had, he said, received a telegraphic despatch from the official authorities at Amsterdam, stating that the daughter of a tradesman here had decamped to this country, and requesting him, as consul, to act *in loco parentis*, and to endeavour to induce the fugitive to return to her natural protector… The young lady, it was necessary to state, seemed to be willing upon the remonstrance made to her to return with her father; but her younger sister, who was married to a tradesman in

London, upon presenting herself, made a complete revolution in the state of circumstances, and the two sisters clung to each other with an earnestness of affection indicating that separation would be intolerable to either.

In answer to questions by Sir R.W. Carden, the married sister, who, although only 18 years of age, had been married at the age of 15, said her elder sister had just attained the age of 21; and, considering that she then became her own mistress, determined to leave her father, under whose tyrannical authority it was no longer possible for her to live. The father said his elder daughter was, he feared, weak in intellect, and required most particularly the guidance of a parent; and, as he was her only parent, he was anxious to perform that duty. The elder girl, with a very intelligent look, shook her head at the imputation of weakness; and the younger indignantly denied that her sister was committing an act of imbecility in going to those from whom she would be sure of receiving nothing but love and tenderness, from one by whom she was considered and treated as a slave. Sir R.W. Carden: Is this young lady entitled to any money, or is there any gentleman concerned in this case? The Younger Sister: No. We don't want money. I know nothing of any gentleman. My sister's wish is to come and live with me and my husband, and she must not go back. I know how she has been treated, and she shall not suffer any more. Sir R.W. Carden, after having asked several questions of all parties, said: I acknowledge I have heard and seen quite enough to lead me to recommend the father to reconcile himself to the choice which his elder daughter, at the full age of 21, so decidedly makes. It appears to me that she is not likely to be unhappy or unprotected by the change. The sisters left the justice-room in ecstasy, the younger pushing the other before her, as it were, to prevent the father from putting a finger on her prize. (1855)

September 2nd

At the Marylebone Police Court [this month], Anne Parker, a married woman, was committed for Attempting to Drown one of her Children in the canal of the Regent's Park. A policeman came up in time to rescue the child, which was struggling in the water. The woman admitted that she had intended to drown her second child, who was with her, and then to destroy herself. It seems that she came from Plaistow: she said her husband, after beating her, had deserted his family. The mother and children exhibited great affection for each other. The children have been sent to the Marylebone Workhouse. (1854)

🕱 *September 3rd* 🕱

Another Accident occurred on the South Western Railway on the evening of the 3rd. inst. Between Esher and Weybridge, the engine-driver espied some moving objects on the line; he therefore shut off the steam and signalled to the guards to apply the breaks; but before they had sufficient time to do so, the engine came in contact with the obstruction in front, which was dashed to pieces, and in an instant portions of flesh and blood were scattered over the driver and stoker, as well as over several of the carriages. It was then ascertained that a great number of sheep had strolled upon the line from one of the adjoining meadows; but owing to the train not being impeded in its progress, the driver proceeded on his journey. Next morning it was ascertained that from twenty to twenty-five sheep had been cut to pieces. The animals, it seems, had obtained an entrance upon the line owing to some defect in palings which surround the meadow where they were at pasture. (1850)

🕱 *September 4th* 🕱

At the Preston Town-hall on the 4th inst., three military officers, named A.G. Onslow, J. Conroy, and Hopton S. Stewart, were fined 40s. and costs, and severely reprimanded by the Bench for Smashing Streetlamps by throwing rabbits against them. The defendants, who, it is said, had been tippling freely, pleaded guilty to the charge. (1855)

🕱 *September 5th* 🕱

A Man has been Murdered by his Wife and Son. The murdered man, David Napper, resided at Trowbridge. On the 5th inst., his son, James Napper, quarrelled with another brother who had lately returned from transportation. The father interfered to separate them, and incurred the displeasure of his son James by striking him. On the following evening they were all drinking together at a public house, when a second altercation took place. James Napper struck his father, knocked him down, and kicked him severely. The wife then fell upon her husband, taking hold of him by the hair and repeatedly striking his head on the ground, swearing she would murder him. They all three then left the inn and went towards home. What occurred afterwards was related by the landlord in his evidence before the Coroner.

He said that the outrage took place in so short a space of time that he had no opportunity to interfere. The son came into the taproom some time afterwards, when he did not appear to be intoxicated. Witness remonstrated with him on his conduct, but he only replied that, 'It served the old — right,' and that if he was not dead already, he would not care about subjecting him to similar treatment again. This statement was corroborated by James Brown, a clothworker, who said he was passing when he saw the deceased on the ground, and saw his wife catch hold of him by the hair, and thump his head on the ground, saying, 'By G—, I'll murder thee!' The deceased was then in a state of insensibility, and the son afterwards took him by the shoulders and threw him backwards on the ground with all his might. Witness lifted the deceased on his knee, but the son still attempted to strike him, and said he would give any one who took his part 'a — good hiding.' The wife and son then left, but, after they had gone a short distance, turned round and said, if the deceased came home that night, they would 'finish him off.' The deceased, however, was shortly after taken to his house, where he soon died. The wife and son have been committed to Devizes gaol for trial. (1854)

September 6th

The journey of the Queen to the North, on the 6th inst. was attended with several Casualties, one of which was fatal ... About six miles north of Darlington, one of the Great Northern Company's 'Fitters' left the guard's van, when the train was at full speed, to lubricate a heated wheel-box: while he was thus engaged, his head came in contact with a girder of a bridge, and he was killed on the spot. (1855)

The village of Cudham, near Bromley in Kent, has been the scene of a frightful Murder. Bagley, a labourer, left his wife and very aged mother in his cottage in the morning: on returning home in the evening with his son, he found the door fastened: when he had forced an entrance he discovered his wife a corpse, and his mother insensible, both having been beaten on the head with a pair of tongs. The cottage had been plundered. Suspicion has fallen on two men, who are in custody. One of them, Robert Paling, a convicted burglar, was arrested near Bristol. He was examined at Bromley on the 6th inst. The discovery of the murder was related; and some witnesses expressed their conviction that Paling was the man they saw running away from the direction of Bagley's cottage early on the morning of the murder. Bagley's son identified some clothes found in Paling's possession as his property. Paling showed great self-possession

147

and considerable acuteness in the cross-examination of the witnesses. He was remanded, and has subsequently been committed for trial. Old Mrs. Bagley is recovering, and may be able to identify the assassin. The other man in custody is Clarke, a native of Hayling Island. He was seized at Havant. Nothing suspicious was found on him. (1855)

September 7th

A Canoe with nineteen naked Savages was picked up on the 7th of September, by the Jeremiah Garnett, Captain Daly, on her voyage from Shanghai to Liverpool. They had, thirteen days before, been blown out to sea from the islands of St. David's, which lie off New Guinea. One of the poor wretches died the same evening. Captain Daly landed the others at St. David's from whence they had been driven.

September 8th

On the morning of the 8th inst. a most singular act of Suicide was committed by Mr. Hall, pawnbroker, of Union street, Middlesex hospital. It appears that, shortly after the shop was opened, one of the young men having occasion to bring into requisition that portion of a pawnbroker's premises known in common parlance as 'the spout', was astonished to find that some pledges which had been thrown down for a customer, who was waiting to take them out, did not reach their destination at the bottom, and, on investigation, it was discovered that the cause of the stoppage was the body of the employer, who was found suspended in the centre by the neck, from the cord employed in pulling up parcels from the shop to the warehouse. Medical aid was procured, but the deceased had ceased to exist. Mr. Hall was of an exceedingly sedate and scientific turn of mind, and no cause is assigned for his committal of the deed. (1855)

September 9th

A poor man named John Carson Died of Hydrophobia, on the 9th, at Banbridge, near Newry. His hand was slightly bit on the 23rd of June by a stray dog which he had found and brought home, and which died two days afterwards. The wound healed in a few days, without giving him any uneasiness of mind, and he continued in the enjoyment of good health up to Sep. 4, when he passed a very restless night. On the morning of the 6th, medical aid was called in, but in vain. On that and the two following days he was quite sensible, and talked seriously about his death with different clergymen who visited him. He changed, became slightly delirious, muttered unconnected sentences, in dread of everything, and thought the different people around him were conspiring to destroy him. When visited by the medical men he said 'they were a parcel of murdering villains, and that they had killed him, for which he would have revenge by day or by night.' He was now secured, but so slightly, that he broke loose, seized a stick, and had no difficulty in clearing the house, as all fled before him. No one dared subsequently to enter, until a police-constable voluntarily came forward, entered and seized him, and was the main hand in properly securing him, while he attempted to bite the people about him. He continued in this until six o'clock on the morning of the 9th, when he, by degrees, became insensible, and, between nine and ten o'clock, death put an end to his sufferings. During the whole time his dread of fluids was excessive, and even bringing a handkerchief near his face brought on the spasms, which prevented an attempt to relieve him by the inhalation of chloroform. (1851)

September 10th

A most brutal and fatal Assault on a Woman, was perpetrated at Shepherd's Bush in the night of Saturday the 10th inst. The woman's husband, James Hays, a bricklayer, was charged with the crime at the Hammersmith Police Court on the 12th. Prom the evidence it appeared that Hays, his wife, and two men named Taylor and George, were in Shepherd's Bush market between eleven and twelve o'clock. Hays had left his wife to live with another woman, but he allowed her some money weekly, and to obtain this she was following him. He replied to her demand with blows. Taylor saw Hays beat his wife with his fists, and when she sought refuge behind Taylor, that person told her to get from behind him, lest her husband might think he was harbouring her. Mrs. Hays ran through the market, her brutal husband running after and kicking at her, and loudly threatening that he would 'do for her' that night. Serle, a policeman, deposed, that about one o'clock he heard a noise which seemed to come from the ground newly dug out for the foundation of some houses, close by the market. He went to the spot, and found Hays standing there, pale, trembling, and much stupified. Serle ordered him to move on: at first he would not move, but stood there sighing and shivering. At length he went away. Next morning, soon after six, a policeman, directed by some women to the spot, found Mrs. Hays lying in a hole, apparently lifeless. On being turned over she opened one of her eyes – that was all. She was taken to the station in Brook Green; thence, later, to the house of her brother-in-law, where she died. She had been kicked and beaten very much. Hays was remanded for a week. An inquest was held on the body of Mrs. Hays, on the 14th; the evidence given in the Police Court was repeated; and the inquest was adjourned. The two men, George and Taylor, who did not protect Mrs. Hays from her husband, gave as an excuse that they feared the hundred Irish within a stone's-throw. Mr. Brent, the coroner, warmly expressed his indignation at their conduct … (1853)

September 11th

On Sunday night, the 11th inst., a Fire broke out in the premises belonging to Mr. Lewne, a waterproof clothing manufacturer in Whitechapel. It originated from some unexplained cause in the front room first floor, in which three men were sleeping at the time. The inmates were saved by the Royal Society's fire-escape, with the exception of a young man named Maurice Abrahams. Upon the conductor entering the room in which the fire began he beheld a fearful scene, for the unfortunate man was found in a corner of the apartment, burnt so frightfully, that when he was touched the flesh came off his body. It appears that he had previously assisted the other two men in effecting their escape, when he became surrounded with flames, and dropped in the midst of them. (1853)

September 12th

At the Worship-street Police Court on the 12th, James Taylor, an elderly man, of respectable appearance, who was stated to be a person in independent circumstances, was charged with an unprovoked and violent Assault upon a Married Woman, named Amelia Manning, residing in Anne's-place, Hackney-road. The complainant, who was in such a state of suffering that she was scarcely able to give her evidence, stated that on the evening of the preceding Saturday, she was proceeding through the Hackney-road in the company of a female friend, when she accidentally met the defendant, who was the landlord of a house formerly occupied by her husband, and she availed herself of the opportunity to apprise him that her husband had been compelled to take out a summons against him to recover the amount of certain rates which they had disbursed on his account during their tenancy. She at the same time expressed her hope that he would liquidate the debt to save him from the expense and annoyance of legal proceedings, but the moment she had uttered the observation, the defendant, who was partially intoxicated, exclaimed, with an oath, 'Yes, I'll pay you at once – take that, you —— ,' and, instantly raising his stick, struck her a terrible blow on the head, which felled her to the ground in a state of insensibility. On recovering her consciousness, she found herself supported in the arms of her friend by another woman who had witnessed the assault, and observing that the defendant was in the act of making rapidly off, she called a policeman and gave him into custody. The complainant added that she had been confined to her bed the whole of the previous day, under the care of a surgeon, and had been ever since in a state of excruciating pain from the effects of the prisoner's violence. A respectable married woman, named Elizabeth York, gave corroborative evidence. The magistrate said that it was a case of such brutal and vindictive violence, that he did not feel himself justified in imposing a pecuniary penalty upon the defendant, but should order him forthwith to be committed and kept to hard labour for six weeks in the House of Correction. The prisoner appeared staggered by the severity of the sentence. He ought rather to have been astonished at its utter inadequacy to the offence. (1853)

September 13th

At Guildhall, on the 13th inst., Thomas Dennis, a boy of fourteen, was charged with Robbery and Attempting to Shoot a Policeman. He had stolen 5l. from his mother, and absconded; a policeman seized him in the Victoria Theatre; he immediately drew out a pistol and attempted to fire – it was loaded with powder and shot, capped, and cocked; when disarmed of this, he produced a second loaded pistol. He said he had bought the pistols and ammunition to shoot his father. He was remanded. (1854)

September 14th

A captain of the National Guard of St. Pierre les Calais, named Millien, now on a visit to this country, has been instrumental in Saving the Lives of two children, who would inevitably have been lost but for his timely and humane conduct. On the morning of the 14th, M. Millien was passing over the Kingsland bridge, and hearing cries for help hastened in the direction whence they proceeded. Finding that someone was at the bottom of the canal, he immediately plunged in and brought up the body of a child, and hearing that there was another, he made another plunge, and another was saved, in the presence of a great number of spectators, amongst whom was Dr. L. Burchell, of Kingsland Road, whose exertions soon restored the children. It has been the good fortune of M. Million to have saved twenty-two persons under similar circumstances, and to have been rewarded with the gold and silver medals of the institutions of his country, as the reward of courage and humanity. (1850)

September 15th

A Case of Affiliation was heard before the magistrates of Dewsbury, on the 15th. The defendant was the Rev. Stephen Matthews, the incumbent of Hanging Heaton, near Dewsbury, the alleged father of an illegitimate child born in May last, by Mary Hellewell, a young girl of sixteen, who was engaged as a paid teacher in the school connected with the church at Hanging Heaton. The rev. defendant is a man verging upon sixty years of age, and has for many years held the incumbency of Hanging Heaton. The case was first heard at the Dewsbury Court House, on the 20th of August, when the justices declined to make an order of maintenance upon the defendant, on the ground that the evidence of the mother of the child was not corroborated in the way required by the Act of Parliament. The decision gave great dissatisfaction in the neighbourhood, where the case has excited considerable attention; and the friends of the girl are determined to have a re-hearing. The court-house was crowded to suffocation during the whole day, the hearing occupying till nearly ten o'clock at night. The magistrates who heard the case had both been present at the former hearing. The evidence went to show that the rev. defendant had seduced the girl, and that a criminal intercourse had continued for two years. The magistrates retired for half an hour; and, on their return into court, still declined to make an order upon Mr. Matthews. The solicitor who supported the application said that he should not again trouble the magistrates with the case, but should, if he had the opportunity, take it before another tribunal. (1851)

🕷 *September 16th* 🕷

A Fire has taken place at Balmoral. Five cottages occupied by the masons and other workmen at present engaged in the erection of the new Palace, were totally destroyed on the 16th inst. The flames were discovered a little after midday, and as the cottages were situated only about 150 yards from Balmoral Castle, the Royal family, and a large number of men were in a very short time on the spot, and using every endeavour to conquer the fire. As, however, the houses were composed of wood, the most strenuous efforts were found unavailing, and by one o'clock the whole were burnt to the ground. When a line of men was formed to convey water to the burning pile from the river. Prince Albert at once took a position, and continued working steadily throughout, shoulder to shoulder with a sturdy Highlandman. The Prince of Wales and Prince Alfred were also actively engaged, while Her Majesty stood by the whole time, and gave such directions as she thought would tend to assuage the fire, seemingly deeply interested by the efforts of the men to save their clothes chests, in which many of them had considerable sums of money. (1853)

🕷 *September 17th* 🕷

A Coroner's Inquest was held on the 17th inst., on the body of Mrs. Catherine Grieve, aged sixty-seven, a lady of fortune, lately residing at Douro Cottage, Southampton-street. It appeared that on the evening of the 15th she had been out to a party, and returned in a state of intoxication. Before retiring to bed, she took nearly a pint of gin, besides other liquor. About ten o'clock the same night, a lady residing with the deceased knocked several times at the bed-room door, but receiving no answer, entered the room, and found that she had fallen on her face on the floor. A medical man was called in, but he pronounced her to have been dead some time, and gave it as his opinion that her death had been caused by suffocation, from falling on her face off the bed. (1853)

🕷 *September 18th* 🕷

At the Thames Police Office, on the 18th, John Murphy was charged with being in the Hutchinson's Arms public-house, Devonport Street, with Intent to Commit a Felony. The curious point in the case was the discovery of the thief by a cat. Murphy was supposed to have left the taproom late at night; the cat was noticed to be uneasy – rushing at the fire-place, mewing, purring, and exhibiting anger. This induced the publican to look up the chimney; whence he succeeded in drawing down Murphy by the heels: a candle and lucifer-matches were found upon him. It would seem that in other cases the prisoner had robbed public-houses by concealing himself in the chimney at night. He was sent to prison for three months for his concealment at the Hutchinson's Arms. (1850)

A Railway Accident of a novel but very shocking character took place on the 18th inst., about nine at night, on the Dinting Viaduct of the Manchester and Sheffield Railway, across the river Etherow, near Glossop. A train from Manchester approached the Hadfield station, which is at the eastern end of the viaduct, and in consequence of a Liverpool excursion train being in advance, and having to discharge passengers at the station, the Manchester train was brought to a stand on the viaduct. The night was very dark, and it appears that some of the passengers in the Manchester train, who had to get out at Hadfield, imagined that the train was already at the station. Three of these persons, two young men and a young woman, succeeded in opening the door of the carriage and got out. The parapet of the viaduct on that side was within a very short space of the carriages, and it is supposed that owing to the darkness of the night, instead of getting down in the narrow space between the train and the parapet of the viaduct, they stepped upon the top of the parapet. Immediately afterwards an alarm was given that they had fallen over, and the shocking fact was soon afterwards confirmed by the discovery of their bodies in the valley below. They had fallen from a height of seventy-five feet. Two of them, John Healy, aged 23 years, and Jane Hadfield, who were lovers, and had been to Belle Vue Gardens, Manchester, were quite dead when found. The other man, Thomas Priestnall, a weaver, aged 29 years, residing at Freetown, was taken up in a state of insensibility, and died in about an hour afterwards. Priestnall had attempted to persuade another young woman to get out with him, but, fortunately, she had not complied with his request. (1855)

🐾 September 19th 🐾

On the 19th, John Gould was tried for the Manslaughter of a child named Towers. The evidence showed that it was the result of accident. Gould, an old soldier, decorated with two medals, is toll-man in the Vauxhall Bridge Road; a window of the toll-house overlooks a lane, apparently little frequented;

Gould had been washing a basin with boiling water, and he emptied it out of the window, having no reason to believe at that time that any one was passing. Unfortunately two children had wandered thither; the scalding water fell upon Towers, and eventually caused his death. Gould offered all the reparation in his power to the parents. Officers in the army gave him an excellent character. He was at once acquitted and discharged. (1850)

🏴 September 20th 🏴

Two Men have been Destroyed by Foul Air in a mine in Cornwall. On the 20th inst. A new steam stamp was being set to work at North Levant Mine, St. Just, and, in order to get 'feed' for the engine, some men were employed to draw a few buckets of water out of an old shaft that was close by. The bucket got jammed between some rocks, and one of the men went down to clear it. After waiting a little while, his comrades called to know why he was so long, but received no answer; upon which another man slid down the rope to see what was the matter. The men at the surface called again, but both below were speechless. The awful truth was then suspected: foul air had been generated in the bottom of the shaft, it is thought by the gas from the coals burning at the engine. Means were immediately resorted to to dispel it, and the two men were soon brought to the surface, but both quite dead. (1853)

🏴 September 21st 🏴

A shocking Accident has occurred at the terminus of the Brighton Railway. On the 21st, a widow lady, named Eastwood, who resided in Edward-street, had arrived at the Brighton terminus from London, and in stepping from the carriage next to the break whilst the train was in motion, she missed the platform, and one foot went between it and the step of the carriage. She was immediately dragged under the carriage wheels, in spite of the attempt to rescue her, and one of the wheels passed over her left foot, and nearly severed it, whilst the other leg sustained very serious injury. She was also much bruised about the body. She was conveyed to the County Hospital, when it was deemed expedient to amputate both legs. The operation was skilfully performed, the patient exhibiting great fortitude; but she died on the following morning. (1852)

💀 *September 22nd* 💀

Lieutenant Annesley of the Scots Fusilier Guards, in a letter to the Countess Annesley, his mother, gives an account of his hair-breadth escapes [at the Battle of Alma]:– 'We were about thirty paces then from the ditch, and the fire was so hot that you could hardly conceive it possible for anything the size of a rabbit not to be killed. I kept on shouting, "Forward, Guards!" to the few men that were not swept away by the —, when a ball came and stopped my mouth most unceremoniously. It entered the left cheek, and went out at the mouth, taking away the front teeth. I instantly turned to the rear, feeling it was about 100 to 1 against my ever getting there, as the bullets were whizzing round me like hail. I tripped, and thought it was all over with me. However, I got up again with the loss of my sword and bear-skin, and at last got into the river and out of fire.' It is melancholy to add that this high-spirited youth sank under his wounds and died a few days after the battle. (1854)

💀 *September 23rd* 💀

Two infants, of three years and fifteen months old, children of Robert Wardell, a labourer at Wetwang, were Drowned on the 23rd. At the inquest on their bodies, their mother gave an affecting account of their death: 'I went to glean in a field of Mr. Hill's, and took my two children with me. I left them under a hedge with some other children, and went off to glean. About one o'clock they both came over to the side of the field where I was. I gave them some cake, set them under a hedge, and told them to wait until I got another glean, and then I would take them home. A pond was near where I left them, but it was fenced off. About a quarter of an hour after I went to the place where I had left them, and I said, 'Have I two little bairns here?' as I usually did. I was surprised at not receiving an answer. I then began to look about, and on going to the pond I discovered the legs of one of the children projecting out of the water.' A surgeon was immediately sent for, but he was unable to restore them to animation. (1850)

💀 *September 24th* 💀

A sickly-looking man, named Garrett, was charged at Clerkenwell Police Court on the 24th, with Assaulting his Wife, a Welch woman. – She stated that she had been twelve months the wife of the defendant, who had neglected to contribute to her support. On the previous day he was skulking about their dwelling doing nothing, and because she told him he was an idle worthless fellow, he took on himself to knock her down, for which offence she gave him in charge. The defendant, whose face was sadly disfigured with scratches, said he was the miserable victim of his wife's ferocity, and since the working of the Act of Parliament for affording a better protection to females, she had served him out with a vengeance, almost daily menacing and otherwise ill-treating him, and daring him by the most aggravating and vile language to strike her, threatening if he did so to give him 'six months at the mill.' Being exceedingly irritated on the evening before, he certainly did give her a slight tap on the side of her head, and she immediately collared him, in the hope that he would suffer hard work in prison for the term mentioned or die there. He had not been free from her scratches scarcely a week since their marriage. – The wife, who had been laughing and otherwise misconducting herself, here called out, 'And it served you right, you wretch, and you shall have six months.' The magistrate said she would be disappointed for once, and, commiserating the husband, set him at liberty. (1853)

September 25th

A grave-digger named Smith met his death at Edinburgh on the 25th of September, by being Buried Alive. He had left his house to dig a grave in a neighbouring church-yard; but, as he did not return, his wife became alarmed, and, having obtained the company of the beadle of the church, proceeded to the place of interment, where, after a search, they were horrified at discovering a hand projecting from a mass of earth which had fallen into the grave where the poor man had been at work. Assistance was immediately procured, and the body of the unfortunate gravedigger exhumed from the receptacle which he had excavated. The body was still warm, but, though attempts were made to restore animation, they proved fruitless, life being quite extinct. (1851)

September 26th

An investigation has taken place before Mr. Wakley, the coroner, respecting the Death of James Walsh, an infant two months old. The child's parents were inmates of Marylebone workhouse in the early part of the year; and left it at their own request. Walsh is a marble polisher, but he is paralysed, and cannot follow his trade. His wife appears almost an imbecile. She was confined on the 26th September. The couple were then in great distress; they received out-door relief, but quite inadequate for their support. Afterwards they became houseless. They applied to be admitted into the workhouse, but were refused, though the out-door relief was continued. One night they were on the workhouse steps for hours, but the porter did not admit them, or inform the master that they were there. On another occasion, they walked the streets nearly all night. At five o'clock in the evening of the 22nd November, the infant died in the mother's arms, in the street, near St. Giles's church. She had covered it up as warmly as she could with ragged garments, and hugged it close to her body to shield it further from the weather – indeed, she seems to have been fatally over-careful of the child. Mr. Joseph, a surgeon, had seen the child some days before; it was then plump and healthy: from a post-mortem examination, he thought that death had been caused by congestion of the lungs from breathing impure air; he presumed the poor mother had caused this suffocation in endeavouring to keep the child warm while wandering in the streets. Of course, if the parents had been in the workhouse the infant would not have been exposed to this fate. The coroner remarked that this was an important case, for if the Poor Law were carried out generally as it had been in this instance, it would be a curse rather than a blessing to the poor, as no man could know his fate if he became utterly destitute: the Poor-law commissioners had decided that even a casual pauper who is houseless is entitled to admission; in this case the Walshes had a settlement, and had actually been in the house six months before. The jury found this verdict– 'That James Walsh died on the 22d day of November, 1853, from congestion and inflammation, caused by cold and exposure to the night-air; and the jury are unanimously of opinion that great culpability attaches to Messrs. Poland and Russell, Directors of the Poor, and to Mr. Messer, Assistant-Overseer, for not admitting the child and parents into the workhouse when application had been made by the parents of the deceased, stating that they were utterly destitute.' (1853)

🕸 *September 27th* 🕸

The Rev. Mr. Holiest, Perpetual Curate of Frimley Grove, was Murdered on the 27th of September, by robbers, who broke into his house in the dead of night. Mr Holiest was in his fifty-fourth year; he had held the curacy for seventeen years, and was universally respected. On the night in question, there were in the house Mr. and Mrs. Holiest, their two sons, youths of fourteen and fifteen, who were at home from school, a man-servant and two maidservants. Mr. and Mrs. Holiest slept on the first-floor. About three o'clock in the morning, they were awakened by a noise in the room; and saw two masked figures standing at the foot of the bed, with lights. Mr. Holiest thought it a trick of his sons, and good-naturedly chided them for the unseasonable hour they had chosen. Mrs. Holiest was not so deceived, and screamed in terror. The men instantly seized them both, and, with pistols pointed at their heads, declared that if they made the slightest noise they would blow their brains out. Mrs. Holiest struggled hard, and at length succeeded in slipping out of bed and seizing a bell-rope; upon which her assailant rushed round to the side of the bed, threw himself upon her with such force as to snap the bell-rope asunder, and continued to stand over her with his pistol pointed to her face. Mr. Holiest, who was a strong and active man, struggled with the villain who stood over him, and getting out of bed, was in the act of stooping down to reach the poker from the fireplace, when his assailant fired, and wounded him in the abdomen. Mr. Holiest was not aware at first that he had been struck, and continued to grapple with the robber, endeavouring to prevent his escape. The report of the pistol alarmed the miscreant who was standing over Mrs. Holiest, and he left her for a moment and joined his companion. Finding herself released, she rushed to the fireplace, and, seizing a large hand-bell, swung it to and fro several times. The villains almost immediately left the apartment; and, descending the staircase, hastened out of the house by the front-door. Mr. Holiest seized a loaded gun, ran down stairs, and fired at three men who were running across a lawn; but, it appears, without effect. On returning up-stairs, Mr. Holiest first discovered that he was wounded. He got into bed, and sent the man-servant for constables and a doctor. Examination of the premises showed that the robbers had entered by a scullery-window, and then forced an entrance into the kitchen. They had set all the doors open, and fastened them back, so that they might easily retreat. They carried off much plunder. When Mr. Davies, the family-surgeon, examined Mr. Holiest, he at once foresaw a fatal issue. The patient's sufferings were intense; and at noon on Sunday, the 29th, it was announced to him that death was approaching. He received the intelligence with Christian resignation; took an affectionate leave of his family and servants; expressed a desire to partake of the sacrament, which was administered to him by a clerical friend and neighbour; and he expired, in a state of almost unconscious exhaustion, between eight and nine o'clock on Sunday evening. (1850)

💀 *September 28th* 💀

On Sunday evening the 28th ult., as Mr. Joel Slater, butcher, of Lower Belgrave-place, Pimlico, was returning home from Richmond, in a light spring-cart, accompanied by his housekeeper, when passing Kew-bridge, one of the Brentford omnibuses, which was coming along at a smart pace, caught the wheel of the cart before Mr. Slater could pull on one side, and overturning the vehicle, precipitated both him and his housekeeper a considerable distance into the road. On being picked up, it was found that Mr. Slater's neck was dislocated, and he expired shortly afterwards. The housekeeper sustained a compound fracture of the leg. (1851)

💀 *September 29th* 💀

An Inquest was held at Bristol on the 29th ult., on the body of Mr. Baker, a tradesman, who, a few days before, committed Suicide by blowing out his brains with a gun, to the trigger of which he had attached a string. It appeared that the unfortunate man took to heart the departure of two sons, his only children, to New York, and became so depressed in spirits, that the apprehensions of his friends were excited. The jury returned a verdict of 'temporary insanity', (1850)

💀 *September 30th* 💀

The Hon. Mrs. Matheson met with her Death on Sunday the 30th ult., under very distressing circumstances. Mrs. Matheson left home at Inverinate early on Sunday morning, in order that she might walk leisurely to church, and saunter along the picturesque coast by the way. She did not appear at church, and not returning to Inverinate, the alarm was given, and search made in the neighbourhood, but without effect. Early next morning, however, as Dr. Maclean was approaching Inverinate, he observed a bonnet and veil on the water, and further search having been made, the body of the unfortunate lady was found in the sea at the base of a rock, which it is supposed she had climbed to enjoy the fine view of Loch Duich which it affords. The deceased lady was sister to the late Lord Beaumont, was married in 1853 to Mr. Matheson, M.P. for Ardross, and has left two children, the youngest only a few months old. (1855)

October

🕷 October 1st 🕷

A Housebreaker has been captured by a lady at Liverpool. On Saturday evening the 1st inst., Mrs. Elliot, wife of Mr. J. Elliot of Camden Street, on going into her bed-room, found that her jewel case on the dressing-table had been meddled with, and that various articles were disarranged. She was questioning the servant, whom she had called into the room for that purpose, about the matter, when she suddenly perceived a man's feet projecting slightly from under the bed. She ordered the girl to go into the street, being careful to shut the front door after her to keep the thief in, and seek for a policeman. The robber, hearing this energetic instruction, sprang from his imperfect place of concealment, and made a rush at the chamber door. Mrs. Elliott, however, threw herself in his way, and grasped him with a firmness and tenacity which resisted the fellow's strenuous exertions to shake her off. The servant girl returned in a few seconds with an officer, and the burglar was given into custody. The most singular part of the matter is, that some time ago the same courageous lady received the thanks of a grand jury in Liverpool for a similar capture of a housebreaker in her premises. The prisoner, J. Tutty, a man well known to the police, was sent for trial at the sessions. (1853)

October 2nd

A daring attempt at Garrotte Robbery was made near Dunfermline on Sunday evening the 2nd inst. About eight o'clock, as Dr. White was on his way to Dunfermline accompanied by his servant boy in his gig, a man and a woman met them. The man sprung forward and seized the reins and drew the horse to the side of the road. The doctor, taking it for a drunken frolic, tried to coax the fellow to let the horse go. He held on, however, and when Dr. White saw he was not disposed to relinquish his hold, he gave the boy the reins and leapt out of the gig. The woman called out, 'Don't be afraid, doctor, he will not harm you.' He then went up to him and requested him to desist, but as soon as they were close together the fellow sprang upon the doctor, tripped up his feet, and threw himself upon, and attempted to choke him by twisting his neckcloth. The woman also threw herself on him and attempted to loosen his great coat, which was tightly buttoned up to the throat, her object apparently being to take what money she could get whilst the man held him down. Fortunately the doctor's neckcloth came away, which relieved him, when he seized the man by the throat, and after a severe struggle succeeded in getting uppermost, when he got out of the fellow's grip and leapt into the gig and drove away. He had gone a very short distance when he met a number of men with whom he returned and overtook the robber, who was secured and lodged in Dunfermline gaol. His name is John Gillon, an Irish coal hewer at Halbeath. The woman is his wife. (1853)

October 3th

An extraordinary Murder has been perpetrated at a lone cottage in the parish of Gayton-le-Marsh in Lincolnshire. On the 3rd inst., a man who was passing some distance from the cottage, heard a gun discharged; and presently Baker, the cottager, ran bleeding from his house, and exclaimed that his wife had been killed and himself wounded by a gun, through the window. The woman was indeed dead; but on a surgeon examining Baker's head no shots could be found in the wounds. The Bakers had not been on very good terms together, and latterly the husband had with difficulty induced his wife to mortgage the cottage, her property, to get money to emigrate. Baker was arrested. But subsequent inquiries showed that there were not sufficient grounds for this proceeding. A surgeon did find a shot in the man's head, on the top of it; there were foot-marks in the garden, marks where a man had knelt under the window, and shots in the window frame; and the marks were in a direction corresponding with Baker's statement of the position of his wife and himself when shot. Several shots were taken from the deceased's neck, and a bit of glass was found in her dress. In the house was a loaded gun: it had not recently been discharged; the cap had rusted on the nipple. In consequence of these facts, Baker was immediately discharged by the magistrates. (1850)

October 4th

Mr. Hatchwell the station-master at Bury St. Edmunds, and Mr. Walton, the station-master at Thurston, on the Eastern Union Railway, were Accidentally Killed on the morning of the 4th. Having some business which required speedy conveyance, they seated themselves on the top of one of the carriages; and in passing under a bridge, their heads struck the arch with a force which caused the instant death of both. At the inquest, the engineer of the line stated that their riding on the roof of the carriage was a breach of discipline, and that they had subjected themselves to dismissal for leaving their stations without order. They had been ten years in the service of the company. (1850)

October 5th

A most terrific and lamentable Railway Accident took place on the evening of the 5th inst. on the Great Southern and Western line at Straffan, within a few miles of the Dublin terminus ... the cattle train ran at full speed into [the passenger train], going clean through a first-class carriage that was last in the passenger train, and driving the remainder into a heap of ruins. The third carriage from the front of the passenger train, a second-class carriage, broke up and turned over, bursting the powerful iron links which held it to the carriage immediately before it. The impulse given to the two forward carriages thus freed was so tremendous that the roof was cut clean off the one next to the ruined train, and it actually fell upon the spot which the carriage just before occupied, the unroofed carriage with the one before it, the tender and engine being sent flying along the line, which they traversed for nearly three-quarters of a mile before they stopped, passing the Straffan station about a quarter of a mile. Of the passengers in those two carriages the greater number were killed, and scarcely any escaped without serious injury ...

[Here is the testimony of one of the survivors, Captain Collis, commander of the Thames Steamer.] 'The first sight I came on was the bodies of two women quite dead. They lay on the bank as if they had been shot out of the door. Near them was a priest, or friar, or monk. He was quite dead, lying close to the rails, as if he had been thrown against the embankment and had rebounded back. I next saw a man, both of whose thighs were broken across. Messrs. Kelly and Connor and I pulled him out from under the ruins of the carriages. He was living, and we laid him upon the bank. We were then attracted by the cries of a lady, whose hand was jammed between the carriages. Her sister lay near her, either dead or insensible. After labouring very hard for some time we failed to extricate them, and had to turn to others while more assistance was being procured. From a heap of ruins, where we saw shawls, hats, and handkerchiefs, we next got out a lady, greatly disfigured, but still alive. We then came to the body of Mr. Jelly, which could hardly be recognised, his head being torn and smashed off – his legs both cut off – his body torn up, and his clothes torn all off him. I adjusted his clothes, and we put the body aside, and from near him we got out the bodies of the English gentleman's wife and sister. Poor fellow! he threw himself madly upon the body of his wife, and kissed her frantically, and then we got the little baby from under her, and the aunt's clothes, alive. We then went to the first-class carriage that had been struck by the engine, and there we saw the bodies of two ladies, apparently cut in two at the waist. They were so jammed in that we could not get at them. Near them was the body of another lady, whose dress only we could see, she was so buried in the ruins. The cries of a little boy then attracted me. He was about eight years old. He was lying under the axletree of a carriage, which had broken both his little legs, and was lying across them. With great difficulty we got him out by raising the axle with a crowbar. I then returned with more help to the two ladies, one of whose hands was jammed, and we got them out. I don't know whether the insensible lady was dead or not, but I think she was. We laid her on the bank. The other was not much hurt. We next discovered the body of a very large man under the train. His head was cut off and gone; we found no trace of it. Both his legs were cut off also from the thighs down. We got out the remains and placed them on the bank. I was at this time a good deal exhausted, having worked very hard. (1853)

🕱 *October 6th* 🕱

A young woman, named Maria Stewart, who resided with her uncle, a person of great respectability, at Crawford, near Bury St. Edmunds, has been committed for trial for two distinct Murders of her own Illegitimate Children. Having been suspected of having given birth to a child, she was apprehended on a charge of concealing the birth. On her road to the station she confessed that the child was buried behind the lodge at her uncle's house. Search was made, and the body of a female child discovered. On being examined by a surgeon, he gave as his opinion that the child had not only been born alive, but that it had sucked. Whilst the prisoner was in the station-house she made a voluntary confession that she was delivered of the child on the 24th of September, that she murdered it on the following day, and kept it in her bed till the 6th inst., when she buried it at the lodge, and that she had murdered one child before. She then indicated the spot where she had disposed of the body, and, search being made, its remains were found. (1851)

🕱 *October 7th* 🕱

John Kelly, a boy of twelve years old, was charged at the Mansion House on the 7th with Stealing in the clothes market in Cutler Street. He had been seen walking along with two 'blinds', a black-and-white dog and a girl, both of which he was in the habit of using in his trade of theft, in which although so young he had been very expert and successful. He carried a whistle, which he blew upon the approach of danger, and the call was immediately answered by a rush from a crowd of Petticoat Lane thieves, and generally a rescue. The girl had been the immediate recipient of the 'swag', and the dog was stated to be the bitter enemy of the police and others who are interested in the preservation of peace and the diminution of robbery. Upon the present occasion the prisoner was disappointed, and his whistle having been secured, he was unable to summon his friends to the rescue. Alderman Gibbs: Let him be taken down stairs and soundly flogged, so that he may remember the day. The prisoner: Oh dear, don't whop me, and I'll promise to cut away from you altogether. Alderman Gibbs: No; you must go away taking with you a wholesome whipping. (1850)

🕱 *October 8th* 🕱

At Kiveton Park station, near Sheffield, on the 8th inst., a boy about fourteen years of age lost his life in a Frightful Manner. He was playing with two other boys on the line, where there is a curve. A great Northern train, travelling at great velocity, was passing along the curve, and got within about a hundred and fifty yards before the boy was aware of it. In a moment he became quite paralysed, and fixing a fascinated stare upon the horrifying engine, there he stood till he was caught up and almost dashed to pieces against a heavy gatepost. (1851)

On the 8th inst. a man named Buffen was cleaning the second-floor window of a house in Torrington square, when the iron rail in front of the window gave way, and he fell backward on to the balcony railings of the first floor, breaking them to atoms. From these he fell on to the railing in front of the house, which, breaking short off, threw him with great force on his head in the gutter. He died shortly afterwards. (1851)

🕱 *October 9th* 🕱

A little boy of seven years old was literally Cut to Pieces at Newton, near Mabgate, in Yorkshire, on the 9th. He was the son of Smith Deuce, a brick-maker, and had gone into the brick-shed where his father worked. The clay in this yard is worked by machinery, being put into an aperture filled with clay-knives, and the whole set in motion by steam-power. The engine on this occasion was at work, and the poor child accidentally fell in amongst the knives, and was instantly killed. (1850)

A child of four years old has been Murdered by a boy at Hungerford. On the 9th inst. the body of a little boy was found on the Downs, with his head fearfully mutilated. It was discovered to be the body of a child named Rosier, whose father is a labourer. It was subsequently ascertained that a boy named Sopp, twelve years of age, was sent on to the Downs by his master to cut some furze, for which purpose he took a billhook. At eight o'clock in the morning he was seen walking hand-in-hand with the child. Sopp was apprehended, and confessed that the billhook slipped out of his hand and struck the child; he was afraid he should be blamed for this, and therefore killed the child outright. Sopp bears a very indifferent character, having been before the magistrates several times for petty offences. An inquest held on the body on Wednesday, resulted in a verdict of 'Wilful murder against William Sopp.' He has been committed for trial. (1855)

October 10th

A most daring Burglary was committed on the night of the 10th inst., in the house of Mrs. Mullett, the George Inn, at Worley Wigorn, in the neighbourhood of Birmingham. About one o'clock in the morning Mrs. Mullett heard a noise; and directly afterwards she heard her chamber-door opened, and saw two men enter. They had a lighted candle with them, were dressed in short dirty smock frocks, having their heads and faces covered with black glazed calico. Mrs. Mullett and one of her daughters occupied this room, and upon seeing the intruders they commenced screaming 'Murder, thieves,' &c. Both the burglars went up to them, placed their hands upon their throats, and quietly threatened that if they did not hold their peace it would fare worse with them. The fellows broke open and ransacked the boxes in the room, and then ordered Mrs. Mullett and her daughter to leave the bed, which the latter did, to allow of the mattress, &c. being searched. A bottle of wine was found in the bed-room, and after drinking part of the contents, they politely asked the landlady and her daughter to taste too, 'as they seemed low and fainty,' but the offer was refused. As they were leaving, Mrs. Mullett made some noise, and one of the fellow's then asked the other for a halter 'to hang them.' The threat had the desired effect, and they left without molestation. In the meantime a similar scene was being enacted by two other burglars, similarly dressed, with the black caps, &c, in another room, where the other inmates of the house slept. They were prevented from making an alarm by being nearly suffocated with a blanket, which one of the fellows held over their mouths. The men, however, were sufficiently merciful to leave behind them, on being entreated to do so, a child's overall and a watch. About 8*l*. was stolen from the bar. Just before leaving they returned also to Mrs. Mullett's room, and asked her if she would know them again. She replied in the negative, and they rejoined that if ever she caused them to be apprehended and was seen from home, she would never return alive. They bade her not to stir for two hours, and then left. The doors were found open by some persons passing at five o'clock in the morning, and it was afterwards found that ingress had been effected through some bed-room windows, which the burglars were enabled to reach by means of ladders which had been left by painters near the house. A 'jemmy' had been used underneath the sash to burst off the fastening at the top. (1855)

🕱 *October 11th* 🕱

A servant-girl of seventeen, named Jane Collins, has Murdered her mistress's child and committed Suicide. She was in the service of Mr. Elliott, a cigar-manufacturer at Mile-End; two children slept with her – an infant twelve months old, and a girl of four. On the morning of the 11th, Mrs. Elliott, receiving no answer when she called the girl, went to her room; the elder child was crying, and the infant was lying on the bed dead – apparently strangled. Jane Collins was not in the room. There was a pool of blood in the wash-house, and an open razor lying on the floor; drops of blood were traced upstairs to a loft; and there, in a small lumber-hole, the girl's corpse was found: there were cuts on the throat, and an apron-string was tightly twisted round it. At the sitting of the coroner's jury, a surgeon stated that the girl had died from strangulation, and not from the wounds on the throat, which were merely superficial. Witnesses deposed that she had not exhibited any signs of insanity; but she was passionate at times, and she was in the habit of saying, 'If my mother was to die, I should cut my throat!' and she had also repeatedly exclaimed, 'When I am in a passion I should kill the child, and then cut my own throat!' (1852)

🕱 *October 12th* 🕱

An atrocious Attempt to Murder has taken place in the county of Cavan. On the 12th inst., Miss Hinds, a lady of property, when returning home about four o'clock, was met in the avenue leading to her home by two ruffians, who dragged her off the car, knocked her down with loaded sticks, and then deliberately fired pistol-shots into her face and head; after which they walked quietly away, leaving her for dead. The unfortunate lady was shortly afterwards carried on a door to her own house in the most excruciating agony, having, besides the beating from the sticks, received no fewer than four bullets in the face and head. Some eighteen months ago, sworn information was given that this lady was soon to be shot; and a communication to that effect was then made to the government, who ordered that she should get a police escort, at all times she might call for such; but she only availed herself of the privilege on one or two occasions. Miss Hinds dared to exercise the rights over the property which she had purchased in the encumbered estates court; she dared to look for and enforce payment of her rents from refractory tenants by ejectment, which would have been tried at the approaching sessions at Ballyconnell. There are many houses near the scene of the outrage, but no person appeared to help the lady; indeed, nearly all the tenants happened to be ostentatiously attending Ballyconnell market that day. The man who drove Miss Hinds says he was fired at too – it is not believed. Government has offered 100*l*. reward for the discovery of the murderer. The Lord Lieutenant has offered a further reward of 50*l*. for the arrest of Patrick Bannon, charged with being one of the criminals; and a reward of 100*l*. has been offered by Mr. Henry Grattan to anyone who shall give him information against the assassins, so as to convict them. Miss Hinds has since died. (1855)

October 13th

A Desperate Attempt at Robbery was made during the night of Sunday the 13th, in the house of Mr. Holford, in the Regent's Park. Several men broke into the house; the servants were alarmed, rose, armed themselves and attacked the robbers, one of whom they wounded and captured. On the following day the prisoner was brought before the Marylebone Police Court, and a number of witnesses were examined. The prisoner called himself William Dyson. Mr. Holford, it appears, is in America. James Paul, the butler, had secured the house on the night in question. About two o'clock in the morning he heard a noise; he got up, and saw the shadow of a man on the lawn; Paul dressed and armed himself, roused the groom and footman and armed them, and then awoke two coachmen in the stables, giving one a loaded gun and the other a pitchfork. These forces were stationed about the house. Three men were seen to leave the banqueting-room, and one of these was Dyson; he was knocked down by a coachman with a pitchfork, and two men grappled him till the police came. Another of the robbers was seen running away; the butler snapped one lock of a double-barrelled pistol, but it missed fire, and as the robber ran behind a bush, Paul fired the other barrel. The undercoachman had fired his gun as soon as he saw the three men descend from a window; one exclaimed, 'O God!' as if he had been struck. Dyson only was caught, the others having disappeared for a time. When search was made, blood was found near the bush at which the butler had fired; and there were traces of blood over some fences, for a considerable distance. Nothing of note was found on Dyson. But at the house the officers picked up some pieces of candle, a crowbar, part of an ormolu ornament broken from a figure in the banqueting room, a sling formed of a large stone tied in a handkerchief, and a hat; there were shot-holes in the hat, and marks of blood on the inside. The robbers had entered by a window, which they had forced open with a crowbar. The prisoner was remanded. (1853)

🕮 October 14th 🕮

On the evening of the 14th a Robbery was committed at Mallow Cottage, near Abbotskerswell, in Devonshire. The proprietor was absent, and had left the care of the house to his three daughters; who had just retired to bed when they heard a noise below, as of some persons breaking into the house. The eldest of them, about fourteen years of age, jumped out of bed, struck a light, which she gave to her sisters, and, arming herself with two pistols, walked down over the stairs, followed by her sisters. On entering the parlour, they found everything in confusion, papers lying about, and the desk rifled. The burglars fled on the entrance of the girl; and the young lady with the pistols jumped from the parlour-window on to the lawn, and fired both after them. The thieves had stolen some money, papers, and plate; but being eager to get off, they dropped some plate on the lawn, which was recovered in the morning. (1850)

🕮 October 15th 🕮

A melancholy Suicide has been committed at Newcastle-on-Tyne. On Sunday morning, the 15th inst., the bodies of two young women were found in the Tyne, above Newcastle bridge. The appearance of the unfortunate girls was most affecting; their arms were clasped round each other, both of them being young and very beautiful. There was no mark of violence on either of them, or nothing to lead to any conclusion, except a determined suicide. From the evidence brought before the coroner on the following day, it appears that the girls were the daughters of a respectable working man, named Ezekiel Robinson. Their names were Ellen and Isabella, and their respective ages 15 and 11 years. Another daughter, with the parents, formed the whole of the family at home. On Saturday evening a serious quarrel took place between the whole of the family, the two deceased, who appeared to have been extremely fond of each other, taking part against the others. The quarrel continued till near twelve o'clock, when Ellen and Isabella went to bed, refusing at the same time to permit the eldest sister to go with them. At half-past twelve or one o'clock the father, on coming in, found his eldest daughter sitting at the fire-side, and, on asking her reason for not going to bed, was told that her sisters would not allow her. The father spoke harshly to the daughters in the bed, and threatened, if it had not been Sunday morning, to 'hammer' Ellen. Ellen immediately jumped up, saying her father always favoured the eldest daughter, and vowing that she would rather sleep in the street than allow her sister to come to her bed. She accordingly dressed herself, and ran out of the house, followed shortly afterwards by her sister Isabella, her father and sister going quietly to bed. On Sunday nothing was heard of the girls, and the family made no inquiry after them; and the first intelligence that was received of the unfortunate young creatures was of their bodies being found in the river. At the inquest, one woman, who refused to be sworn, was committed to prison, and the evidence of the daughter Jane was so prevaricating that the coroner found it necessary to caution her. The inquiry was adjourned. (1854)

🕸 *October 16th* 🕸

On the 16th inst. Dr. George Hindes was Accidentally Shot by John Baker, Esq., of Ashgrove, at Rainfield, near Killeshandra, the residence of Dr. Hindes's brother. The deceased, who resided in England, was on a visit to his brother, Dr. Hindes; and Mr. Baker, having dined there, after dinner, took down a blunderbuss from the gun-rack over the mantelpiece of the room in which they were sitting, and playfully presented the butt-end of it to the breast of Mr. Baker, and said he would shoot him. Mr. Baker struck aside the weapon with a cane which he had in his hand, and in so doing touched the trigger, when the gun, which unfortunately was charged, exploded, and the contents lodged in the chest of the unfortunate gentleman, who almost instantly expired. (1851)

🕱 *October 17th* 🕱

Two omnibus-drivers have been committed for trial on the charge of Manslaughter by furious driving. On the night of the 17th inst., a Chelsea and Islington omnibus and a Hackney omnibus, were racing along Great Portland Street, when one of them ran over a man named Mason who kept a shell-fish stall, and injured him so much that he died soon after. Mason's son was also severely hurt. After a protracted coroner's inquest, the two drivers, Titus May and John Wood, were committed for trial. (1853)

🕱 *October 18th* 🕱

Mr. Jackson, a respectable painter, of College Street, Chelsea, has Lost his Life in a humane attempt to save the lives of fellow-creatures. On Saturday afternoon, the 18th, as he was walking along Sloane Street, along with his wife, he saw a poor woman with two children attempting to cross the road immediately in front of a cab, which was coming along at a furious rate. Thinking that they must be run over, he tried to stop the horse, but was knocked down with great violence, and the wheels of the cab passing over the lower part of his body, he was taken up in a state of insensibility. He was conveyed to St. George's Hospital, where he died shortly afterwards, plunging a wife and seven children into the deepest distress at their sudden bereavement. (1851)

🕱 *October 19th* 🕱

An attempt has been made to Burke a young woman at Yarmouth, named Mary Ann Proudfoot. She was found at night by the wall of a mill, all but suffocated; her clothes were torn, and there were marks of a struggle on her person; while over her face was fastened a plaster made of pitch and tar. She stated that the man who had beaten her and placed the plaster over her mouth was Samuel Howth, a corn-porter, by whom she was with child. She was a servant in the family of the merchant who employed Howth. The meeting was sought by Howth on pretence of providing money for the woman's lying-in. Howth was apprehended by the police, and examined by the magistrates on the 19th. He is a man of forty, with a wife and family. Mary Ann Proudfoot is thirty-six; she has had two illegitimate children. Her appearance produced a sensation of horror in the court. Her head and face were swollen to nearly twice their original size; the features appeared to be completely destroyed, the face presenting a blackened pulpy mass, produced by fearful blows inflicted by some blunt instrument while on the ground. She was greatly exhausted and almost bent double. From the poor creature's evidence and that of other witnesses, it appears that the plaster was a very large one, sufficient to cover the face, head, and neck; it was made of Stockholm pitch and coal-tar spread on canvass. The woman stated that she tore off the plaster when Howth first threw it over her face; but he replaced it. Her screams brought persons to the spot in time to save her life. At Howth's house a kettle was found containing tar and pitch, and a piece of canvass similar to that used for the plaster. One of his hands had a smear of tar upon it. A brace was found near the woman; Howth had but one brace to his trousers when arrested. The prisoner was remanded for a week. (1852)

🦇 *October 20th* 🦇

Another dreadful case of Child-murder has been discovered at Wakefield. About 5 o'clock on the morning of the 20th inst. one of the porters, named Jackson, employed at the railway station of the Lancashire and Yorkshire Company, went to his work as usual, for the purpose of seeing the government train despatched to Manchester. A young man named Park, employed as a clerk in the telegraph office, was also in attendance, and booked four persons to go by the train, two men and two females. On the departure of the train, Jackson, as was his usual custom, went into the passage leading from the railway yard on to the platform, where passengers were booked to go by the trains, and proceeded to extinguish the gas-lights. The passage at this time was perfectly clear; but when he returned, after an absence of a few minutes, he found a common blue band-box, rather clumsily tied with cord, lying in the passage. He took up the box and carried it into the booking-office to show it to the other clerk, and their curiosity or suspicion being aroused by the weight and appearance of the band-box, they opened it, when they found it contained a child, wrapped up in a white cloth, with its throat cut from ear to ear, the head being almost severed from the body. It appears from the statement of the booking clerk that about ten minutes after the departure of the train a man and woman came to the booking-office window, and requested to know if the train had gone to Thornhill. On learning that it had, and that there was no other train until half-past eleven, they went away, and he saw nothing more of them until they were afterwards taken into custody, when he positively identified the woman as the person who made inquiries respecting the trains at the booking-office window. The man and woman were also identified by a porter, who met them in the railway yard, on their way from the station, as he was going on duty, about twenty minutes before six o'clock. The man and woman, whose names are James Doyle and Ann Smith, were taken into custody about 7 o'clock the same morning. They were brought before the magistrates at the Court-house, and remanded for a week, to give the police an opportunity of obtaining further evidence. (1851)

🕸 *October 21st* 🕸

Sir Robert Clifton, Bart, was brought before the Marlborough Police Court on the 21st, apprehended in consequence of information, given by Mr. Samuel, a silversmith in the Strand, that a Duel was about to take place between him and Charles Law Fox, Esq., of the Guards. Mr. Samuel now said that, since he had made the application, he had reason to believe that he had been misinformed, and Sir R. Clifton said, that to the best of his belief, the quarrel, he expected, would be amicably settled. The magistrate called him to give his own recognizance to keep the peace for twelve months. As soon as the parties had left the court, one of Sir Robert's military friends suggested the expediency of giving the reporter 10*l.* to keep the matter out of the newspapers, but the defendant's solicitor said that would not do, as 10*l.* had been offered on another occasion, and had not only been refused, but the circumstance had been mentioned in the papers. (1853)

🕸 *October 22nd* 🕸

On Saturday night, the 22nd inst., a brutal Murder was committed in Charles-street, Williamson-square, Liverpool (a place almost entirely frequented by the lowest prostitutes, thieves, &c.). Two sailors, named Crispin and Crimp, were standing with two females, and were slightly intoxicated, when they were suddenly attacked by a foreign sailor, named Emanuel Montero, a Spaniard, who stabbed both men in the left groin, almost in the same place, and without the slightest provocation. Crispin died from the effects of the wound shortly afterwards, and Crimp lies in a very dangerous condition. The ruffian made off after inflicting the wounds, but was arrested on Sunday night. A coroner's inquest has returned a verdict of wilful murder and he has been committed for trial. (1853)

🕸 *October 23rd* 🕸

At the Central Criminal Court on the 23rd, Elizabeth Gilday, a decent, careworn looking woman, with an infant in her arms, surrendered to take her trial for Bigamy. The evidence proved that in June, 1835, the prisoner was married to her first husband, who turned out to be a habitual felon, and she suffered brutal ill-treatment at his hands. Subsequently he was transported for seven years, leaving her with one child quite destitute, whom it appeared she had honestly brought up by hard labour, and her conduct had been most exemplary. Once during her husband's period of transportation he had written to her, and hearing no more of him she married again in August, 1847, John Fletcher, with whom she still lived, and had two children. Her second husband was a most respectable man and much attached to her, and they lived comfortably until the return of the first husband from transportation about three months ago. The jury found her guilty, but recommended her to mercy, and she was sentenced to one month's imprisonment. (1850)

On the night of the 23rd, a bailiff named Andy was Shot Dead at Newtown, in Tipperary. He went to serve an order from the Tipperary bank on Luby, a farmer who, on seeing him enter, deliberately laid hold of his gun, and advancing to within two or three yards of him fired, and literally tore open the belly and side of the unfortunate man. It is needless to say he died instaneously. The poor man had sent his wife to America last summer, and expected to join her as soon as she would be able to send him a remittance. (1850)

🕱 *October 24th* 🕱

At the Huntingdon Assizes, on the 10th, John Titman, James Stokes, and John Hall were indicted for burglariously entering the house of Thomas Fairley, at Great Raveley, on the 24th of October, 1851, and Stealing a quantity of Property. It appeared that Mr. Fairley who is the bailiff of Mr. Hussey, at Great Raveley, was awoken during the night by a crash against his back door, and, arming himself with a revolving pistol, he went to the top of the stairs, when he saw by a light below the face of a man at the foot of the stairs. The man then blew out the light and retreated, when Mr. Fairley discovered there was another man in the kitchen, at whom he fired; the fire being returned. He then saw other men, some of them with masks, and fired again, when several shots were fired in return. They then set fire to the parlour, and Mr. Fairley, becoming overpowered by the smoke and by the wounds he had received, and the men threatening to shoot his wife, who came to his assistance, was compelled to submit. After this they ransacked the house, and collecting a number of valuables they made off, having previously regaled themselves with such spirits and eatables as they could find. Titman and Stokes were found asleep on the side of a road in the neighbourhood, in the course of the morning, and apprehended, and Hall, having been implicated in the matter by Stokes, was subsequently taken into custody. A quantity of the stolen articles were found strewed about the road, and Mr. Fairley now distinctly identified Titman and Stokes. The jury returned a verdict of Guilty against all the prisoners, who were known to belong to a notorious gang. They were sentenced to be transported for life. (1852)

🕱 *October 25th* 🕱

An atrocious Murder was perpetrated on the morning of the 25th near Stafford, at a house on the road to Wolverhampton, down a secluded lane. The house was occupied by an aged couple named Blackband, who, in addition to the land and buildings adjoining, were also the owners of several fields of land. About eight o'clock information was sent to Stafford that a cottage at Moss Pit was on fire, and engines were immediately despatched to extinguish the devouring element. On breaking open the door of the house the fire was discovered to have originated in one of the bedrooms, but the smoke and flames prevented any one from ascending the staircase. Ladders were immediately procured and holes made in the roof of the building, and the fire-engines having subsequently arrived, the flames were extinguished. On ascending the stairs, the old man and woman were discovered at the further end of the room on a bedstead, still burning. Upon examination, it was discovered that the head of Blackband had been cloven with some heavy weapon, the frontal bone being completely smashed, and the back of the head opened. The body was reduced almost to a cinder with the exception of the head and one of the legs. Across the bottom of the bed lay the burnt trunk of his wife's body, arms and legs being entirely gone. She had received a heavy blow over the right eye. For many years the old couple, through infirmities, had slept apart in different rooms in the house, the stairs to the old man's room ascending from the house-place, and those to his wife's bedroom at a distant part of the dwelling from the pantry. At the bottom of the pantry stairs was a large pool of blood; and it is supposed, that after the murderer had despatched the old man, he proceeded to the other part of the house, where his second victim was descending the stairs, when he immediately dealt the fatal blow which deprived her of life. Having committed this twofold deed, he must have carried her through the house to the bedroom of her husband, and placing her on his bed, have set fire to the clothes, intending to destroy every vestige or mark which would tend to his detection by burning the house and all that it contained; and thus lead to the supposition that the fire was one of accident. The dog, which was kept in the house, was found in the well opposite to the door, a heavy blow on the head having, no doubt, previously deprived it of the power of making any alarm. The murder must have been perpetrated after daylight. At half-past seven o'clock a gentleman passed the house when there was no sign of fire, but he observed a man walking through an adjoining field, as if leaving the house. (1852)

October 26th

On Wednesday morning, the 26th, about nine o'clock, a gentleman committed Suicide at the Bridge-house Hotel, London-bridge. About that time a report of a pistol was heard to proceed from the bath-room, and the attendant on entering found that a gentleman had shot himself through the heart. (1853)

💀 *October 27th* 💀

Two Alarming Fires took place on the 27th inst., between twelve and
one o'clock in the morning; the one in Lambeth, and the other in
the Hampstead-road. One occurred on the premises of Mr. Lovesay, a
chandler and general dealer, in George-street, Lambethwalk. At the time
of the outbreak the various inmates of the house were in their beds asleep.
They were quickly aroused by the police, and those sleeping in the lower
part of the house were enabled to effect a safe retreat, but not until they
were nearly suffocated with smoke. Two lodgers, living in the top part of
the house, had to jump through a skylight, and, in so doing, it is feared
that they were badly cut by the glass broken by their weight. Engines
were promptly obtained, but the fire could not be subdued until the
whole of the contents of the shop were consumed, and much damage
done to the upper portion of the premises. The other fire took place on
the premises of Mr. Lang, a tailor, Hampton-terrace, Hampstead-road. As
in the previous case, the inmates were all in bed and asleep when the
alarm was given, and it was only by forcing their way through the smoke
that they escaped with their lives. The fire could not be got under until
the stock in the shop was all but consumed. Both fires, it is presumed,
arose from an escape of gas. (1853)

💀 *October 28th* 💀

A shocking Accident occurred on the Manchester, Sheffield, and
Lincolnshire Railway on the night of the 28th ult., to a man named
Oldham. The locomotive depot is about a mile west of the Sheffield
station, a tunnel, 120 yards long, intervening. The men employed at the
depot are allowed to traverse this tunnel in proceeding to and from
their work, though there are no lights in it, except one at the east end.
About eight o'clock in the evening, Oldham went to his supper and
passed safely through this tunnel. About twenty minutes to nine he was
seen by the pointsman to re-enter on his return, and a few minutes
after two trains, one from Manchester, and the express to Manchester,
passed through the tunnel. They experienced no obstruction, nor were
any indications of the fatality observable. At nine o'clock the driver of
a locomotive was passing cautiously through the up line and observed
by the light of the engine fire the body of a man lying partially across
the down line. It was a frightful object. The upper part of the head was

completely cut away below the eyes, and his cap, which lay close by, was
filled with bone, brains, and blood. Between the time of his entering the
tunnel and the approach of the trains there was ample opportunity for
passing through, yet he had not proceeded more than half-way when
the calamity overtook him. The conjecture is that he loitered on the
way, and when the trains approached was unable to escape. An inquest
being held, the jury returned a verdict of 'Accidental death,' adding to it
their unanimous opinion that lights ought to be forthwith placed in the
tunnel for the prevention of future accidents. (1853)

🕱 *October 29th* 🕱

A poor old widow, named Withers, was Accidentally Killed on the 29th
ult., on the Reading and Basingstoke branch line of the Great Western
Railway. The old woman, who was very deaf and partially blind, lived
close by the line, over which there is a crossway. She got on the line with
the intention of going to her daughter's who lived near, and while crossing
it, the train from Reading was passing on the down line, and, coming up
at the moment, struck her. About half an hour afterwards, the wife of a
labourer, perceiving something lying on the line, went up to it, and was
horror stricken at beholding the old woman quite dead, her brains being
scattered about, her legs both broken, and her body mutilated. On being
struck on the head by the engine, she must have been carried some little
distance, as the body was found more than a dozen yards' distant from the
crossing. She had repeatedly been warned of her danger in going across
the railway without an attendant, which caution appears to have been
but little heeded by her. Formerly, however, gates were placed on either
side of this crossway, and a policeman was stationed at the spot on the
approach of the trains; but both had been removed – it is said on the score
of economy. (1852)

🕱 *October 30th* 🕱

A boy of 14, Richard Medhurst, has Met a Mysterious Death. He worked
with his father at a factory in Clerkenwell. On the evening of the 30th
October, he left the factory with another boy. A man who was in a chaise-
cart, in Old Street, said he wanted a boy to go with him to hold his
horse; the boy said he would go; he got into the cart, and the man drove

off towards Shoreditch. Nothing more was heard of Richard Medhurst for several weeks, and at length his naked corpse was found in a ditch at East Acton. His father said that when the boy left home he was stout and healthy: the corpse was very emaciated; there were marks as if the hands and feet had been tied with a cord; there was a bruise on the nose, and a more extensive one over the right eye; on the body were scratches and scars; the back and hips were sore as if from lying long in one position. There was no food in the stomach; and the left lung was extensively diseased, though when last seen alive, Richard, it was said, exhibited no signs of such disease. Medical evidence, however, described the disease as of long standing, and the boy's constitution as of a highly scrofulous character. It was inferred that, from some unaccountable motive, the boy was decoyed away, imprisoned, starved, and beaten; and when death resulted, his body was conveyed to Acton to mislead those searching for the murderers as to the locality of the crime.

The Coroner's jury, after two sittings, adjourned to allow of further inquiries, and to enable the Coroner to apply to the Home Secretary to offer a reward for the conviction of the murderer. Mr. George Wildbore, keeper of the New Inn at Waltham Cross, a man of respectable character, was apprehended and brought before the Clerkenwell Police Magistrate, charged with having carried away the boy from Old Street. The chief witnesses against him were two young boys, who said they saw Medhurst taken away in Mr. Wildbore's chaise-cart, but their statements were vague and self-contradictory. The magistrate remanded Mr. Wildbore, and refused bail. Mr. Wildbore was again brought up, when the case against him entirely broke down. A third boy came forward to give evidence about seeing the accused in Old Street at 7 o'clock on the evening of the 31st October: the magistrate entirely disbelieved this boy's story, which was impugned by his own father, while he repeatedly contradicted himself. Witnesses were called to prove that Mr. Wildbore was not in London on the evening of the 31st of October with a chaise-cart: he came to London on that day by rail, and returned at 20 minutes to 6: the alibi was complete. The magistrate said he should have discharged Mr. Wildbore even if no exculpatory witnesses had been called, for there was really no evidence against him. When liberated, Mr. Wildbore was loudly cheered by his friends. (1854)

🕸 *October 31st* 🕸

George Anderson, well known as a clown at the theatres, committed Suicide, on the 31st ult., by throwing himself from a second-floor window in Fetterlane. So determined was he upon self-destruction, that, previous to his leaping from the window, he called to a woman that was underneath to move away as speedily as possible; he then fell headforemost upon the pavement. Upon being taken up, it was found that he had sustained a considerable fracture of the skull, and other extensive injuries, and he died almost immediately. The poor man had for a long time been afflicted with consumption, and was much embarrassed. (1852)

November

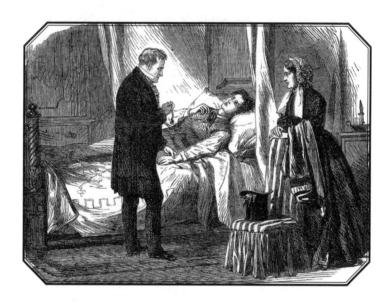

💀 November 1st 💀

A dreadful Murder has been committed near Shotleybridge in the County of Durham. Mr. Robert Stirling: a young surgeon, having completed his studies in Edinburgh, was spending a short time with Mr. Watson, surgeon, at Byer's-green, whom he was assisting in his practice; but he intended shortly leaving for the East as he was under orders to join the Turkish Contingent. On the 1st inst. he left Mr. Watson's residence to visit some patients residing in the out-lying districts of Thornley, Barlow, and Low-Spen. He had completed his last visit about one o'clock in the afternoon at Spen, and that was the last time he was seen alive. He never again returned to Mr. Watson's residence; and on the evening of the 6th his body was discovered in a copse near Derwent-bridge, a short distance from Gibside-park. His face was dreadfully beaten in and bruised, and it was found that he had been shot through the abdomen. His watch had been stolen, and his pockets had been rifled. It appears that on leaving the farm house he had proceeded down a lane leading past Derwent-bridge, which is somewhat solitary, and in passing a clump of trees had been shot by some one lying in ambush, and then dragged through a hedge to the plantation, where his body was found, and there either despatched by being beaten about the head with the butt-end of a gun or with two large stones that were found near. He had then been robbed of all he had. This fearful outrage was committed upon a public road not far distant from some houses, and several labourers were working in a neighbouring field, and they state that they neither heard nor saw anything unusual. The day of the murder was the rent day at Gibside-park, and some of the farmers belonging to the estate had to pass down the lane where the murder was committed to go to the hall with their rents; and there is reason to think that Mr. Stirling being observed to come from a farm-house, was taken for one of them, and so robbed and murdered. (1855)

November 2nd

A Disastrous Collision at Sea occurred off the Norfolk coast on Sunday morning, the 2nd inst. The *Alert* schooner, of Ipswich, ran into the sloop *Samuel and Eliza*; the master of the sloop boarded the schooner to learn her name; in attempting to return, he was so crushed between the vessels that he died in a short time. Both vessels were greatly damaged, and in a short time the crews were obliged to quit them in their boats, as they were fast foundering. The mariners were picked up by passing ships. (1851)

November 3rd

A Town-and-Gown Riot, more than usually serious, has taken place at Cambridge. A person attempted to give a lecture in the Town-hall, on the 3rd, against the use of tobacco. The under-graduates mustered in great strength, provided with pipes, cigars, squibs, and crackers. They soon interrupted the lecturer by calling for 'Three cheers for Sir Walter Raleigh;' they smoked their pipes and cigars, set fire to crackers and squibs and threw them about, and created such a disturbance that the lecturer could not make himself heard. The Mayor and the police were sent for; the lecturer retired; and the under-graduates passed a resolution 'that tobacco was anything but pernicious.' The riot would have ended here probably, had not a scholar begun to destroy a seat; the police interfered, a general combat ensued, and some of the gownsmen were apprehended. The senior Proctor now arrived, and the disturbance was quelled. Two under-graduates have since been fined for assaulting the police. (1854)

🕱 *November 4th* 🕱

On the 4th, a man named Owen, keeper of a coffee shop, in Bear Street, Leicester Square was Killed on board the *Queen of the Thames* steamer, near Erith Pier. He was going to see a boxing-match, and was much intoxicated. He was sitting on the frame-work surrounding the engine, when he lost his balance, and fell among the machinery. He laid a desperate hold of the side ledge; but the cylinder rising at the moment, the arm was chopped off, and he was dragged down between the engines. The engineer stopped the vessel as soon as possible, and then a sight, the most appalling, presented itself. The head of the unfortunate man was completely cut off, as were a leg and an arm; the brains and portions of the body were scattered amongst the machinery. The scattered remains were gathered together, and having been tied up in a sail-bag, were rowed ashore in the custody of a waterman and some of the passengers. The deceased, who was a man of middle age, has left a wife and two young children.

🕱 *November 5th* 🕱

A Fatal Steamboat Explosion occurred on the evening of the 5th at Conham Ferry, near Bristol Bridge. A small steam-tug, on the screw principle, the property of the Kennet and Avon Canal Company, was engaged in towing one of the barges of that company laden with general merchandise from Bath to Bristol. When it arrived at the place named, the boiler burst with a terrific noise; and on the smoke and steam clearing off not a vestige of the steamer could be seen. The deck had been blown out and hurled into the air, descending to the fields on both sides of the water; while the hull, shattered and torn asunder, had sunk to the bottom of the channel, which in that place is more than twenty feet deep. The crew of the John and Sophia barge, which was a short distance astern, immediately commenced an active search for the poor fellows, four in number, who were on board the steam-tug, when suddenly they observed a person in the water calling for help. He was immediately rescued, and proved to be a man named Eacott, who had been steering at the moment the explosion took place, and was blown clear off the deck into the air. The poor fellow was dreadfully injured, his left foot hanging to his leg by the skin, just above the ankle, and his body being shockingly mutilated. The bodies of the other men were subsequently found in the river, from which they were taken out and landed. At the inquest on the bodies, it was made highly probable that the boiler burst from excessive steam-power, negligently or recklessly got up by the engineer; but an open verdict was returned. The jury said, that if the engineer were living they would heavily censure him; and the coroner thought, that if he were living a verdict of manslaughter ought to be returned against him. (1851)

A Gallant Deed has been done by a young Cambridge under-graduate. On the 5th inst., a party of students went down the river to Ely, and, there being a flood and strong current, it was late when they reached the locks on their return, eight miles from Cambridge. A young man named Clarke (being short-sighted, and it being dusk) stepped into the lock, and being unable to swim, sank several times before anyone was able to assist him. At length an undergraduate of Sidney College, named Ellis, came up, and hearing from the cries, &c, what had occurred, although unable to see from the darkness, he plunged at once into the lock, though encumbered with his clothes and two heavy coats. Being an expert swimmer, after a severe struggle, and when nearly exhausted, he succeeded in dragging his almost lifeless companion to shore. Mr. Ellis is a native of Merionethshire, and is said to be as distinguished for high scholastic attainments and good conduct as for intrepidity. (1855)

🂢 *November 6th* 🂢

Several Fatal Railway Accidents have occurred this month. On the 6th inst., Mr. Summerhays, stationmaster at Guildford, was superintending the work of shunting a coal-train on to a siding, and while thus engaged stood upon the narrow space between the up and down lines. The view of the pointsman was obstructed by a break van standing on the line, but, hearing a noise, he said to Mr. Summerhays, 'I think the express is coming.' The deceased replied, 'Is it?' and moved, but the engine was upon him. The buffer struck his back, knocking him on the line, and the whole of the train passed over him, cutting him in two. He had held the appointment of stationmaster at Guildford for about twelve months, and had by his conduct gained the esteem of the inhabitants. He has left a wife and seven children. (1855)

A fatal accident occurred the same afternoon on the North Woolwich Railway. Near the Barking-road station a pathway communicating with Messrs. Mare's factory crosses the railway, and here two children were knocked down by a train. The elder child, between seven and eight years of age, had her head smashed to pieces, and the body was shockingly mutilated. The younger was carried on the line for upwards of fifty yards, and although dreadfully injured, was taken up alive. No hope, however, is entertained of its recovery. This makes the fifth or sixth accident which has happened at this spot. (1855)

November 7th

Robert Martinson, the cashier of the Newcastle-on-Tyne Bank, who absconded after Stealing nearly 5,000*l*., was apprehended on the 7th inst., at Southampton, on board the United States mail-steamer *Washington*, just as she was about to leave that port for New York. He had been advertised for, and 100 guineas reward offered for his apprehension, and a detective officer had been in Southampton for some time on the look-out for him. Mr. Hillier, a clerk to Messrs. Croskey and Co., agents for the *Washington* steamer, recognised him amongst the other passengers onboard the *Washington*, and gave him into custody of the detective. The delinquent cashier had been living at an inn in the town pretty freely. In the morning, two or three hours before the *Washington* sailed, he gave the landlord of the inn two 100*l*. Bank of England notes to get changed. The latter took them to a bank in the town, where some demur was made as to giving change for them. The presenter of the notes stated that they belonged to a gentleman who had put up at his house. This caused the banker to decline changing them, unless that gentleman could give a reference. When the landlord returned to his house, he found that the owner of the notes had gone on board the *Washington* to arrange about his berth, and he then thought that he would take the notes to Messrs. Croskey and Co., to endeavour to obtain change for them there. Mr. Hillier, the clerk in the office, hearing the landlord mention the circumstance about the notes, and having read the advertisement about Martinson, went on board, saw him, and also saw that he answered the description given in the advertisement, and he then very quietly put himself in communication with the detective, and gave the delinquent into custody. In less than an hour afterwards the latter was on his way to London instead of to New York. (1855)

❧ *November 8th* ❧

A shocking Murder has been committed at a place called Lype, in the parish of Cutcombe, near Dunster, on the old Minehead-road. The victim was a fine girl about eleven years old, named Eliza Coles, who lived with her mother, a widow, and her brother, a youth of about eighteen, in a lonely house, part of which was also occupied by an aged woman named Norman. In the neighbourhood was a barn, which had not been used for many years. The mother of the poor girl left her house on the morning of the 8th inst., to go to work, and shortly afterwards the son also went to his work at a neighbouring quarry, the girl being left at home. About 10 o'clock the old woman, Mary Norman, saw the girl sitting on one side of the fire-place, while a man named James Bailey, who lived at Luxborough, was seated on the other. She was not seen alive after that time.

About eleven o'clock a man named Sedgebeer, who was working opposite the entrance to Lype, saw Bailey advancing towards the place at which he (Sedgbeer) was, in a hurried manner; and on arriving at the spot where he stood he observed that Bailey was labouring under some excitement. Bailey then went to the quarry at which the girl's brother was working, and remained there, occasionally working for a short time, during which he partook of Coles's dinner. At four o'clock Bailey left the quarry, and soon afterwards he called at the cottages at Lype, and inquired if 'the old woman (Coles) or any of them' had returned? Mrs. Norman replied in the negative, and he then went away. About seven o'clock the boy Coles returned, and missing his sister, he went to meet his mother, who returned with him and made inquiries for the poor girl at some neighbouring cottages. Failing to obtain any information they searched their own premises, and ultimately the barn, the door of which they found closed, the mother went in, and on going to a dark part of the barn she discovered the lifeless body of her child. She carried the body to her house, and then it was seen that her throat had been cut in a most horrible manner.

Information having been given to the constables, they went to the house of Bailey's father, who lives at a short distance from the cottages. They found the son in bed, and having stated that they were come to take him into custody on a charge of murder, the prisoner exclaimed, 'I didn't murder her;' but he admitted that he had been at the house on his way from work, and stated that on his leaving she accompanied him a short distance, and then returned. On him was found a knife, which was of course taken from him. On examining the barn, blood was found on some ashes near the door, and also part of a buckle strap, which was identified as belonging to the prisoner; the other part was found upon him. Near the barn is a stream of water, and a little beyond this from the barn, was discovered a footprint, which corresponded with one of the prisoner's boots. This mark was in a place which a person would pass over in proceeding from the barn to the spot at which the man Sedgbeer was when the prisoner went towards him. On examining the prisoner's clothes, blood was found in different parts, which had been partially washed out. On the girl's body being examined, marks of two severe blows were found on the top of the head, and also the mark of a violent blow over the left eye. There were two stabs in the neck, one on each side, and these correspond with the blade of the knife found on the prisoner. There was a horrid gash right across the neck, from left to right, which divided all the principal parts, down to the bone, and at the bottom of this cut was the mark of another stab, between two of the vital vertebra; or neck bones. From the appearances there could be no doubt that the murderer first stunned his victim by striking her on the head, and then dragged her to a darker part of the barn, where placing her head on one of the stone sleepers, he completed the horrid crime. The prisoner was brought before the magistrates of the district, and fully committed for trial; and a verdict of wilful murder was also returned by the coroner's inquest. (1853)

🕸 *November 9th* 🕸

A most daring Burglary was committed on the morning of the 9th inst. in the house of Mr. Hampshire, a respectable tradesman, residing at Tingle Bridge, near Barnsley. The robbers, five in number, effected an entrance at the kitchen door, with an instrument which cut a hole in the door, by means of which the door was unbolted. The robbers proceeded to the bedroom of Mr. and Mrs. Hampshire, and threatened to murder them if they made any alarm. Mr. Hampshire was covered with the clothes, and almost smothered; while an instrument was placed round Mrs. Hampshire's neck, resembling, as she thought, a piece of hoop iron, which a man held at both ends, almost strangling her. Mrs. Hampshire presented a very disfigured appearance, her neck being very black, and her eyes protruding from the fearful injury she had received. Meantime the other villains were ransacking the house for money, and about 30*l.* fell into their hands. They all had their faces covered with black crape, or marks of some description, so that their features could not be discerned. The entrance was effected about half-past one o'clock, and they departed about two, saying they would go down stairs and have some refreshment, telling Mr. and Mrs. Hampshire that it would be at the peril of their lives if they made any alarm. However, the burglars did not make any long stay, but hastened away. Mr. Hampshire is a grocer and horse dealer, and the thieves, in addition to the money, took a quantity of tobacco, cheese, sugar, and other articles. The door of a cottage house, under the same roof, was securely fastened by the robbers before Tentering Mr. Hampshire's, so that he might not receive any assistance from his neighbour. (1855)

A Tragic Incident occurred on the 9th of October on board a steamboat on the Missouri. Among the deck passengers were Mrs Lydia Miller and her husband. They had been married only three weeks, and were on their way from a visit to Minnesota. While asleep in the night Mrs. Miller was awakened by a person behaving rudely to her. The person went away, but renewed his conduct. She awoke her husband, and told him what had happened, at the same time asking him for his pistol. He gave it to her, and went himself in search of the ruffian who had molested his wife. During Mr. Miller's absence the villain returned again, when Mrs. Miller levelled the pistol at him, and shot him through the heart. It proved that he was a watchman of the boat, named Bugg. Mrs. Miller was examined by the coroner at St. Louis, but was exonerated from all guilt. (1853)

November 10th

At the Middlesex Sessions, on the 10th, Henry Martin, a young man of twenty-one, was convicted of inciting Charles White, a boy of twelve, to Rob his Master. White was employed as an errand-boy; Martin accosted him in the street, induced him to purloin a pistol, and then by threats of making this crime known, compelled him to steal a silver fork, a sovereign, and a watch. Martin, who had previously been thrice convicted of felony, was sentenced to fourteen years' transportation. (1851)

November 11th

Houghton Pit, near Newbottle, in Durham, the property of the Earl of Durham, has been the scene of an Accident, still more fatal. The colliery is said to have been considered in a good general condition. On the 11th, while one hundred and fifty miners were in the workings, a very violent explosion of fire-damp occurred; many of the people were blown to pieces or destroyed by the flames, but the great majority were in a safe spot. They occupied a position where the air was respirable, while they were hemmed in on all sides by the fatal choke-damp. Some who attempted to gain the shaft perished by suffocation, and others with difficulty regained their refuge. Here one hundred and twenty persons remained for hours in utter darkness, and momentarily expecting to be suffocated by the foul air. Fortunately a communication was at length opened, and all the living miners were got to the shaft. It was found that no fewer than twenty-six men and boys had been killed. (1850)

November 12

A Fatal Accident occurred on the London and South Western Railway on the 12th inst., to William Wallace, a plate-layer in the employment of the Company. Wallace was engaged with other men at his vocation, between the Waterloo-road and Vauxhall terminus, when the train was approaching, from Windsor. The driver of the engine blew his whistle and shut off the steam, and his mates called to him, but it is believed he became confused. He was knocked down and the train passed over him, cutting his body in half, and severing his legs from his body. He was conveyed to the vault of St. John's Church to await an inquest. (1853)

November 13th

A melancholy case of Hydrophobia has occurred at Lochend, near Edinburgh. About seven weeks ago, a boy named Weston, between eight and nine years of age, a family servant, was bitten by a little dog belonging to the neighbourhood, which had been observed on the day of the accident howling and roaming about the place in a rather unusual manner. The boy's father, in consequence, cautioned him not to approach the dog, but, heedless of the advice, he stole out unobserved, and ran to caress the little favourite, when the animal immediately leaped upon him and bit him above the eye. Having told what had taken place, the dog was immediately killed, and medical aid having been procured, the wounded part was cut out of the boy's brow, and other measures taken to prevent the virus from spreading. The wound healed up, and all seemed well, but on the 13th symptoms of hydrophobia began to appear, and although the most eminent of the medical faculty of both Edinburgh and Leith were consulted, all was unavailing, and the unfortunate sufferer died two days afterwards. (1850)

🕱 *November 14th* 🕱

A frightful and Fatal Accident was the subject of an inquiry before the county coroner at Torquay on the 14th inst. Two men, named Robert Richards and James Brown, were employed blasting rocks on the Braddons, at Tor, for the erection of some houses in the neighbourhood. They bored two holes in the rock, about two yards apart, which they charged in the usual way with gunpowder. Instead of providing the necessary apparatus for firing the train, Richards had recourse to an invention of his own, which was the substitution of a common reed, one end of which he inserted in the hole he had bored in the stone, having previously put in a heavy charge of powder; and, as he was in the act of attaching a lighted fuse to the other end of the reed, by some means the powder exploded, and the unfortunate man was blown some distance into the air, and then fell over the cliff, a depth of upwards of 100 feet. He was taken up frightfully mutilated, and conveyed to the infirmary, where he died soon after his admission. His companion, Brown, had a most miraculous escape, having only left the spot a minute before the explosion took place. (1853)

🕱 *November 15th* 🕱

Another extraordinary case of Suspected Poisoning has occurred. The death of Mr. John Parsons Cook, a gentleman of Rugeley, who kept race-horses and was a betting-man, is attributed by a coroner's jury to poison, administered by William Palmer, a surgeon of that place. It appeared from the very extended investigation before the coroner, that Palmer and Cook were at times partners in betting on horses, and also made bets against each other; there was a bet pending between them at the time of Mr. Cook's death; what was their general position towards each other in money matters is not clear – Mr. Cook's betting-book has mysteriously disappeared. On the 13th November, Mr. Cook was at

Shrewsbury Races; his horse Pole-star won a race; Mr. Cook received some 800*l*. Palmer was with him. While drinking grog at night, Mr. Cook complained that his liquor burnt his throat – there was 'something in it;' Mr. Palmer took up the glass, drank about a tea-spoonful of the liquor that remained, and said, 'There is nothing in it;' then he asked another person to taste it – when none was left. Soon after, Mr. Cook was seized with sickness: he told a Mr. Fisher that he believed Palmer had 'dosed' him; he gave Mr. Fisher 800*l*. to take care of, saying, 'Take care of it, for I believe I have been dosed.' Mr. Cook got better. He afterwards hinted to a Mr. Herring that Palmer– 'that villain' – had put something in his liquor, and that they had had betting transactions: he added, 'You don't know all.' Mr. Herring asked him how he could continue to associate with Palmer. 'He again replied in an absent manner, and, walking towards the door, "Ah! you don't know all."'

Cook and Palmer returned to Rugeley on the 15th November; Cook lodged at the Talbot Arms; he continued to associate with Palmer. On the 18th he was seized with sickness; Palmer attended him; Palmer sent for Mr. Jones, a surgeon at Lutterworth. Mr. Jones could not see any symptoms of bilious diarrhoea, which Palmer said Cook was suffering from. Mr. Bamford, surgeon, of Rugeley, was also in attendance at Palmer's request. Mr. Bamford prescribed medicines for the patient. On the night of the 21st, soon after he had taken pills administered by Palmer, Mr. Cook was very ill. Palmer was sent for by Mr. Jones; he came with extraordinary speed, bringing two pills which he said contained ammonia. They were given to Mr. Cook. Mr. Jones describes the sequel– 'Immediately after taking the pills, Mr. Cook uttered loud screams, and threw himself back on the bed in very strong convulsions. He then requested to be raised up, saying, "I shall be suffocated." We endeavoured to raise him up; but he was so stiffened out with spasms that it was impossible to do so. When he found that we could not raise him, he said, "Turn me over;" and I turned him over on his right side. I listened to the action of his heart, which I found to gradually cease, and in a few minutes he died. I never heard of his having a fit before. I have never seen symptoms so strong before. They were symptoms of convulsions and tetanus; every muscle of the body was stiffened. I cannot say what was the cause of convulsions. My impression at the time was that it was from over excitement.' The local surgeons made a post-mortem examination to ascertain the cause of death – but in vain; there were no signs of disease of a mortal nature, nor any of poison having been administered. The viscera were sent to London, and examined by Professor Taylor and Dr. Rees. They could find no traces of poison; they detected antimony in small amounts in the various organs and their contents; but antimony is a safe medicine, though enough may be given to kill: the viscera presented no appearance to account for death. But how did the antimony get into the system? Mr. Bamford, who made up the medicines which Mr Cook ought to have taken, did not use any antimony. Mr. Bamford had sent pills containing calomel; yet no mercury was detected by Professor Taylor and Dr. Rees. After hearing the general evidence, and especially that of the chambermaid who waited on Mr. Cook, Professor Taylor said he was fully prepared to give his opinion of the cause of death – Mr. Cook died from tetanus, caused by medicine given a short time before death; and his opinion was that the medicine contained strychnine. A chemist's apprentice deposed that he sold six grains of strychnine to Palmer on the 20th November.

Remarkable evidence was given of Palmer's conduct after Mr. Cook's death: he was seen by the chambermaid looking under the bolsters and pillows of the bed, and searching the pockets of the deceased's coat. Mr. Jones said – 'Shortly after deceased's death, I left the room; and on my return I found Mr. Palmer with Mr. Cook's coat in his hand. I did not see Mr. Palmer take anything from the coat. He said to me, "You, as his nearest friend, had better search his pockets, and take possession of what there may be in them." I searched his pockets, and all I found in them was a purse containing a five pound note and about 5s. Some conversation took place about the betting-book, and Mr. Palmer said that all the bets were void, and that the book was of no use to any one. Both of us made a slight search for the betting-book, but we did not find it. On Friday, on my return from London, I searched for Mr. Cook's betting-book, but could not find it.' Other persons searched in vain. Mr. Cook, a druggist of Stafford, said that Palmer had recently asked him what dose of prussic acid would kill a dog. Palmer did not attend the inquest – he was confined to his bed by indisposition.

The jury deliberated for a few minutes, and then found that 'the deceased died of poison, wilfully administered to him by William Palmer.' Suspicions of foul play are entertained with regard to the deaths of Palmer's wife and brother. The wife's life was insured for 13,000*l.*, which was paid by the office. Palmer induced his brother to insure, and then got possession of the policy; he tried also to insure his brother's life himself, but failed. The brother died. The life-office had inquiries made; and the claim of Palmer seems to have been resisted. It is also said that Palmer tried to insure a 'gentleman's' life for 25,000*l.*, – the gentleman was his occasional groom. (1855)

💀 *November 16th* 💀

A Daring Robbery has been committed in the house of Miss Morris, at Weston Beggard in Herefordshire. At three o'clock on the morning of Sunday the 16th, three men entered the house, ransacked the lower rooms, and then ascended to Miss Morris's bedroom; when she awoke and screamed, one thrust the bedclothes over her head, pressed on her chest, and threatened to murder her. They had their faces blackened, or wore crape over them; one had a gun, and another a bludgeon. The noise aroused the servant; but as he opened his door, the leader, a stalwart fellow, presented a gun, and completely cowed him. The house was rifled, and among other plunder carried off was a large and heavy piece of bacon. After the robbers had left the house a few minutes, they returned, and fired the gun through an upper window – it was heavily charged. The neighbourhood was quickly alarmed, but the robbers got clear off. The carrying away of the bacon, and some other facts, have suggested that they were neighbours. (1851)

💀 *November 17th* 💀

A Shocking Accident occurred on the 17th, at Carnarvon. In a cottage built under the town wall, there was an aged woman, the wife of John Jones, a blacksmith, working in Mr. Smith's quarry, and seven of her children, including a married daughter, and her child, who had come to visit their parents. In a moment a portion of the scraping at the summit of the wall, measuring about ten yards long and three feet deep, and weighing about eight tons, fell on the roof, and crushed it in at a stroke. One of the children who was on the threshold was thrown at a distance from the house. The old woman and the other children, with the exception of the married daughter and her child, were speedily rescued from their perilous situation with a few bruises. The others remained, however, under the rubbish until about five o'clock, notwithstanding all the exertions made to recover them, and when found she was bent down in a sitting posture with the child in her lap, and the lives of both extinct. The rain, it is supposed, by moistening the earth and destroying the adhesive power of the mortar, caused the stones to unloose. (1851)

November 18th

Another barbarous Murder, with Highway Robbery, has been committed in Norfolk. The victim was Lorenzo Bella, a silversmith, who resided in Norwich. He had two assistants in his shop, to whom he left the care of his business while he travelled through the county to obtain orders and to sell his jewellery. He usually carried a box of gold and silver watches and other jewellery in a bag, suspended from a stick on his shoulder, and his custom was, when he sold goods to the country people, to take payment in small instalments. He was last seen alive, walking towards the village of Wellingham, about one o'clock on Friday, the 18th inst. About three o'clock the same afternoon a person named Robinson, who resided in the neighbourhood, while walking along the road, observed a great quantity of blood, and noticed that some portions of it had been partially covered by dirt scraped from the road. At this moment two young gentlemen, sons of the Rev. Mr. Digby, of Tittleshall, came riding up on ponies, and two ladies in a gig, a Miss Shepherd and Mrs. Digby. The whole party stopped, and their attention was directed to the blood. One of the young gentlemen observed that there was a trail of blood to the hedge, and Robinson jumping upon the hedge, saw that the trail was continued through the fence into the ditch, on the other side, where a horrible spectacle presented itself. The body of Mr. Bella was found with the legs towards the hedge, and the coat collar turned up as if the murdered man had been dragged by his coat through the fence. By the side of the body lay Mr. Bella's box of jewellery, unopened, but removed from the bag, and his stick and umbrella, and also a large hatchet, such as is used for felling timbers. The blade of the hatchet was covered with blood and hair, and it was evidently the weapon by which the unfortunate man had been murdered. His trousers pockets were turned inside out, and rifled; but in his waistcoat pocket a watch was found, still going. His head had been nearly severed from the body by a blow at the back of the neck, and there were four deeply-cut wounds across the temples and face, any one of which must have caused instantaneous death. The right eye was also driven inwards to the depth of nearly an inch. Indeed the poor man appeared to have been felled like an ox, and dragged through the fence into the ditch. On searching the clothes of the deceased more minutely his account-book was found, soaked with blood, in one of his pockets, but the keys of his box were gone. No suspicion was entertained as to the perpetrator of the murder until late in the evening. A man named William Webster, while driving in his cart from Tittleshall to Wellingham, shortly before one o'clock on the same day, had seen a man in the plantation adjoining the ditch where the body was found, and he observed that the man stooped down to hide himself as he (Webster) approached. He communicated this circumstance to the parish constable, stating that the man was William Thompson, a labourer, who lived with his father in the neighbourhood. Thompson, the same night, was apprehended in bed; and parts of his clothes were found to be stained with blood. On further search, a silver watch, with the name 'L. Bella' as maker, another watch with the same name, a canvas bag with a third watch, and money in notes, gold, and silver, were found in different places. On the 19th the prisoner was taken before the county magistrates. Several witnesses having been examined he was remanded till further evidence could be adduced. Thompson is about twenty years of age; and his appearance is superior to that which is generally characteristic of his class. He listened attentively to the evidence, but appeared to be quite calm and unconcerned. (1853)

🕱 *November 19th* 🕱

A case of Suicide, followed by a verdict of *felo de se*, has occurred at Oldham. On the 19th inst,, the house of Mr. Stott, a farmer, near Oldham, was robbed; a man named John Mills was soon afterwards apprehended on the charge, and hanged himself in Oldham lock-up. On the 14th inst, an inquest was held on the body, and the above verdict returned. The coroner said he quite concurred in the decision, unusual as it was. The law required that the body should be interred within twenty-four hours of the finding of the jury, and between the hours of nine and twelve o'clock at night. The verdict having been delivered before nine o'clock, it became imperative that it should take place on that night. He therefore issued his warrant to the police authorities, requiring them to see to its fulfilment. A coffin, the best that could be put together in the short time, was procured. The circumstance soon became noised abroad, and shortly before twelve o'clock a great number of persons had assembled in the churchyard and about the house where the body lay, many seeming greatly excited. The body was removed in a cart procured hastily, and followed by the father and a few other relatives, a large crowd following at a distance. The body was interred in the lower part of the churchyard, about a quarter to twelve, without any ceremony or observance whatever. At this moment the excitement seemed so great, that it was feared an attempt would be made to take it up again; but the grave was quickly filled, and the police all at their posts, so that shortly after twelve the whole had dispersed without disturbance. (1853)

November 20th

An inquest was held on the 20th at Guy's Hospital, touching the death of a young woman, named Joanna Hern, who had committed Suicide by taking prussic acid. It appeared that on the evening of the 18th, she was at the house of Mr. Littleton, in Long-lane, whose wife she had been caring for, and that a young man, named Henry Thomas, who was paying his addresses to her, came to see her home. They had been joking together, when she said she would go up stairs in the bed-room, previous to going to her aunt's in the Kent road, with whom she lived. She went up-stairs, and Mrs. Littleton's sister, who was in the bed-room with her, soon after gave an alarm, which called up all the inmates of the house. The girl said she had taken poison; she then exclaimed, 'Oh, Henry, Henry!' alluding to the young man, and immediately afterwards, 'Oh, my poor mother!' Immediately afterwards she expired. A bottle containing prussic acid was found in the bed-room, and it was proved by medical testimony that her death was caused by prussic acid. The deceased was generally in excellent spirits, but would sometimes complain about her father and mother having left her to go to America. Verdict, temporary insanity. (1851)

A frightful Accident occurred on the 20th inst. on the Hull and Selby Railway. Mrs. Bolding, wife of William Bolding, who resides in a cottage closely adjoining the railway, and between Hamerton and the Old Junction Station, had crossed the line to hang out some clothes. A train happened to come up at the time she was crossing the line for safety, when, owing to the noise of the train, and the whistle of the engine, she got confused, and did not observe a luggage train close upon her on the other line of rails until it was too late to escape. The engine of the goods train struck her on the head, just above her nose and mouth, and nearly took off one side of her head. Her brains were dashed out, and besprinkled the shutter of her own house. Of course death was instantaneous. No blame appears to have attached to the driver of the luggage train. (1855)

💀 *November 21st* 💀

On the 21st inst. an inquest was held at Bethlehem Hospital, on the body of William Campion, a criminal lunatic, who had committed Suicide. He was tried at York in July 1854, for stabbing, and acquitted on the ground of insanity. He was a sailor, and a native of Whitby, in Yorkshire. He was admitted into the above hospital on the 23rd of November, 1854, was of a dissatisfied and sometimes very violent disposition, and had been treated as an invalid ever since his admission into the institution. On the 19th, in the evening, he was seen by one of the attendants standing near a stove with four or five other lunatics. There was then nothing peculiar in his manner. Ten minutes afterwards he was found hanging by his neck in the water-closet, he having suspended himself by means of his neckerchief and braces. The jury returned a verdict of insanity. (1855)

💀 *November 22nd* 💀

At Guildhall, on the 22nd, Charles Clark was charged before Alderman Humphery with Stealing a Watch the previous morning in the Old Bailey. Robert Pollard, the prosecutor, said: I was present yesterday morning at the Execution of the man Mobbs. I was in front of the scaffold, when I felt something at my pocket, and then missed my watch. Alderman Humphery: I suppose you were there to see the man hung? Were there many persons there? Witness: Yes, sir, a great many. Alderman Humphery: Did you miss your watch before the execution or afterwards? Witness: The condemned man was just coming on the scaffold, and before he was hung I saw the prisoner moving from my side. I followed him; but perceiving me behind him, he ran up St. Clement's Innyards, in Old Bailey, and threw himself on some matting. The watch produced by the officer is mine. It is engraved with my own name. Prisoner: I did not throw myself down, I fell down. Alderman Humphery: There is one thing very clear. The awful sight of a man being hung has no fear for you. William Gardiner saw the prisoner, on reaching the top of Clement's Inn yard, throw himself on some sacks and drop something down the iron grating. The witness went below and found the watch produced. Prisoner: I never took the watch. Alderman Humphery: You came out to witness the execution of a fellow creature, but it does not appear to have done you any good, for your intention in being there was to pick pockets evidently. It is quite clear that you committed a highway robbery, and that too under the gallows, an offence that was punished at one time with death. It is too serious a case for me to deal with summarily, and I shall therefore commit you for trial. (1853)

💀 *November 23rd* 💀

William Baker, a boy of eleven, was tried at the Central Criminal Court, on the 23rd, for the Manslaughter of his brother, a lad of thirteen. This lad had been eating his dinner, and had just finished when the prisoner came in, and he was about to sit down to the table to eat his dinner, and took up a knife and fork, when his brother scolded him for coming home so late, and also said that he should not have the knife and fork. The prisoner said he should come home when he pleased, and he should have what knife and fork he liked. He then sat down to his dinner, when the brother took up the lid of a saucepan and struck him on the back with it, and then went to the other end of the room. The prisoner at the same instant threw a knife at him, and it entered his left side and stuck there. The brother pulled the knife out of his body and gave it to the prisoner, and he laid it on the table and exclaimed that he did not mean to do it. The wounded lad ran into the room of a lodger, and was conveyed to the hospital; but the hurt was mortal, and he died two days afterwards. The judge told the jury that if they thought that the prisoner in a moment of passion had thrown the knife at hazard and with no deliberate intention whatever, they would be justified in acquitting him; and even if they had any doubt upon the point, the prisoner was equally entitled to the benefit of that doubt. The jury, after a short deliberation, returned a verdict of Not Guilty. The boy was discharged and delivered to the care of his father. (1852)

💀 *November 24th* 💀

On the morning of the 24th, a man committed Suicide by throwing himself from Waterloo-bridge. He was observed by several persons to climb over the balustrading, but from being in his shirt-sleeves, with a leather apron on, they fancied he was going to do something to the gas-pipes. No sooner did he reach the ledge or shelving, than after pausing for an instant, as if for reflection, he jumped into the Thames. All this had been seen by one of the officers of the Thames police force from the deck of the floating station, off Somerset-house, and a boat, manned by some of the constables, was immediately put off in hopes of saving the man's life. The tide at the time was running down, and the boat, having to row against it, could not arrive in sufficient time to rescue him. (1851)

🕸 *November 25th* 🕸

A Dreadful Murder has been committed at Leighton Buzzard. Abel Burrows, a married man of thirty-seven, was the criminal; and a poor old woman, Charity Glenister, seventy-six years of age, the victim of his wanton ferocity. Burrows is a man of dissipated habits; once an ardent follower of Primitive Methodism, and accustomed to talk of sacred subjects under the influence of drink, he had left his wife, and lived with another woman. On Friday morning, the 25th ult., he went to his father's cottage, where Charity lodged. Soon afterwards Charity ran into a neighbour's house, pursued by Burrows, armed with a large hammer of the kind used by road-men to break stones. The door of the house had been closed, but Burrows broke it open. Charity ran up the stairs to an upper room: Burrows followed, seized her by her gown, and struck her three times on the head with the hammer, smashing her skull. Burrows was subsequently apprehended by a constable. He exclaimed that Charity had ruined him and his mother – he was glad he had killed her. He was committed to prison by the magistrates; and a coroner's jury returned a verdict of wilful murder against him. The murderer subsequently confessed his crime, and said he had committed it because the woman had often breathed the devil into his mother. He knew when she was in the room because it always smelt of brimstone. When he was told that the poor woman was dead, he exclaimed exultingly, 'Ah, I am glad of that, it is a very good thing; Glory to God – glory, glory, glory; Hallelujah, Amen!' (1853)

🕸 *November 26th* 🕸

On the same day, a scaffold at the tower of the new church of St. Matthew, Bedford New-town, St. Pancras, now in the course of erection, suddenly gave way, and five of the men upon it were thrown to the ground from a height of sixty or seventy feet. One of the poor fellows, named Donnes, about twenty-five years of age, lived only a short time afterwards, but the rest escaped with trifling injuries. A sixth caught a rope in his descent, and hung by it till he was rescued. (1853)

🕸 *November 27th* 🕸

At the Marylebone Police Office, on the 27th ult., George Bellamy, a young man of twenty-one, was committed for Stealing jewellery worth 500*l*. A girl who was arrested with him was liberated, as there was no evidence to prove her connexion with the robbery. Mrs. Goodwin of York Place, Portman Square – a very aged and infirm lady – on leaving England for the continent, deposited her jewellery in a cellar, the door of which was secured by two locks, and seals were attached. The butler was left in charge of the house. Bellamy had formerly been in the lady's service; he visited the butler, got possession of the keys, furtively opened the cellar, seized the box of jewellery, relocked the door, joined the broken seals with Chinese glue, and returned the keys to their usual place. Nothing amiss was observed, and the criminal got away from the house unsuspected. One day the butler was startled by the police informing him that the valuable property had been stolen. Bellamy, after selling some of the plunder in London, went to Dublin. There he attempted to dispose of a quantity of broken gold settings; the police were informed; and he was arrested with the remainder of the jewellery, whole or broken, in his possession. He confessed the crime and described the manner in which the robbery had been committed. (1852)

🕸 *November 28th* 🕸

Innumerable private letters describe the condition of the army and the privations and sufferings of the men. The correspondent of the *Morning Herald* writes, on the 28th November: 'We sleep in rain and mud, get up in rain and mud, walk about in rain and mud, and in the evening retire to our oozy beds with feelings of grim dissatisfaction that we were not born tortoises or alligators, so that we might look forward with something like satisfaction to the prospect of passing the next six months in a puddle. If there is any truth in the virtue of a cold-water cure, assuredly we ought to be the healthiest army in Europe. Of course our readers, thinking of the dirty crossings in Bond Street and Pall Mall, will soliloquise over a comfortable breakfast, and say, "Yes, the camp must be very muddy"; but let me entreat them to believe they know nothing about it. During the course of my wanderings I have seen some dirty places, but I never saw mud, sheer, deep, tenacious mud, till I came to the Crimea.' (1855)

💀 *November 29th* 💀

More disastrous accidents from the Explosion of Engine-boilers have occurred. At Halifax, on the 29th ult., the boiler of a manufactory exploded while the people were all at work in the afternoon: the boiler was the centre one of three; above was a part of the premises occupied by the workers, and this became a heap of ruins, which the fires of the boilers set in a blaze that was with difficulty extinguished. Many were buried in the rubbish, and it was a long time before the debris could be cleared away to get at the unfortunate people. Nine were taken out dead, and others were found very much hurt. Another explosion subsequently occurred at Bilston, in Messrs. Baldwin's colliery. Though very violent, large masses of iron flying to a long distance and destroying buildings, no one was killed. The engineer was scalded, but is going on favourably. (1850)

💀 *November 30th* 💀

A Burglary with Violence was committed at Frencham Common, near Farnham, on, the evening of the 30th ult. About eight o'clock, Mr. Marshall, who lives with his sister alone, was aroused by a loud knock at his front-door. On opening, he found a group of seven men standing round it; and as soon as he presented himself, one of their number inquired the road to Guildford. Mr. Marshall was in the act of stepping out to direct them, when he was suddenly knocked down, it is supposed by a life-preserver. The men immediately entered the house; but they were encountered by Miss Marshall, who, with great presence of mind, rushed up stairs to procure a gun which her brother always kept loaded, calling out at the same time, 'I'll fire at them.' The villains caught her upon the staircase, and presenting pistols at her, dragged her to the front-door, where the pointed out her brother lying in an insensible state on the ground, and cautioned her to be quiet. They then ransacked the house of everything of a valuable character it contained, taking off amongst other property a number of old guineas. Before leaving, they abused Miss Marshall in good set terms for not having more property in the house. Mr. Marshall was insensible for two hours, and has suffered much since. (1850)

December

💀 December 1st 💀

An Extraordinary Escape from the Pentonville Prison was made by a convict named George Hacket on the evening of Sunday the 1st inst. Having lately escaped from a cell at the Marlborough Police Court, and also attempted to escape from Newgate, he was removed to Pentonville, and placed under the surveillance of the prison officers. After service on the above evening he was missing, and it was by finding the sheets of his bed, a rope, and his clothing on the parapet-wall that his mode of escape was detected. It appears that he had wrested off the spring of the door of his cell, which he formed into a 'jemmy,' and concealed about him a weight and the sheets and rope of his bed, which he must have wrapped round his body under his clothes. As soon as he was conducted to his seat in the chapel he must have slipped down off it on to the flooring, and by the 'jemmy' and weight forced out the boarding, thus enabling him to descend to a small closet beneath. A window with trifling protection afforded him access to the parapet-wall some few feet below. Gaining it, he proceeded along to one of the main walls, 50 or 60 feet long, communicating to the governor's house, on the north side of the prison. Reaching the end, he must have got on to the roof of the house, a height of more than six feet from the wall. He then must have divested himself of the prison clothing, save his trousers and blue shirt, and with the 'jemmy,' rope, sheets, &c. left them on the roof, and by sliding down one of the gable-end walls got clear of the gaol. The governor despatched officers to the different police stations with a full description of his person, and the inspector of prisons instituted an inquiry into the circumstances attending the convict's flight. Next evening the governor received by post the following note:—

Monday, Dec. 2, 1850. George Hacket presents his compts. to the Governor of the Model Prison, Pentonville, and begs to apprise him of his happy escape from the gaol. He is in excellent spirits, and can assure the Governor that it will be useless for his men to pursue him; that he is quite safe, and in a few days intends to proceed to the continent to recruit his health.

All endeavours to discover and recapture him have been unavailing. (1850)

December 2nd

An Explosion took place on the 2nd inst. in a rocket factory, near Dartford, belonging to a Mr. Callow. The factory was levelled with the ground, and seven workpeople were destroyed. The body of a man named Haggard was found with the whole of the clothing consumed, portions of the flesh stripped, and the brains protruding. The remains of five persons were soon collected together, and two others were picked up alive. One had both his arms broken, and the other (a woman) had her legs and thighs fractured, and her eyes blown out. The man lingered for an hour and a half. The woman only lived half an hour. An inquest was held on the bodies, and the jury, in their verdict, declared themselves to be 'unanimously of opinion, that gross carelessness had been displayed on the part of Mr. Callow, in suffering blasting cartridges to be manufactured in a building quite unfitted for the purpose, having imperfect floors of wood and gravel; in suffering the men employed to work in nailed boots and shoes; and in not having any defined rules or regulations, either written or printed, for the guidance or protection of the persons employed in the premises.' (1851)

🕱 *December 3rd* 🕱

An action for Criminal Conversation was tried in the Court of Common Pleas on the 3rd inst.. The plaintiff was Mr. Hawker, a Devonshire gentleman; the defendant Sir Henry Seale, a major in the Devon Militia. Mrs. Hawker, formerly Miss Rolkinghorn, married Captain Murray, who was killed in the Caffre war. On her return to England she married Mr. Hawker. Unfortunately, although much attached to each other, they perpetually quarrelled about trifles, and separated in the end. In 1854, however, Mrs. Hawker made advances toward a reconciliation, and wrote a tender appeal to her husband, promising that there should be no more temper on her part, and that she would try to win back that affection that seemed to be gone from her. Friends were deputed to bring about a reunion of husband and wife; but in the meantime, Sir Henry Seale, a married man with a family, appeared on the scene, and won the wife's affections. Mrs. Hawker lodged at the house of a Miss Spurling at Clifton. Here Sir Henry paid her frequent visits; occupied a dressing-room adjoining her bedroom; dined with her; staid in the house until midnight, sometimes all night. On one occasion his red sash was found on Mrs. Hawker's bed. Miss Spurling said, that so long as her rent was paid, what went on did not concern her. The evidence, in one instance direct, led to the belief that the husband had been wronged. He only sought damages sufficient to enable him to obtain a divorce. The defence was limited to the efforts of Sir Frederick Thesiger to make out that the evidence for the prosecution was weak and inconclusive. The jury found a verdict for the plaintiff, and awarded him 100*l.* damages. (1854)

🕱 *December 4th* 🕱

Another dreadful Agrarian Murder has been committed in Ireland. Mr. Thomas Bateson, the brother of Sir Robert Bateson, and manager of the estates of Lord Templeton in the county Monaghan, was returning home on the evening of the 4th inst., from his model farm to Castleblayney, when he was attacked by three men, who lay in wait for him in a hollow of the road near some small plantations which afforded a cover. A little boy named Baillie, age thirteen, was driving home his father's cows, and saw the onset. A shot was fired; then three men rushed on Mr. Bateson, and beat him down with pistols, or with bludgeons. Mr. Bateson rose against them three times, but at last fell as if dead; and the men escaped through the plantations. The Armagh omnibus passed immediately afterwards, and Mr. Bateson was found insensible, but not dead. He lingered till the following evening, and then expired. His skull had been fractured in many places, and a portion of the brain carried away. Two pistols were picked up near the scene of the attack, both of them clotted with blood, and carrying portions of Mr. Bateson's hair. One had been fired, the other was still loaded, but the cap had been flashed. A large stone covered with blood and hair was also found. Two persons have been arrested on suspicion. Mr. Bateson was proverbially kind to the poor, and gave constant employment to a great number of labourers; but he had lately taken some eviction proceedings against dishonest tenants of Lord Templeton. (1851)

December 5th

Mademoiselle Julie, a girl of eighteen, an actress and dancer, died lately at Plymouth after lengthened sufferings, from the effects of burns and nervous shock; her Costume having caught Fire from a lamp on the stage while she was dancing before the audience. She supported her mother and a little brother by her exertions, and much sympathy has been excited for her and them. (1855)

December 6th

Union Hall, in the Borough, was Destroyed by Fire on the evening of the 6th inst. For many years it was the chief police office for the district, and, since the removal of the magisterial business, the premises have been occupied jointly by Messrs. Pickford and Co., the railway carriers, and Messrs. Smith and Co., hat and cap manufacturers. The outbreak was exceedingly sudden. The clerks of Messrs. Smith were engaged in the counting-house, when they were startled by a flash of light on the opposite side of Union Street, and, going out to ascertain the cause, they were astonished to find that their own place was on fire. So rapid was the work of destruction, that it was impossible even to save the books, and in less than a quarter of an hour, the whole building was in flames. A number of engines were quickly on the spot, but it was some time before a supply of water could be procured. The firemen succeeded in preventing an extension of the flames, but all efforts to save the Union Hall proved abortive, and it was completely consumed by eleven o'clock. (1851)

December 7th

There have been many Affrays between Game-keepers and Poachers [during this month], some of them of a desperate character. One of these was on the preserves of Sir Arthur Clifton, at Barton Wood. The keepers were only three, and the poachers were at least forty; but the keepers had powerful aid from a mastiff named Lion, of great local fame. The keepers first met three men: they immediately let loose the dog – which, however, was half-muzzled – and rushed on. The foremost poacher drew his clasp-knife and ripped open the belly of the dog; but the keepers were on the point of overpowering the three poachers, when one of them gave a shrill whistle, and poachers poured in from every side. The odds were fearful; but the keepers still continued to fight valiantly. All attempts at capture were given up, and it was now merely in self-defence that Sir Arthur's men fought. In a short time they were completely overpowered, the poachers leaving them in the preserves frightfully mutilated. No one has been taken. The keepers are recovering, but Lion died on Tuesday morning. (1851)

December 8th

A Double Murder was committed on the evening of the 8th inst., in Warren Street, Fitzroy Square. A man named Bartlemy, accompanied by a young woman, called upon Mr. Moore, a soda-water manufacturer in Warren Street. After he had been there some time, Moore's servant heard a scuffle, and the cry of 'Murder!' and running into the passage, arrived in time to see Bartlemy shoot Moore dead. The assassin at once made for the front door; but he there found that a neighbour, one Collard, barred the way. Locking the door, Bartlemy sought to fly by the back garden in the New Road. Collard, anticipating this, ran round, and finding

Bartlemy leaping from the garden wall, seized him as he alighted. The ruffian, however, drew another pistol, fired, and Collard fell. Fortunately another person was near, and he secured the assassin. Collard was carried to the University College Hospital; but it was found that the wound was mortal, the ball having entered the belly and passed through the body. He was able, however, to make a dying deposition of the facts, and to indentify Bartlemy as the murderer. There were indications of a severe struggle in Moore's back parlour – blood spattered about, furniture smashed, and on the floor a broken cane loaded with lead, which had been used by Bartlemy. It would seem that the young woman who accompanied him has escaped. After a protracted investigation, which has thrown no light on the motives of the crime, the murderer has been committed for trial. (1854)

🕱 *December 9th* 🕱

The Rev. H.F. Hewgill, curate of Crofton, near Fareham, Hants, was brought on the 9th inst. before the magistrates, at Fareham, on a charge of Obtaining Money under False Pretences. On the 17th of November last the accused, who has resided in the parish about eighteen months, and is a married man, thirty-four years of age, having a wife and four children, suddenly left Crofton with a young woman named Macfarlane, the daughter of a pensioner living in the village, who has lately filled the office of mistress at the village school. During the absence of the rector for the benefit of his health, at Bournemouth, the general duties of the parish and the superintendence of the village school devolved upon the curate, who had, therefore, frequent opportunities of conversing with the schoolmistress, and a close intimacy sprang up between them. The missing pair were traced to Boulogne, where they remained for about a week, living in the first style, and frequenting the theatre and other places of amusement. From Boulogne they returned to England, and having spent some time in London, afterwards visited various parts of the country, until at length the young woman was deserted by the clergyman, in the metropolis, without a penny in her pocket. Soon afterwards the seducer was apprehended in London, and sent to Fareham, where a crowd had assembled at the railway station, and expressed their indignation by hooting, hissing, and groaning. The young woman was brought to Fareham and handed over to her relations. On Mr. Hewgill's examination before the magistrates, several tradesmen preferred charges against him of having obtained money from them on false pretences; and he was committed for trial at the next assizes. (1853)

December 10th

In the Dublin Commission Court, on the 10th inst., Mr. Kirwan was found guilty of the Murder of his wife and sentenced to death by Mr. Justice Crampton. The evidence was circumstantial. Mr. Kirwan was an artist, living by sketching. He had been married twelve years; but the whole of that time he had been living also with another woman, by whom he had eight children. Neither of the women knew of her rival, until six months before her death, Mrs. Kirwan learned the fact. On the 6th of September, the Kirwans went to the little island called 'Ireland's Eye,' in Dublin Bay, to sketch. Kirwan had a sword-cane with him. Another party visited the island, and at four o'clock saw Mrs. Kirwan alive; the couple being then left alone on the island. At seven o'clock cries of distress on the island were heard. When the boatmen returned at eight o'clock according to their instructions, Mrs. Kirwan was missing; and after a search her body was found on a rock. The incident is thus described by one of the boatmen – 'Her bathing-dress was up under her arms, and there was a sheet under her; her head was lying back in a hole, and her feet were in a pool of water about the full of my hat – about half a gallon. I saw cuts on her forehead and under her eye; there was blood coming down by her ears, from her side and breast, and other places.' Kirwan told the boatmen that his wife left him to bathe at half-past six o'clock; but the continued fall of the tide proved that she could not have been drowned or carried by the water to the spot where she was found. The boatmen found her clothes in a spot which they had previously searched, *after* Kirwan had been a short time absent from them. The body showed marks of violence; but a Coroner's inquest found a verdict of 'Accidental death;' and the body was buried in a part of Glasnevin cemetery, so wet that in two months the body was decomposed. Since the trial, the correctness of the verdict has been questioned, and Mr. Kirwan has received a reprieve. (1852)

December 11th

At the Surrey Sessions, on the 11th, the Revd. Daniel Donovan, a Roman Catholic priest of Bermondsey, was tried for Assaulting Mary Murphy.

The woman had been confined three weeks, and was sitting by the fire with her infant when Mr. Donovan came in. He was very angry with her. She and her husband had become Protestants; and the infant had been baptised by Dr. Armstrong, an Irish Protestant clergyman, who has converted many Roman Catholics in Bermondsey. Mr. Donovan inquired about the infant's baptism; and then abused the woman, and struck her three times with his umbrella. Further, he incited the landlady to turn the Murphys out of the house; and the landlady subsequently took away the bed on which the woman slept. The witnesses called for the defence in some measure corroborated Mrs. Murphy's statement, though they softened it. It appeared also from Mrs. Murphy's admissions that she obtained money and other relief from Catholics as well as Protestants – Donovan had given her money. The jury convicted Mr. Donovan; but both they and the prosecutrix recommended him to mercy. On that recommendation, the sentence was not imprisonment, but a fine of 5*l*. The fine was immediately paid, amid the execrations of the mob and the dreadful howling of the women. They were in a state of such excitement that it was found necessary to send out both the priest and his accuser privately through the gaol. (1852)

🕱 *December 12th* 🕱

There was a fatal Boiler Explosion, on the 12th, at the Lower Soundwell Pit Colliery, Kingswood, near Bristol. A number of men had just been hauled up, when, without any warning, the boiler blew up, and scattered to an immense distance the materials of the massive masonry into which it was built. Thomas Waller was killed on the spot; Francis Fowler, John Palmer, and a boy not named, were dreadfully scalded and wounded. Waller has left a widow and five children. (1851)

On Sunday morning, the 12th inst., T. Martin, aged twenty-four, H. Burton, aged seventeen, and W. Sheen aged twenty, assistants in the employ of Mr. Elliot, a cheesemonger, of Portman-place, lost their lives from Suffocation by Carbonic Acid. They had retired to rest at an early hour on Sunday morning, in a room where a tripod charged with candent charcoal was standing under an opening in the skylight, there being no chimney in the apartment. Their non-appearance on Sunday at breakfast time led to a search, when two of them were found dead in their beds, while the third, Burton, was unconscious, and died in the morning. A verdict has been returned of 'Accidental death.' (1852)

🕱 *December 13th* 🕱

A Fatal Accident took place during the progress of the three o'clock down train on the South-Western Railway. As the train was proceeding at its usual pace, between Basingstoke and Andover-road stations, when it had reached near Oakley-park bridge, a man was observed by the engine-driver and stoker walking downwards on the up line. The engine-driver instantly blew the whistle, and made every effort to shut off the steam; but it was too late. The engine and train passed over the body of the unfortunate man, which was cut to pieces. His name is Thompson, and he was in the employment of the Telegraph Company, and resided at Basingstoke. (1852)

🕱 *December 14th* 🕱

In the Abergwydden colliery, Monmouthshire, the gearing of the lifting apparatus having gotten out of order, the heavy 'carriage' ran down the shaft with frightful rapidity. A man stood beneath; panic rooted him to the spot, and he was crushed to death. (1850)

🕱 *December 15th* 🕱

Mr. Lacy, cabinet-maker, of Whitechapel, was Burnt to Death in his own house, on Monday evening, the 15th. He was nearly eighty years old; he had been out in the evening to see his daughter, and returned to his house about eleven. Soon after he entered his house fire was seen to rise in the shop, and when the door was broken open the old man was heard crying out, 'Oh save! For God's sake, save me!' but a body of flame intervened which could not be passed through, and he perished. After the fire was subdued, his charred remains were found on the floor of the workshop. It is supposed that he let a spark fall from his candle amongst some thin wood-shavings. (1851)

Mrs. Marshall, wife of a hosier in Regent Street, committed Suicide in a Cab on the 15th inst. From the inquest on the body it appeared that Mrs. Marshall, who was a remarkably fine woman, elegantly dressed, left home on Thursday afternoon and proceeded to Camden-town, where she hired a cab and directed the driver to take her to London Bridge. On arriving at the tollgate in the Old Pancras road, the man at the toll bar receiving no reply, opened the cab door and found the occupant bleeding from a wound in her throat. She was immediately driven to the nearest surgeon's, and almost immediately expired. The evidence of the surgeon, Mr. Waldegrave, also went to show that the deceased had taken essential oil of almonds – sufficient to cause death. The wound in the throat was inflicted with a pocket knife, which was found upon deceased, and which was quite new. The deceased having been for some time in a desponding state of min mind, the jury returned a verdict of 'Temporary insanity.' (1853)

🕱 *December 16th* 🕱

At the Central Criminal Court, on the 16th, Henry Horler, a young man, was convicted of the Murder of his Wife, by cutting her throat while she was in bed. The man's counsel could only suggest that he was not a responsible agent when he did the deed, his mind having been unhinged by injuries which he imagined he had received from his wife's relations. Sentence of death was pronounced by Mr. Justice Wightman, amidst the wretched prisoner's screams for mercy. On the same day, Amelia Elizabeth Burt, a married woman of thirty, was tried for the Murder of her Child, by throwing it from Hungerford Bridge. In this case it appeared that the poor creature was of unsound mind, and she was accordingly acquitted on that ground. (1852)

🕱 *December 17th* 🕱

On the morning of the 17th inst., as a goods train from York and Leeds, on the Great Northern line, was proceeding to London, one of the axletrees of the fourth truck broke soon after the train had passed Bawtrey; but the coupling chain connecting the truck with the next wagon held up the hinderpart of it, and thus prevented an immediate stoppage of the train. The detached axle and wheels, however, worked their way under the other carriages, and in a short time threw off the line the wagon next the break-van, as well as that vehicle, and broke them both almost to pieces. The iron chairs of the line and the plates were also torn up for some distance. The guard, Graham, was slightly bruised. The up-line was quite blockaded, but fortunately the down-line was comparatively clear, otherwise the consequences might have been very serious, for in a few minutes after the break down, the night mail train from London came up at full speed. (1853)

🕱 *December 18th* 🕱

Another case has occurred of Robbery attempted by means of Strangulation. Mr. Adolphe Dubois, a dentist in Princes Street, was passing through Norton Street, near Portland Place, about half-past nine o'clock on the night of the 18th, when he noticed three men in a doorway, as if they were there to get out of the rain. As he was passing, one of them ran down the steps and rushed against him, at the same time throwing a rope or gag over his head, which was instantly forced round his neck, and tightened so as nearly to choke him. Mr. Dubois endeavoured to give an alarm; but the rope was twisted tighter, a man being at his back, using something like a lever to effect this compression. He contrived, however, to call out; upon which the other two men ran down the steps and held his hands. By the time he had nearly lost consciousness, he felt the pressure removed, and then saw the three men running off by different ways. He called out 'Murder! Police!' and he then noticed that his outside coat was torn, and that his watch and chain had been taken from him. In a minute or two afterwards, a man who called himself William Thompson was brought to him, and he instantly identified him as the man who had used the gag or rope to him. The watch was soon afterwards produced in a shattered condition, having been found in an area close to where the prisoner was stopped. He had marks on his neck from the violence to which he had been subjected; and he suffered a kind of spasm every five minutes from the same cause. Thompson was brought before the Worship Street Police Court, next day, and remanded on a statement by the police that they expected to capture his accomplices. (1850)

🕱 *December 19th* 🕱

The *Isabella Anderson*, of Inverness, has been wrecked and all on board have perished. A bottle, containing a letter written in pencil, found by a young fisherman on the beach of Golspie, has disclosed the melancholy catastrophe. The sheet was rolled crosswise, as if done hurriedly, and put into the bottle in such a manner that it could not be taken out without breaking the bottle. The letter will be read with a mournful interest:– 'December 19 – ship *Isabella Anderson*, of Inverness. Our canvas has given way! The raging waves dash with fury round our helpless barque! The rocky coast of Norway will soon tell our fate. This is my last work, and I accomplish it with the braveness of a British sailor. My love to my affectionate wife. The same to my beloved family. Evermore farewell! John Sanderson.' (1855)

🐾 *December 20th* 🐾

At Winchester Assizes, on the 20th inst., Abraham Baker was tried for the murder of Naomi Kingswell, at Southampton ... The young man was very much in love with the girl; they lived in the same service; she appears after at first returning his affection to have trifled with him; and, annoyed at his jealousy, to have intimated that she no longer loved him. She would not speak to him. In a passion of jealousy and despair, he bought a double-barrelled pistol, one Sunday morning, went behind Naomi in the kitchen, in the presence of the cook, and fired the pistol – the charge entered the girl's brain. Both Baker and Naomi were well-conducted and very religious persons; Baker was a Wesleyan. His counsel pleaded that he must have been insane when he killed Naomi; but the only witness he called made out no case of insanity. Mr. Baron Parke laid down the law very carefully to the jury: strong passion or jealousy was not insanity. The jury – many of whom were in tears, touched by the simple eloquence of the murderer's confession – returned a verdict of 'guilty.' The judge, who was also much moved, passed the capital sentence. The prisoner was in a dreadful state during the trial, and after the sentence he was carried out 'more dead than alive.' The whole trial was a very painful one. (1855)

🐾 *December 21* 🐾

A frightful and most distressing accident has happened at New York, whereby nearly Fifty children have Perished, and many more have been irrecoverably injured. Ward School, in Greenwich Avenue, is a large building of four stories, with a winding stair-case. Each storey opens upon the landing, and is occupied by different departments of the institution. The girls were in the third storey, and in the fourth storey was the male department. One of the teachers in the female department was taken with a fainting fit, and was carried out into the passage-way, where a cry was raised of 'Water, water,' by one of her companions. This cry was not understood, and the next moment the cry of 'Fire!' was raised, and spread through the building. The children from the primary department rushed to the stairs, as did also the scholars on the floor above them. The stairway was soon filled, and the press against the banisters so great that they gave way, precipitating the children to the ground floor. Two of the female teachers made an effort to stop the children; but their efforts were vain, and they were themselves hurried along with the current. In the upper room – the boys' department – Mr. M'Nally, the master, took his stand with his back against the door, and forbade any one to go out – thus saving the lives perhaps of hundreds. Some of the boys jumped out of the windows, and one of them had his neck broken by the fall. There were altogether in the building but a few short of 1,800 scholars. Hundreds went over the stairs, until there was a mass of children, eight feet square and about twelve feet in height. The alarm was now given outside, and the police were soon at hand to give assistance. Those that were on the top were, of course, but slightly injured; but as soon as these had been removed the most heartrending spectacle presented itself. Body after body was taken out in a lifeless state. Some recovered when brought into the air, but no fewer than fifty of the children had ceased to breathe. Of the female teachers five were injured, some of them very seriously. The dead and dying were carried away in litters, amid a scene of grief and agony which beggars all description. (1851)

December 22nd

A Double Accident occurred on the Railway near Harrow, on the night of the 22nd. When some little distance to the South of the station, the tyre of the near leading wheel of the engine became detached, and left the rails. The speed at which the train was travelling had the effect of keeping the carriages on the line, and the engine ran along the ballast in a parallel line with and about six inches from the rails, for nearly a quarter of a mile. At this point the line suddenly curves, and there being no flange to keep the engine on the rails, it ran down the embankment, a distance of six or seven feet, and buried itself deeply in the earth. At the same instant, the coupling-chain between the tender and the guard's break snapped, and the carriages, taking an opposite direction from the engine, ran across the down line of rails. The guard's break caught the end of the tender as it left the line, and, after turning completely over, was literally crushed by the carriages which followed. Bartholomew, the guard, was frightfully mutilated, and killed on the spot. This disaster had scarcely taken place when the down goods-train, leaving Camden at eleven p. m., arrived at the spot, and in the absence of any warning signal, ran directly into the debris; striking a composite carriage with such force as to cut it completely in half, throwing the engine and several trucks off the rails, and creating a frightful scene of destruction and confusion. The driver of the express was thrown completely over the hedge into an adjoining field, where the wet soil protected him from serious injury. The fireman fell between the rails, and escaped most miraculously – several of the carriages having passed over him without inflicting any personal injury. The driver and stoker of the goods-train were much shaken, but not otherwise hurt. (1852)

December 23rd

At the High Court of Justiciary, Edinburgh, on the 23rd, George Christie, an old pensioner, belonging to Aberdeen, was convicted of the Murder of a widow named Ross, and her grandchild, a boy about five years of age, on the 4th of October last. The old woman lived in a small cottage along with her grandchild, about a mile from Aberdeen. She kept a few cows and sold milk. It was supposed that she had a little money, and as far as the evidence went, the sole motive for the murder on the part of the accused was to possess himself of the property. The murder appears to have been committed in a very atrocious manner; no fewer than nine blows – any of which were sufficient to have caused death – having been inflicted on the woman, while the skull of the child was split open down to the nose. The prisoner was seen in the house on the night of the murder, and was afterwards apprehended with several articles, including a purse with a small sum of money, and a gold ring, belonging to the deceased. Blood was also found on his person. His guilt was quite clear, and the jury had no hesitation in convicting him. His execution is appointed to take place at Aberdeen on the 19th of January. (1852)

December 24th

A very Serious Accident took place on the 24th, to one of the up trains on the Bristol and Exeter Railway. Until very recently the communication between the Yatton station and Clevedon was accomplished by means of coaches and omnibuses, but some time since the company laid down a branch-line to that place, worked by means of a small steam-engine.

On the above morning, the man who has the charge of the switches having neglected to properly turn the points, the train was diverted from its proper course, and ran directly onwards, coming into violent collision with the engine-house, knocking away the ends of the walls and a portion of the roof, and then running away into a field adjacent. The train was very full, as it carried third-class passengers, and a great number of holiday-seekers were availing themselves of the convenience it afforded to visit their friends in Bristol, and the utmost consternation prevailed among them. Many of them received contusions, and one lady had her front teeth knocked out. The engine driver, a very steady man, named Oxford, was literally buried beneath the debris of the fallen building, and upon his being got out it was discovered that be had received a severe injury of the leg, and other hurts, which rendered it advisable to remove him to his home. The engine was also disabled. (1852)

🕱 *December 25th, Christmas Day* 🕱

On Christmas night, a Dreadful Occurrence took place near Kilrush, in the county of Limerick. Bridget Haugh dressed herself in man's clothes, and, having blackened her face, went to her father-in-law's house to have some diversion. Her brother-in-law was taking care of the house, as his father was not at home; he had a loaded gun in his hand, and when he saw, as he thought, the man blackened, he presented his gun at his sister-in-law and fired, and lodged the contents of it between her shoulders. She died at once. There was an inquest held on her body, and the verdict returned was manslaughter against Michael Haugh, her brother-in-law. (1851)

On Thursday morning, the 25th, Mr. J. Douglas, a special pleader, who resided in Garden Court, Temple, was Found Dead in his chamber, having a deep wound in his head. It appears that on his return home on Christmas Eve, he remained in his sitting-room for some time, and it is supposed that on retiring to his bed-room he was seized with vertigo, and fell against the key in the door lock, when the key inflicted the wound. He was about sixty years of age. (1851)

🕱 *December 26th* 🕱

A man named James Holman, a labourer, living in the parish of Crowan, in Cornwall, has been committed to take his trial for the Murder of his Wife on the 26th of December. On that day Holman went to a neighbour's house, and implored him to accompany him to his cottage, saying that he believed his wife was dead. On going thither the woman was discovered lying under the grate, with her face part buried in the ashes. She was lifted up and removed into the kitchen. On washing her face it was discovered that she had received some frightful wounds on the head; there were also scalds on the back of both her hands, but not any on the palms, nor were her clothes burnt. Blood was also noticed on the sleeve of Holman's coat, and some on his trousers, as well as several spots of blood about the room. In the chimney corner, when the body was lifted, a lighted candle was found stuck in the ashes. Two days afterwards, a well belonging to his house was examined, in consequence of some suspicions that had been excited, and at the bottom a hatchet was found. Holman strongly denied any knowledge of it, but it was identified by one of his neighbours as having belonged to him. He was then apprehended, and an inquest having been held on the body, he was committed for trial at the assizes. Subsequently he expressed a wish to see two of the jurors, and said to them, 'I left home on Monday morning, and returned in the evening. As I came in, I called out, "Phillipa, where are you?" and she replied "What is that to you?" I then said, "You are drunk again I see," upon which she threw the firehook at me. I thereupon gave her a push, and she fell into the fireplace. I left her there, and went out to feed the cattle; but finding her in the same position when I returned, I lifted her up, and found her dead, with a cut overhead. Seeing the hatchet on the floor covered with blood, and fearing I might be suspected of murder, I took it away to throw it into the well.' (1854)

December 27th

A most daring Murder was perpetrated on the 27th of December at Belper by a man named Anthony Turner, who had been for some years in the habit of collecting rents for a widow lady named Barnes, who lived with a relative, the Rev. J. Bannister, a clergyman of the Church of England, at Field House. Having been a defaulter to a considerable amount, Mrs. Barnes sent him a note a few days previously to say that he would not be allowed to collect any more rents, and that he was to consider himself discharged from his situation. On the above evening he went into a provision shop at Belper and borrowed a large carving knife, such as is used for cutting bacon. He then went to Mrs. Barnes's house; she refused to see him, on which he pushed the servant-girl aside, and rushed up stairs. The servant, very much alarmed, ran to fetch the Rev. Mr. Bannister, who was in an adjoining building. He immediately ran into the house, and met Turner coming down with the knife in his hand, which was covered with blood. Turner made a desperate attempt to cut the reverend gentleman with the knife, but after a sharp struggle between them the murderer was precipitated down stairs. Mr. Bannister immediately went into Mrs. Barnes's room, where he found her lying upon the ground, with her head almost severed from her body. One of her thumbs had been cut off, as if in struggling with the murderer. Turner after passing Mr. Bannister on the stairs, on leaving the house met the servant-girl coming in, and he made an attempt to strike her with the knife, but she turned her head and evaded the blow. The murderer then ran off at the top of his speed, and for the time escaped pursuit. The electric telegraph at the Belper station was immediately set to work, and the news conveyed in a few minutes to Derby, Nottingham, and other midland towns, but it was not till the evening of the 29th that he was captured, in his mother's house, where he had taken refuge. Two constables, who had been on his track, went into the house together, and on seeing them Turner retreated up stairs, and made an attempt on his life by cutting his throat with a common table-knife; but the wound was a very slight one, a constable having struck him a blow on the arm before he had time to do himself much injury. He was immediately secured, and conveyed to Belper. An inquest having been held, a verdict of 'wilful murder' was returned against Turner, and he was committed for trial. (1852)

☠ *December 28th* ☠

A Railway Accident [this month] has been attended with the destruction of pictures to the value of 14,000*l.* Mr. Naylor. of Leighton Hall, Montgomeryshire, lent them to grace the opening of St. George's Hall at Liverpool. To avoid danger by rail, the pictures were sent home in a van; as the van was attempting to pass over a level crossing of the Shrewsbury and Chester Railway, it got entangled with a gate; a train rushed up, drove into the waggon, and smashed it and the pictures to pieces. (1854)

🕱 *December 29th* 🕱

Four persons have been Suffocated by a furnace, at Elscar, in Yorkshire [during this month]. At that place there are some extensive smelting furnaces, at the back of which stands a row of cottages occupied by the workmen. In the cottage next to the furnace lived a woman named Phoebe Sadler, whose husband absconded about three months ago. Her family consisted of two sons, of the ages of fifteen and seventeen, a daughter aged eighteen, and a lodger who had only gone to reside there on the previous Sunday night. Soon after ten o'clock the family retired, the mother, son, and daughter sleeping together in the front bedroom, and the lodger in a room at the back, into which the stairs opened. In the morning the eldest youth returned from work, and after repeatedly knocking without obtaining any reply, he entered through the kitchen window. A strong sulphurous smell pervaded the house. Having opened the house door, he hastened up-stairs, and came in contact with the lodger, who lay dead on the room floor. In the front chamber lay his sister, brother, and mother, all dead. His mother and his brother lay on the floor, at the foot of the bed, clasped in each other's arms, whilst his sister was stretched upon the bed, having died to all appearance unconscious of danger. Not so the mother. She had evidently been fully roused to the sense of her position, and was endeavouring to escape with her boy, a poor cripple, when she was overcome by the poisonous exhalations which filled the house. The lodger, too, had evidently tried to escape. The rooms were filled with white vapour, which was exuding in copious volumes from the wall next to the furnace; and such was its deleterious influence that it was found impossible to remain in the house for many minutes together, even with the doors and windows open. At the inquest on the bodies, it appeared that there was a large crack in the wall of the adjoining furnace, through which vapours of cyanide of potassium, a deleterious gas, were discharged, and found their way into the dwelling-house. (1853)

🕱 *December 30th* 🕱

William Henry Marshall, a servant out of place at Brighton, attempted to Murder his Wife, and afterwards committed suicide, on the 30th of December. At three o'clock in the morning his wife was awoke by a knocking at the door, on opening which she observed that her husband was almost in a state of nudity. 'Why did you return home in that state?'

she inquired. He replied, 'To kill you,' and suiting the action to the word, he seized her by the shoulders, and then grasped her throat. Nearly naked as she was, she rushed into the street, followed by her husband, who caught her in the middle of the road. They then struggled together till she fell, and he upon her. She raised the cry of 'Police' and 'Murder,' and then effected her escape. As she ran off she saw a razor in his hand, and he having raised himself again fell. She then returned to him and found the blood gushing from his throat and a razor lying beside him. By the time that several persons, alarmed by her cries, reached the spot, the man was dead. A coroner's jury gave a Verdict of Temporary Insanity. (1851)

A barbarous Murder has been committed in Leitrim. Three armed men entered the dwelling-house of a poor man named John Curran, residing at Corduff; and, having placed him on his knees, one of them discharged the contents of a loaded gun through his heart, leaving him a lifeless corpse on his own floor! They quietly departed; and although there were two of the deceased man's daughters present at the time, one of whom was a married woman, neither of them as much as raised the cry of murder, or endeavoured by any means to obstruct the escape of the assassins. This crime, it appears, was not connected with the possession of land, but was caused by some family quarrel, and the murderers, it is probable, were the victim's near relations. An inquest was held, but the jury were unable to return a verdict against any particular persons. (1852; happened in 1851)

🕱 *December 31st, New Year's Eve* 🕱

On New Year's Eve a horrible Murder was committed in Paris. Two old ladies, Madame Ribault and Mademoiselle Lebelle, jointly occupied an apartment in the Rue Bourbon Chateau, Faubourg St. Germain. The former has published several successful works on education, but has latterly devoted her time to writing articles for periodical publications, and more particularly for the *Journal des Demoiselles*. The directors of this publication are always in the habit of sending one of the clerks to settle the monthly accounts of the parties who contribute articles to the work. A man named Laforcade, who was sent to settle the old lady's account, had some months since a violent altercation with her, he having made a mistake on his own side of 5f. On this occasion the amount due to Mme. Ribault was 400f., when Laforcade offered her 200f., saying that she had already received 200f. on account. This she denied, when the clerk presented her with a receipt for that sum with her name affixed to it, but which signature she immediately declared to be a forgery. On this a violent altercation ensued, when the clerk suddenly attacked Mme. Ribault, and struck her several blows on the head and chest with a sharp instrument, which he had concealed about him. She fell to the ground senseless, and apparently dead.

The noise of her fall attracted the attention of Mdlle. Lebelle, who was in another room, and she hastened to ascertain the cause of it. The moment she entered the room, the clerk flew at her, and in a few moments she was lying on the floor a corpse. The murderer then returned to his residence at Montmartre. Madame Ribault, after some time, recovered from her state of insensibility, and although exhausted from loss of blood, managed to crawl to a table on which was a small bell, with which she hoped to bring assistance. The noise of carriages in the street prevented the bell from being heard, and it was not for some hours after that some persons ascending the staircase entered the apartment.

The commissary of police was immediately sent for, and received from the lips of Madame Ribault a recital of what had taken place. A warrant for the arrest of the murderer was immediately issued, and he was taken at the office, to which he had gone as usual, in the belief that no one could appear against him. It appears that after the assassin had gone away, Madame Ribault, whilst lying bleeding on the floor, feared that she would die before assistance should arrive; she accordingly attempted to trace in blood on her chemise characters which would indicate the assassin; but, reflecting that they would not be legible, she, by a great effort, managed to crawl to a chimney-board, where she traced with her finger, dipped in blood, the letters 'Commis de M. T .' These letters are very irregular, but are perfectly legible; some others that follow the letter T. are illegible. After this Madame Kibault began to make as much noise as her failing strength would allow, in order to attract assistance, and at last the door of her apartment was forced open. The courage displayed by this old lady was extraordinarily great; for eight hours she remained lying on the floor in a pool of blood, and every hour became weaker and weaker, and, during all this time, the corpse of her murdered companion was lying near her. After Madame Ribault had been stabbed by the assassin in different places, he attempted to thrust a piece of cloth into her throat, but she succeeded in dragging it away. The cloth in question – a napkin – was found; it bore the marks of teeth and blood. It was believed that Madame Lebelle had been strangled; but, on examination of her throat by medical men, none of the contusions caused by strangulation could be discovered. In examining her mouth a black pin was found, and afterwards a piece of black riband was seen in the throat. By the aid of instruments this was pulled up, and to it was attached the cap which Madame Ribault had worn on the previous evening. It had been pressed into a sort of ball, and thrust violently into the throat of the deceased by a stick, or some such sort of thing. The assassin attempted suicide by opening a vein with a piece of glass which he took from the window; but he was discovered in time. (1851)